Commitment
to God's
World

Ans van der Bent

Commitment to God's World

A Concise Critical Survey
of Ecumenical Social Thought

WCC Publications, Geneva

Cover design: Rob Lucas

ISBN 2-8254-1162-0

Printed in Switzerland

Contents

Introduction

To write an account of social, political and economic thought in the ecumenical movement might be seem to be an audacious enterprise — not for lack of material (though much of it needs to be brought to light from archives and many scattered places of publication), but because of the very nature of the social-ethical enterprise within the ecumenical movement. The context in which the 20th-century ecumenical movement was born differed completely from that of today, and the shifts in central social concerns and in the political and economic landscape have been so rapid that any attempt to keep up with the demands on social ethics is almost futile.

In that sense ecumenical social thought does not differ from other attempts to develop social ethical paradigms. However, it is at the heart of Christian witness that we are to respond to the needs of our neighbours, the needs of the world in which we live. The more this world has become integrated, the more the old power structures of colonialism have broken down and the formerly colonized nations have demanded the right to participate in decision-making, the more the discussion on social-ethics has become a conflictive one. From one side comes the demand for thorough and careful analysis; from the other, cries for change in situations of anguish. Both positions have their right and need to be reconciled in the process of dialogue. This process is still underway, which explains why a book such as this must remain open-ended.

Nevertheless, there are two reasons why the attempt must be made. The reconciliation just mentioned cannot take place apart from historical insights. The ecumenical movement is in danger, due to the fast-changing world, of forgetting its past. Preserving the ecumenical memory is a vital task for ourselves and the ecumenical generations to come.

Second, no concise but inclusive documentary survey of social, political and economic thought in the 20th-century ecumenical movement has ever been published. This book tries to fill that gap. Its fourteen chapters are a modest experiment in inter-relating a vast number of ideas, concerns and commitments in order to make a relatively coherent and consistent whole accessible to readers interested in the development of ecumenical social thought. The bibliography lists many official and important secondary sources, historical and contemporary, but this is only a selection of major publications. The total literature — books, pamphlets, articles and archival documents — is extremely vast, widely scattered and often very specific, dealing only with one or another aspect of social ecumenism.

In assembling this mosaic of insights, positions and opinions, I have selected only the most obvious and relevant parts of official documents, as well as reactions to and commentaries on them. Wherever texts are quoted the number of the document in the bibliography is indicated in parentheses, and at the end of the quotation the page reference is given. For sources not listed in the bibliography, the relevant publication data are given in parentheses after the title. A chronological list of assemblies, conferences, consultations and committee meetings of the World Council of Churches and international conferences from 1924 to 1991 offers a more systematic overview of the most important gatherings in the field of ecumenical, social, political and economic ethics during this century.

It goes without saying that the complexity of the evolution of ecumenical social thought is extremely difficult to unravel and explain in all its agreements and disagreements, certainties and uncertainties, ups and downs, commitments and abstentions. Moreover, it must be acknowledged at the outset that it would have overburdened this book to give account of all the areas in which social-ethical thinking has been significantly developed in the ecumenical debate. To mention only one area which has had to be left out: the churches' mission in health, with its studies on Health, Healing and Wholeness and more recently the study-process related to HIV/AIDS.

This leads to a further comment. Any analysis and evaluation of ecumenical social ethics is liable to take insufficient account of the historical, cultural and confessional factors behind the documents and in the mind of the one doing the analysis. A certain measure of subjectivity is inevitable; and other interpretations, depending on other experiences and other insights, are needed. This subjectivity also characterizes the author's observations and comments made between the citations in this book. Some of them may seem one-sidedly critical. Yet they are meant not to bias issues but to encourage readers to make their own independent evaluation from their own perspective.

Whatever the variety of the points of view, I hope this reference work will sharpen the ecumenical memory, identify present ecumenical trends and assist in the elaboration of future ecumenical options.

The ecumenical movement has not yet fully developed the theological undergirding of its ethical commitments or drawn out the theological insights implicit in them. This is due in part to the pressing nature of the challenges and the intensity of the commitments they invoke, in part to theological one-sidedness and the complexity of intercultural theological debate. It is indeed a gigantic theological-ethical enterprise to come to grips with two major factors of the present era in particular: the revolutions in science and technology and the demands of peoples for social justice.

The task of relating the church intimately to the world is even more difficult than putting in order the church's "internal affairs" of unity and mission, which is the prerequisite of all sound practice of ecumenical social ethics. Only out of manifold confrontations and discussions can the churches and their faithful become more alert to their responsibility to witness in word and deed to the worth of every human being and the sustainable well-being of all society and all creation. The actual practice of the Christian community in the world and a permanent critical encounter with human sciences and social and political ideologies should foreshadow the transforming power of the kingdom of God, which embraces the whole of humanity ever more closely despite its most serious setbacks and failures.

About the visible or invisible presence of that kingdom there is a persistent ecumenical division of conviction, and therefore tension and conflict. Some suggest that the "elitism" of "sophisticated academics and theologians", mainly from the North, so colours all ecumenical documents on social ethics as to render them meaningless and irrelevant, at least for "ordinary and unsophisticated" Christians, especially in the South. But the latter in turn are criticized by the so-called ecumenical "experts" for being too passionate and inclusive about engagement in society and thus falling prey to illusion and incompetence.

To put this dilemma in other terms: a small minority of ecumenical Christians are incessantly asking why the Christian church should be involved in matters of society and how its involvement can be convincingly expressed. A larger group of ecumenical Christians takes for granted that there is ample room for reflection and action and that the real needs of real people can best be met by methods which stand a good chance of being effective. They reject the charge that their idea of what Christian communities can actually do is inflated. Throughout this book it will be seen that only by living in continuous local and worldwide dialogue can the tendencies towards utopian, sceptical or defeatist thinking be avoided and the possibilities of making sensible ethical choices enhanced.

There is an obvious difference between "official" ecumenical texts emerging from deliberative and decision-making processes within the World Council of Churches and its worldwide constituency and individual commentaries on these documents. At the same time, it should not be overlooked that every conference document is drafted by knowledgeable, sometimes visionary individuals before being endorsed by the participants in an international gathering. Committees responsible for producing reports cannot do so without theological and ethical experts. That is why this volume includes a considerable number of statements made by these same experts on their own account. They are to be valued both in their own right as well as in relation to collective ecumenical positions. Where these comments focus on disagreements over priorities, those disagreements are themselves rooted in different ways of construing how the total Christian ethical venture hangs together. Thus they serve the particular purpose of introducing the reader to the ongoing debate on ecumenical social ethics. Often it will be helpful to read these comments against material produced by one's own church and in the wider ecumenical family.

Such a procedure helps to enrich the diversity of engagement with social-ethical issues.

For almost two millennia the church — and after the Reformation, the churches — showed little concern for the well-being of society. They were even less prepared to criticize and to correct the state in its exercise of social responsibility. Increasingly, too, the churches were extraordinarily ignorant of each other's life, suspicious, much given to the unreflective use of labels, unwilling to learn from one another, at best ill-equipped for any kind of international cooperation.

Ecumenical leaders realized from the start that if the movement were to make headway, there must be a sustained effort of education, study and practical activity: education in expounding the ecumenical idea and in interpreting the churches to one another; study of the manifold problems in economic and industrial life; practical activity in applying social principles to the churches' life and witness.

For many years, moreover, there was a tension between what may be roughly called the North American and European points of view: the former more concerned with immediate practical applications and construing thought in terms of collecting factual data to apply to urgent reforms; the latter more interested in principles and looking to research for the elucidation of how to apply Christian principles to complex modern problems. North Americans tended to sit somewhat loose to the existing churches, Europeans were more conscious of the diversity of confessions and their widely differing approaches to social problems. North Americans were more "empirical", Europeans more theoretical (or, as they themselves would perhaps have said, more thorough). But this became apparent only at the beginning of the activities of the Life and Work movement from 1920 onwards.

A final observation, which relates to a major shift in the perception of ecumenical social ethics. As the following chapters will show, two elements have particularly shaped ecumenical social thought from the late 1960s onward: the increased participation in the ecumenical debate of churches from outside the North Atlantic region, and the growing importance given to what the Faith and Order conference in Edinburgh in 1937 termed "non-theological factors" of unity. This development has led to a conflict between different approaches in social ethics, which can briefly be described as the deductive and inductive approaches.

At the same time, this discussion is taking place on the ground of the conviction of the unity of the church. More and more in recent years, the concept of unity has been challenged by developments in society. On the one hand, we see unifying factors in economy and politics; on the other hand, we observe growing disintegration and fragmentation in societies.

This book is thus also an account of the struggle to come to terms in ethical discourse with God's intentions and people's desires in turbulent social situations.

I

Early Beginnings 1850-1925

Such classic religious reference works of the early 20th century as the *Encyclopaedia of Religion and Ethics* (New York, Scribners, 1922) or *Die Religion in Geschichte und Gegenwart* (Tübingen, Mohr, 1909) do not contain entries on "church and world", "society", "the world" or "humanity". Terms like "social ethics", "international affairs" and "human rights" were not yet widely used in church circles. After the 1920s a number of works begin to analyze and to evaluate relations between the church and the world, the church's impact on society and Christian obligations towards humanity, but they are limited in scope, content and method, conditioned by the theological, ethical and cultural wisdom of their time.

The nineteenth century

Only during the last few decades have systematic attempts been made to look back critically at the churches' lack of response to the human oppression, exploitation, deprivation and wretchedness caused by the industrial revolution and Western colonial expansion. The conviction has grown that it is essential to reflect on the relations between church and world during the 19th century and at the beginning of the 20th century, when attitudes which directly affect the nature of the problems faced today first developed. *Separation Without Hope?* **(149)** is a striking ecumenical example of such reflection. This volume of essays on the relation between the church and the poor is written from the point of view that a completely coherent synthesis of historical developments is impossible and that a tension between the social sciences and theology must be maintained. Yet it points out in considerable detail that the Christian churches were both the source and the victim of events.

For almost an entire century, most Christians and theologians remained passive about the development of industrial society and the human dramas to which it gave rise. They were unaware that "they actively contributed, both by their own individual daily political, economic and commercial activities and by their ignorance of the collective effects of these activities, in promoting more and more intensely an ill-considered and irresponsible development under cover of the alleged neutrality of their spiritual and church life" (p.6).

Failing to recognize the need for state intervention to emancipate the working classes, Christian communities were indifferent, conservative and often reactionary, not only in Europe and North America, but also in Africa, Asia and Latin America. The churches did try desperately to serve the marginalized, destitute and poor, initiating vast service programmes and creating organizations to implement them. But in general their efforts did not go beyond works of charity. "The poor were served, but the social reality of poverty and its underlying causes went practically unchanged. The service offered, mainly emotionally inspired..., while helping to mitigate the symptoms of poverty, did nothing in the majority of cases to eradicate poverty itself." Church welfare organizations were incapable of removing poverty and its antecedents: "they offered palliatives without, in most cases, making any attempt to attack the root causes" (p.174).

The structures of church institutions, with minor adjustments, continued to be those of the pre-industrialized world. Christianity failed to grasp the many facets of increasing secularization. Instead of listening to the pleas and protests of the new working classes, the forces now moving history forward, most church organizations opted for the past. Wishing to halt social change, they insulated themselves from important aspects of what was happening and neglected to adjust their life and mission to take account of the demands made on them by new social, economic and political conditions.

> The link with capital inevitably hindered their attempt to move nearer to the working classes which regarded the churches as institutions of the rich. The most they offered was a basis for efforts by those from the lowest levels of society to climb the social ladder. Their participa-

tion in the life of the church was seen as an endorsement of efforts in this direction, making it possible for them to be accepted as socially respectable (p.180).

A small minority of Christians realized that the appropriate response to the social ills connected with mass poverty was to urge legislative reforms. But even they addressed their exhortations to church opinion and met with no wider response among the marginal sectors of society they wanted to defend. Because the churches' attitude towards these people continued to be paternalistic and patronizing, the estrangement between those inside and those outside the community of the faithful was aggravated and the divorce finally sealed. Only much later did it dawn on the church that instead of trying to "control" or "win back" the poor, it must stand solidly with them and plead for them.

Charitable institutions and social movements

Nevertheless, the value of the long tradition of generous Christian charity should not be minimized. As Christian social action developed in the 19th century in service ministries, home mission and settlements, it often broke through denominational and national barriers. In Germany the Lutheran Inner Mission began an activity of reclamation among neglected children in the slums and established homes for epileptics and work colonies for the unemployed. Similarly, in England and Scotland the Settlement movement began educational services for the poor and young people. In the United States indigenous and African-American people became objects of compassion and service. Roman Catholic religious orders and congregations, regarded as an adaptation of monasticism to modern conditions, were esteemed for their work in orphanages, hospitals and homes for the deprived and afflicted.

In his essay "Movements for International Friendship and Life and Work 1910-1925" **(14)**, Nils Karlström presents such Christian charitable institutions and movements as a prelude to international and interdenominational cooperation. He also describes the Christian socialist movement created in the late-19th and early-20th centuries. Though rejecting the Marxist worldview and its hostility to Christianity, it nevertheless recognized much of the socialist criticism as justified and thus sought to awaken public opinion in favour of social reform carried out in a Christian spirit.

In England the Christian Social Union was established in 1889. Later, social service unions were started by the English free churches. In 1911 representatives of these different unions founded the Inter-denominational Social Service Council, which drew up a common Christian "Statement of Social Principles". Out of such earlier social efforts grew the 1924 Conference on Christian Politics, Economics and Citizenship (COPEC) **(1)**, whose impact would later be felt in the Life and Work movement.

In Germany Adolf Stoecker, Adolf von Harnack and others, uniting various ecclesiastical and theological tendencies, founded the Evangelisch-Sozialer Kongress in 1890. In France Tommy Fallot is regarded by the Christian social movement as its founder. Two of his disciples, Elie Gounelle and Wilfred Monod, became leading personalities in the Life and Work movement. In Switzerland the Christian social movement was characterized by serious efforts to forge contacts with socialists. According to its spokesmen, Hermann Kutter and Leonhard Ragaz, the demand by the labour movement for reconstruction of the economic order was essentially a Christian demand.

Social gospel

In the United States the social gospel movement began to attract notice at the turn of the century. Its most outspoken theological advocate was Walter Rauschenbusch, a prolific author whose most systematic work was *A Theology for the Social Gospel* (New York, Macmillan, 1917). The social gospel movement was influential in the creation of the US Federal Council of Churches in 1908. The "Social Creed of the Churches" endorsed by the FCC in 1912 declared that the churches must stand for the principles of conciliation and arbitration in industrial disputes, abolition of child labour, reduction of working hours, a minimum standard living wage in every industry, the most equitable possible division of the products of industry and the abatement of poverty.

Social gospel leaders looked for the "real" Jesus, whom they believed could be known by historical scholarship. They understood his central message of the nearness of the kingdom of God as an historical possibility to come on earth in some fullness, bringing social harmony and eliminating gross injustices. Great emphasis was put on the law of love. God works in and through human beings towards the kingdom of love, a cooperative commonwealth in which socialized and enlightened men and women will work for the good of all. Sin was considered to be primarily selfishness, but human beings can be educated to prefer social good to private advantage.

Aware of the collective transmission of sin through human institutions, the social gospel movement believed that social salvation would come as institutions as well as individuals come under the law of love. Through determined moral efforts the day of the kingdom's coming can be hastened. By self-sacrifice Christians can be heralds of the coming dawn. Much of social gospel thought was pacifist, especially in its later phases between the two world wars.

Social gospel theology has been charged with having an over-optimistic view of the human being and a naïve strategy of preaching and pronouncement. Among those to make this neo-orthodox critique was the young W.A. Visser 't Hooft, whose dissertation on the *Background of the Social Gospel in America* **(20)** criticized its emphasis on God's immanence rather than transcendence and its misleading belief in the perfectibility of the human being and society. The central idea of humanity's gradual progress towards higher stages of moral and spiritual development contradicts the realistic biblical affirmation of our sinful predicament.

Yet Visser 't Hooft also noted that "the social gospel is in a sense the first expression of American religious life which is truly born in America itself" and that "this ethic constitutes the one most important attempt to transcend the individualistic notions of the last centuries by a solidaristic conception of social life... May it therefore not be that America is yet at the beginning of the process of finding itself?" (p.186). It will be seen that the basic social responsibility expressed in the social gospel has continued to influence the ecumenical movement until today.

International movements

There was a spectacular proliferation of national and international movements and bodies for unity, cooperation, friendship, fellowship, peace, service and relief around the turn of the century. This burgeoning of internationalism took place within the framework of 19th-century colonial expansion and technological development. Among the various organs of cooperation were the Universal Christian Council for Life and Work, the World Conference on Faith and Order, the International Missionary Council, the Federal Council of the Churches of Christ in America, the Church Peace Union, the World Alliance for Promoting International Friendship through the Churches, the World Student Christian Federation, the Young Men's Christian Association and the Young Women's Christian Association.

The origin, nature and scope of all these organizations and movements are succinctly described by Charles S. Macfarland in *International Christian Movements* **(17)**. He points to the religious motivation and ethical orientation of an era characterized by an evangelical, liberal, progressive, reformist and moderate mainstream within Christianity:

> It is not by the exchange of political ambassadors that Christianity will perform its mission, but rather by the interchange of good will and service. The influence of the church and of Christianity upon governments must be that of moral and spiritual power. It surely cannot be gained by following the same sort of political diplomacy which has shown its weakness and its inability to regenerate political institutions. This influence must come, therefore, not by diplomatic negotiations between ecclesiastics and government leaders, but by bringing the peoples of the world together in Christian sympathy and mutual service. Following this principle, evangelical churches and Christian institutions throughout the world have been coming together in a simple, natural and quiet way — much like the coming of the kingdom of heaven, without observation (p.8).

In a later book, *Pioneers for Peace through Religion* **(127)**, Macfarland described the history of the Church Peace Union and its auxiliary, the World Alliance for Promoting International Friendship through the Churches. Their conviction of the need to apply Christian principles to international relations, to promote mutual understanding between the nations and to develop and strengthen international law found expression in their supportive attitude towards the League of Nations, the World Court and the Kellogg-Briand Pact. Macfarland, then general secretary emeritus of the FCC in the US, pointed out: "Unfortunately, age-old national suspicions and jealousies denied them adequate support. They did not fail, but the nations failed to adequately support the machinery created" (p.8).

The World Alliance and Life and Work

Nils Karlström **(14)** gives a detailed account of Christian institutional efforts towards international understanding, especially the World Alliance for Promoting International Friendship through the Churches.

Two members of the British parliament, J. Allen Baker, a Quaker, and Willoughby H. Dickinson, an Anglican, were prompted by church peace conferences at The Hague in 1899 and 1907 to promote peaceful relations between the churches in Great Britain and Germany by a large-scale exchange of visits between church representatives. A German church delegation, led by Friedrich Siegmund-Schultze, visited England in 1908, and the next year an English delegation went to Germany. In the US, the Federal Council also played an important role in working for closer understanding between US and European churches.

In 1914, Protestant, Roman Catholic and Jewish organizations founded the Church Peace Union. The $2 million it received from industrialist Andrew Carnegie served to finance most of the future activities of the World Alliance. Created a day after the first world war broke out, the World Alliance started functioning through national councils in the US, Canada, India, Japan and several European countries. At a post-war conference in Oud Wassenaar, near The Hague, in 1919, the German delegates made a declaration that they personally considered Germany's violation of Belgian neutrality an act of moral transgression. The profound impression left by this declaration made trustful cooperation within the World Alliance possible for the national committees. Several resolutions were passed on how the Alliance could best develop its work for peace, and Archbishop Nathan Söderblom of Sweden introduced the idea of an international Christian conference and suggested creation of an "ecumenical council" which would represent Christianity in the spiritual realm.

As this proposal could not be taken up by the World Alliance, it was followed through at a conference in Geneva in 1920 which ultimately led to the Universal Christian Conference on Life and Work in Stockholm in 1925, whose basis was shaped by the COPEC conference of 1924, the greatest undertaking thus far to focus Christian thought and action on the urgent problems of the day.

Darril Hudson's *The Ecumenical Movement in World Affairs* **(13)** considers the Hague peace conference of 1907 the beginning of political, social and economic action by the Christian churches on an international scale. He analyzes the global role of Protestant Christianity as an important pressure group which became a decisive factor in the growth of the ecumenical movement.

A 1929 peace conference of 500 delegates at Prague climaxed the history of the World Alliance. Asserting the "paramount duty of the Christian church to strive for the mental and moral disarmament of the people in all countries and to lead them at the same time to insist upon a rapid and universal reduction of armaments and the adoption of methods of arbitration and mediation in the settlement of all international disputes", the Alliance encouraged the churches to support wholeheartedly the work of the League of Nations.

From 1931 to 1937 the World Alliance and the Universal Christian Council for Life and Work were closely related through common offices in Geneva, a joint general secretary, joint youth work and a common bulletin, *The Churches in Action* **(4)**. In 1938, however, the World Alliance decided to remain "an autonomous movement which serves the churches" rather than to join Faith and Order and Life and Work in forming the World Council of Churches.

Tentative evaluations

Several essays written in the 1930s, collected in *The Church through Half a Century* **(10)**, take stock of the gradual unfolding of Christian social thought. In "The Social Interpretation of Christianity", John C. Bennett summarizes the attitude of Christian thinkers towards the kingdom of God and its relation to human progress in three stages:

> The first was a stage of lyrical optimism, though... Rauschenbusch saw deeply into the stubbornness of the forces making for social evil. The second was a stage of restrained optimism haunted by the immediate tragedy of the war and by the possibility of future catastrophe. The third stage, in which we are now, is one of profound puzzlement and social fear. Hope is not dead but eager expectation is

dead. Our sense of what is possible in history is being revised. Many of us are seeking a basis for loyalty to the purposes of God in history which does not depend upon expectation of results in our time (p.119).

An equally realistic note is struck by Henry Smith Leiper in his essay "Ecumenical Christianity". Aware of the need for simplifying the ecumenical movement in order "to secure a much more consolidated front", he states:

There are complex tasks to be accomplished by the uniting churches. They are varied tasks; they require different techniques and appeal to men of unlike gifts and temperaments. Much could be lost as well as gained by pooling these interests too completely. An omnibus ecumenical movement to which was committed the missionary enterprise, as well as all the other world tasks, for each of which there has grown up a unique organization, might easily break down under the sheer weight of its responsibilities and the limitations of time, intelligence, ability and mere physical strength which nature imposes on the men and women who have to do the work (p.389).

In his essay on "The Development of Ecumenical Social Thought and Action" **(22)**, Paul Abrecht observes that

in the beginning co-operation was hampered by the lack of substantial agreement concerning the theological foundations of Christian action in society and also by disagreements about the method by which Christian thought should proceed in determining the Christian's role in society. It has been well said that, in the first ecumenical discussions of social questions, "there was no common body of social thought, no common experience in dealing with these issues, not even any agreement as to which issues were of primary importance. There was only a common concern about the urgency of the world's need for social reconstruction... and a common conviction that Christians and the Christian churches were called to play a part in that reconstruction" (p.235).

The quotation is taken from *Statements of the World Council of Churches on Social Questions* **(25)**, p.6.

Contending that the church must recover lost ground after abandoning the whole area of human activity for several centuries, Archbishop William Temple insisted in *Christianity and Social Order* **(19)** that the task of the Christian community is to work out a scale of values for the socio-political field:

> In this enterprise we shall be censured for departure from our own contention that the church is concerned with principles and not with policy. For the framing of policy, knowledge of contemporary facts and that power to estimate tendencies which comes only from specialist study are indispensable. But a statement of principles will carry us to ground commonly left during the last few centuries to purely secular forces; it is bound to seem like an intrusion into practical politics, even when it scrupulously stops short. And the line of demarcation is not very clear.
>
> It may be possible to draw it with more definiteness when we have reviewed the history of the church's enterprise or lack of it in this field, and we have set out some of the principles concerned. The aim, however, is clear throughout. The Christian citizen is required in his civic action (e.g. voting) to promote the best interest of his country with a Christian interpretation of the word "best"; the aim of any formulation of Christian social principles is to provide that Christian interpretation or at least the means of reaching it (pp.27f.).

In his analysis of the understanding of humankind in ecumenical discourse, Gert Rüppell shows the extent to which ecumenical social thought took shape in a phase of global political and economic expansion of Europe on the one hand, and of internal economic restructuring on the other. The churches were confronted with the need to adapt to new realities. Most of the process of adaptation in the realm of social thought took place in movements rather than in the mainstream churches. Thus there was not a sufficient response to the challenges arising in social thought outside the Christian thinking. The churches' concern was to Christianize culture and respond to the new realities within the framework of familiar ethics and the ideology of a *res publica christiana* (*Einheit ist Unteilbar*, Rothenburg, Ernst Lange Institut, 1992, pp.119ff.).

As we shall see in the next chapter, the process of seeking a basis of loyalty to the purposes of God in history, the creation of a common body of social thought, the awareness of the sheer weight of Christian responsibility and the courage to challenge purely secular forces was slow and uncertain. Yet this process has been fundamental to the development of ecumenical social thinking.

II

From Stockholm 1925 to Edinburgh 1937

Nils Ehrenström offers a detailed historical record of institutional ecumenical developments from the mid-1920s to the outbreak of the second world war in his essay on "Movements for International Friendship and Life and Work 1925-1948" **(11)**. Another important source is Charles S. Macfarland's *Steps toward the World Council* **(18)**. Several recent books and articles deal more objectively and critically with the reservations and frustrations, frictions and misunderstandings which hampered the churches in their effort to define and carry out their common social responsibility. After a long period of self-centred isolation during which each church went its own way and concentrated on its own immediate tasks, difficult and concerted efforts were needed if a common voice was to be heard in a time when the grave human issues had taken on a global dimension.

Stockholm 1925

It took more than five years of preparation to assemble over 500 delegates in Stockholm in August 1925 for the first Universal Christian Conference on Life and Work. From 1920 onwards an arrangements committee, constantly enlarged, held six preparatory meetings, each making a distinct step forward. It may have sensed the sinister forces developing in the political life of the world, but it was far from seeing clearly the issues which would face the next world conference on Life and Work in Oxford in 1937.

The letter inviting the churches to Stockholm stated that "the world's greatest need is the Christian way of life, not merely in personal and social behaviour but in public opinion and its outcome in public action", a goal which involved "putting our hearts and our hands into a united effort that God's will may be done on earth as it is in heaven". It continued with an outline of the agenda of the conference:

> To this end... we will consider such concrete questions as that of industry and property, in relation to the kingdom of God; what the church should teach and do to help create right relations between the different and at times warring classes and groups in the community; how to promote friendship between the nations and thus lay the only sure foundation upon which permanent international peace can be built [*The Stockholm Conference 1925* **(2)**, p.18].

The message of the conference was its only official utterance. It contained expressions of penitence for the churches' failure to do their duty and affirmed their obligation to apply the gospel "in all realms of human life — industrial, social, political and international". But it described the primary mission of the church as "to state principles and to assert the ideal, while leaving to individual consciences and to communities the duty of applying them with charity, wisdom and courage"; and it looked beyond the churches for "allies in this holy cause" — youth, those seeking after truth by whatever way and the workers of the world, many of whom "are acting in accordance with these principles". Thus Stockholm did not offer "precise solutions" or put the results of its "friendly discussions" to a vote.

Nevertheless, its scope was wide-ranging, as the message summarizes:

> We have set forth the guiding principles of a Christian internationalism, equally opposed to a national bigotry and a weak cosmopolitanism. We have affirmed the universal character of the church and its duty to preach and practise the love of the brethren. We have considered the relation of the individual conscience to the state. We have examined the race problem, the subject of law and arbitration and the constitution of an international order which would provide peaceable methods for removing the causes of war — questions which in the tragic conditions of today make so deepan appeal to our hearts. We summon the churches to share with us our sense of the horror of war, and of its futility as a means of settling international disputes (pp.727f.).

Like the preparation of the conference, its follow-up was due almost exclusively to Archbishop Nathan Söderblom's personal initiatives and surpassing breadth of vision. In his introduction to *Nathan Söderblom: A Prophet of Christian Unity* by Peter Katz (London, J. Clarke, 1946), George Bell stated that Söderblom "did more than any other Christian leader or teacher of his time to unite Orthodox and evangelical churches of all nations and communions in a common fellowship" (p.10).

Though Stockholm is well known for the slogan "doctrine divides, service unites", the conference was in fact confronted by a profound theological difference which made full agreement on social responsibility impossible. Despite the tragedy of the first world war and a deep moral frustration because of its results, representatives from the Anglo-Saxon churches adhered to the social gospel and remained optimistic about realizing aspects of the kingdom of God in history as a result of human progress. A few, like William Temple, had a more sophisticated theological understanding of the church in relation to society, but they too were rather confident about possible Christian achievement. Voices from continental Europe, particularly from Germany, stated an opposite conviction; that there is no relation between the kingdom of God and human efforts to achieve justice and peace in this sinful world. Though a rather small minority at Stockholm, their view was widely held in Protestant churches, and it was the sort of theological difference that made cooperation on social issues extremely difficult. At a much later stage the Faith and Order movement would deal with this difference in its own way.

The International Christian Social Institute of the Life and Work movement, which was founded in 1926 and later became the Study Department of the World Council of Churches, was rather successful in laying down principles, lines of activity and methods which have since become essential parts of the ecumenical movement. Hampered throughout its life by inadequate financial support, especially after the economic depression of the 1930s, it was not always able to put its purposes into effect.

In his article "Breakthrough in Ecumenical Social Ethics" **(211)**, John C. Bennett observes that

in the two decades before Oxford there had developed on the European continent a revival of historical Protestant theology with

Karl Barth as the great leader and stimulus. This theological revival stressed the transcendence of God, the prevalence of sin in persons and in human cultures and institutions, the uniqueness of the biblical revelation with its centre in Christ and the contrast between it and human wisdom and moral understanding. The relation between the kingdom of God and history was chiefly the contrast between them (p.135).

Nils Ehrenström summed up the clash of the different theological-ethical convictions in his essay cited above **(11)**:

> The tension between the different conceptions of the kingdom of God came to dominate much of the discussion and, because not squarely faced, led to continual misunderstanding. This misunderstanding was not eased when the theological issue was confused with national and confessional categories — such as American activism versus German other-worldliness, or Calvinism against Lutheranism. Here an anti-thesis was revealed — partly theological, partly geographical and cultural — which in changing manifestations was to preoccupy the movement for many years to come (p.547).

Comparing developments in ecumenical social thought with Roman Catholic social thinking as reflected in the social encyclicals from *Rerum novarum* (1891) to *Quadragesimo anno* (1931), Paul Abrecht **(22)** suggests that

> whereas in later years Roman Catholicism had to overcome an uncompromising rejection of socialism and Marxism, non-Roman social thinkers were obliged to rid themselves of some illusions about man and society which an idealist socialist reading of the Bible had fostered. The economic depression in Western capitalist countries and the rise of the totalitarian political systems in Europe showed the inadequacy of some of the theological and ethical ideas with which the church was working. A deeper theological basis was needed (p.238).

Chapter XIII will be devoted to a more systematic attempt to compare pronouncements on social questions by the Holy See and the World Council of Churches.

The greatest weakness in the composition of the Stockholm conference was the level of participation of the younger churches outside the Western hemisphere. Only six nationals were present from

India, China and Japan. But this weakness did not characterize Stockholm alone. Not until the world conference on Church and Society in Geneva in 1966 did social and political ecumenism cease to be an essentially Western phenomenon. In 1925 travel and finance were major obstacles, and these churches were still considered to be the province of the International Missionary Council.

From 1910 onwards the ecumenical missionary movement had also found its attention ineluctably drawn to the social environment in which the churches live and speak, particularly to the conditions of society in countries where missionary work was being done. The subjects of "The Christian Mission in the Light of Race Conflict", "Christianity and the Growth of Industrialism in Asia, Africa and South America", and "The Christian Mission in Relation to Rural Problems" were major focal points at the conference of the International Missionary Council in Jerusalem in 1928 (*Report of the Jerusalem Meeting of the International Missionary Council, 1928*, London, Oxford UP, 1928, vols 4-6).

After the Jerusalem conference, the International Missionary Council set up a Department of Social and Industrial Research and Counsel in Geneva, in order "to collect and distribute information on the economic and social developments which challenge the gospel of Christ and limit the growth of his kingdom among the younger churches". Ten years later its next world conference in Tambaram, India, included sections on "The Economic Base of the Church", "The Church and the Changing Social and Economic Order" and "The Church and the State" (*Tambaram Series*, London, Oxford UP, 1939, vols 5-6).

Between 1925 and 1937 the Universal Christian Conference for Life and Work grew from a rather amorphous continuation committee into a close-knit organization with an ecumenical council, active sectional units for geographical areas and a permanent secretariat in Geneva under the direction of Henry Louis Henriod. Much energy went into preparing for a second world conference, more authoritatively representative and wider in scope than Stockholm and involving far more intensive preparatory work than was possible in 1925.

The biennial meeting of the Council in Fanø, Denmark, in 1934, was a critical and decisive one. Here the Council resolved to throw its weight on the side of the Confessing Church in Germany — against the so-called German Christians and, by implication, the Nazi régime. It was decided to focus the world conference in 1937 on the theme "Church, Community and State" and to seek to mobilize the forces of the churches for a combined investigation of these issues.

A key figure in the International Missionary Council from 1921 to 1938, Joseph H. Oldham became the chief architect of the Oxford conference. Oldham invested in this new venture all his wisdom and experience, his rare knowledge of human beings and world affairs and his gift of imparting his own missionary zeal to others. The preparatory study programme he organized for the conference on the spiritual-ethical basis of the church's task in the world became a model of ecumenical common study. This brought the Life and Work movement out of its early tendency towards idealism and utopianism and provided it with carefully thought-out positions on various social and political matters.

Oxford 1937

The Oxford conference took place in a year of deep crisis and international disturbance. The global economic and social situation had been steadily worsening since the beginning of the 1930s. The effects of the economic depression in the advanced industrial countries had spread around the world, and the resulting social tensions convulsed practically every society. The danger of a worldwide clash between church and state, which at Stockholm had appeared only as a small cloud on the horizon, had spread over the sky by Oxford.

The débacle of the Orthodox Church in Russia and the reverberations of the church struggle in Germany were a pervasive presence during the two-week conference. The inevitable absence of delegates from the German Evangelical Church was an unmistakable sign of threat and upheaval, but there was scarcely a nation represented where the possibility of conflict between church and state was not observable.

With 300 delegates, named by more than 120 churches in 45 countries, Oxford was more a working conference than Stockholm. The impressive preparations presented an adequate consensus of opinion of the different ecclesiastical traditions. The attendance of distinguished scholars and persons experienced in political affairs guaranteed a note of actuality and proportion in the conference's pronouncements. The study volumes, especially on the Oxford theme, served to stimulate thinking in theological faculties, in forums and among lay groups. While the direct comment on the reports solicited from the churches was "disappointingly meagre", according to Visser 't Hooft, he attributed this to the fact that "most churches had as yet no corporate and relevant teaching on the problems of society and felt, therefore, unable to express an official opinion on the findings of Oxford" (*The Ten Formative Years 1938-1948*, Geneva, WCC, 1948, p.28).

The delegates were divided about whether it is morally permissible to bear arms under modern conditions of warfare, though unanimous in seeing war as a fruit and manifestation of sin. The message of Oxford urged the unity of Christians in an unbroken fellowship of prayer "if war breaks out". Unity in Christ, as an actuality already illustrated at Oxford, was the central affirmation of the message; and the conference, noting "the efforts of those movements which are working for the cause of international understanding through the churches", rejoiced in the recommendation to create a World Council of Churches. The conference chose a committee of seven members who, together with a similar committee named by the Faith and Order conference in Edinburgh in 1937, met in Utrecht in 1938 to begin the process of uniting these two branches of the ecumenical movement into a World Council of Churches.

The report of the Oxford conference remains to this day the most comprehensive statement on problems of church and society and Christian responsibility. The following excerpts from the report, *The Churches Survey Their Task* (3), taken from the sections on "Church and Community", "Church and State" and "Church, Community and State in Relation to the Economic Order", are models of ecumenical statements on social issues.

Church and community. The difficulty of deciding how far in particular instances the Christian should go in cooperation with ways of life which are in greater or less degree contrary to God's will is often great; and the danger of self-deception is always present. No general principle of guidance can be laid down. That the ways of the community or nation may reach such a pitch of evil that there is no option for the church but to repudiate them altogether, and even at times refuse cooperation with them, can hardly be questioned in view of contemporary events, but just where that point is must be left to the guidance of the Spirit... This is the tragic and continuous tension in which the church is always placed, the tension between the pure ideals of the kingdom and the unredeemed community of men in which it has to live and bear its witness. But so soon as it seeks peace by becoming unconscious of that tension then it is traitorous to its Master and Lord (pp.70f).

Church and state. We recognize that the state as a specific form and the dominating expression of man's life in this world of sin, by its very power and its monopoly of the means of coercion, often becomes an instrument of evil. Since we believe in the holy God as the source of justice, we do not consider the state as the ultimate source of law but rather its guarantor. It is not the lord, but the servant of justice. There can be for the Christian no ultimate authority but very God (pp.78f.).

Church, community and state in relation to the economic order. Industrial expansion and technical progress have tended to defeat their own ends. In place of free trade and free competition, which were characteristic principles of the earlier expansionist period of capitalism, protectionist measures were adopted by the state and monopolies were established in many fields of economic enterprise... The consequent contraction of markets accentuated the competitions of nations for the remaining markets of the world. Through this development, the earlier stage of competitive capitalism has been gradually replaced by the monopolistic stage, and this economic change has brought with it corresponding political consequences. On the one hand, the economic process has been increasingly subjected to state control and interference; and, on the other hand, leading industrial and financial groups have been tempted to obtain the support of the state for their particular interests, and the original ideal of modern democracy has thus in practice become increasingly difficult to achieve (pp.100f.).

The competitive superiority of large-scale production has gone far to destroy the old traditional society of craftsmen and farmers, and thereby has created a society which is characterized in many countries by the concentration of wealth on the one hand, and the existence of large urban masses on the other. The progressive mechanization of industry has periodically thrown large numbers of workers into long periods of unemployment. The cycle of industrial fluctuations has caused a tremendous waste of productive power and, in consequence, "poverty in the midst of plenty" (p.99).

The phrase "Let the church be the church", often cited as a summary of the spirit of Oxford, does not in fact appear in the report. The Message says: "The first duty of the church, and its greatest service to the world, is that it be in very deed the church — confessing the true faith, committed to the fulfilment of the will of Christ, its only Lord, and united in him in a fellowship of love and service." As Bennett notes **(211)**, "those words do not express the spirit of triumphalism which might be read into the shorter phrase, but call for the freedom of the church from false authorities of state or culture and for the self-criticism that pervades these reports" (pp.136f).

The ecumenical social witness of church leaders like Bell, Oldham, Temple and Visser 't Hooft and theologians representing new trends in Christian thought like Barth, Emil Brunner and Reinhold Niebuhr insisted that it was an error to identify any particular social system with the will of God or to equate it with God's kingdom. Stressing the egoism, pride and hypocrisy of nations and classes, Reinhold Niebuhr strongly argued for a Christian realism and insisted on the support of political policies that carefully delineate the limits of power.

The Oxford section report on the economic order echoes this stance:

> Every tendency to identify the kingdom of God with a particular social structure or economic mechanism must result in moral confusion for those who maintain the system and in disillusionment for those who suffer from its limitations. The former will regard conformity with its standards as identical with the fulfilment of the law, thus falling into the sin of pharisaism. The latter will be tempted to a cynical disavowal of the religion because it falsely gives absolute worth to partial values and achievements. Both errors are essentially heretical from the point of view of Christian faith. The one denies the reality of the kingdom of God in history; the other equates the kingdom of God with the processes of history. In the one case, the ultimate and eternal destiny of human existence, which transcends history, is made to support an attitude of indifference towards historical social issues; in the other case, the eternal destiny of human

existence is denied or obscured. [*Foundations of Ecumenical Social Thought* **(212)**, p.35].

From this it follows that a Christian social order is impossible and that social problems cannot be solved by a direct application of Christian "moral principles". A Christian ethics of justice derived from the love commandment must face both the difficulty of directly applying this commandment and the reality of evil. Thus, the Bible offers no direct solutions for contemporary political and social conflicts. Moreover, the place of power in the struggles for justice must be acknowledged. The state is necessary, but its dependence on power relativizes its authority. Finally, Christians must both critique liberal democracy, without repudiating the democratic principle, and reject atheistic and totalitarian communism, while not joining the self-righteous Western anti-communist crusade.

Countering certain Lutheran interpretations of social ethics, Oxford emphasized that

> the laws of justice are not purely negative. They are not merely "dikes against sin". The political and economic structure of society is also the mechanical skeleton which carries the organic elements of society. Forms of production and methods of cooperation may serve the cause of human brotherhood by serving and extending the principle of love beyond the sphere of purely personal relations (p.33).

The conference used the expression "middle axioms", which had been introduced by Oldham in the preparatory material, though without elaborating extensively on it. This was an attempt to define an orientation for participation in the life of society by churches and Christians that was concrete enough to give direction in specific situations without becoming a rigid law. According to José Miguez Bonino:

> Theologically, the quest for such criteria originates, on the one hand, in the crisis of both the natural law and the "creation orders" foundations for social ethics and, on the other hand, in the crisis of the idealism of the social gospel and the kingdom of God. Oldham locates this criterion in his distinction between an ethics of "ends" and an ethics of "inspiration" which struggles to discern God's marching orders for God's people at particular points in history. Siding with this second line, he tries to combine a strong Christological orienta-

tion on the lordship of Christ — closely bound to the biblical revelation — and an understanding of the present conditions of society. In this double context he speaks of the church's "discerning the signs of the time and in each crisis of history fulfilling its appointed task" (*Dictionary of the Ecumenical Movement*, Geneva, WCC, 1991, p.675).

After Oxford 1937

Abrecht **(211)** sees the major achievement of the Oxford conference as its resolution of the theological-ethical disputes which blocked progress at Stockholm:

> By emphasizing the provisional character of all Christian efforts at social and economic policy-making, the Oxford conference helped avoid the danger of churches making ecclesiastical/theological commitments to contemporary social-ideological fashions. By its emphasis on cooperation with the social sciences and on the contribution of the Christian laity, it helped to prepare the way for a new type of Christian social thinking, avoiding... ecclesiastical pontification and moralizing...
>
> What is remarkable is how long the consensus of Oxford endured, indeed how much of it still applies... It remains... an influential option in ecumenical social thought despite subsequent challenges from other theological-ethical views. Yet the emphasis on the Stockholm pole also persists and is very much to the fore today, particularly... in the contemporary period of liberation ecumenism" (p.150).

Even as the second world war raged, preparations for peace and reconstruction became a priority for the World Council of Churches in process of formation. The understanding of interchurch aid quickly broadened from the traditional social and economic help that one church gives to another of the same communion, to joint action in Christian solidarity crossing confessional and geographical boundaries, to common Christian stewardship towards the human family assisting people in need whoever and wherever they are. Rescuing Jews threatened with deportation to concentration camps, providing material and spiritual care to refugees, organizing chaplaincy services to prisoners of war, building relations with resistance movements, shipping food, clothing and medicines to large groups of suffering people — these were, during those years, virtually the sole raison d'être of the World Council of Churches.

This is confirmed by Visser 't Hooft's *Memoirs* **(226)**, whose chapters on the "Swiss Road", relations with the German resistance, the extermination of the European Jews, preparing for peace and reconstruction and the post-war task of reconciliation are the most moving part of his recollections. It was as if reflections on unity, witness and the relation between church and society receded into the background in face of the daunting challenges of interchurch aid then facing the whole ecumenical family, which in turn knitted it more closely together.

In *The Genesis and Formation of the World Council of Churches* **(224)**, Visser 't Hooft notes:

> The war years strengthened the determination of the churches to manifest their fellowship. This is shown most clearly by the fact that, in this period of crisis and uncertainty, so many churches decided to participate in the establishment of the World Council. At the first meeting after the war, it was reported that ninety had already accepted the invitation, and thus expressed their confidence in the future of the Council (p.59).

The formative years of ecumenical social thinking were, as we have seen, shaped by the contextual questions of the North. Not only was there little participation of persons from the South, but where they were present there was little understanding of their problems and their critical evaluation of the movement's Eurocentric approaches. This foreshadowed the relationship that would increasingly emerge at a later stage, especially after the integration of the International Missionary Council into the WCC in 1961, broadening the worldview within the movement and beginning a discussion on social ethics that would take into account the life-and-death concerns of the majority of humankind.

III

General Developments 1948-1968

When the ecumenical discussion on social thought resumed after the second world war, the global situation had completely changed. Europe was in ruins, vividly illustrating the human "disorder" identified in the theme of the Amsterdam assembly. Colonial empires were breaking down, and the years to come would see the independence of former Asian and African colonies. "Rapid Social Change" was thus not only a preoccupation of the decolonized countries, but an issue for the colonizers as well. States and churches had to adapt to a situation in which most of the previous paradigms of social thought had to be re-evaluated and most of the discussion of social concerns would be influenced by the ideological undercurrent and hostilities emanating from the East-West conflict.

In 1946 a commission was appointed to prepare the third section of the Amsterdam assembly on "The Church and the Disorder of Society". Many of its members had been leaders at the Oxford conference in 1937: Oldham, Niebuhr, Brunner, Ehrenström, Bennett and Nicolas Berdyaev. Among the newcomers were M.M. Thomas, Jacques Ellul and C.L. Patijn, all of whom were to play a substantial role in the development of ecumenical social thought in the ensuing decade.

The Amsterdam assembly's report recommended that the WCC and the churches focus on three key areas: (1) the social concerns which should guide post-war political and economic reconstruction; (2) the churches' response to the Cold War and its ideological character; (3) the human problems associated with rapid technological change, especially in relation to the meaning of work.

In 1948 the WCC Study Department initiated an enquiry into "Christian Action in Society" which included two major sections:

"The Responsible Society" and "The Meaning of Work". Since the former topic is dealt with extensively in Chapter V, mention will be made here only of four particular projects which were significant in the pursuit of it: (1) Moral Problems in Economic and Political Life Today; (2) The Responsible Society and European Problems; (3) The Witness of Christians in Communist Countries; (4) The Responsibility of Christians for the Social Problems of the Underdeveloped Countries.

A WCC study of economic and social justice began in 1952 with the publication of a study paper by Denys Munby, an Oxford economist, on "Moral Problems in the Economic Situation Today" (later expanded into a book, *Christianity and Economic Problems*). Munby's work initiated a discussion of economic justice issues in preparation for the Evanston assembly, which continued in the 1955-61 "Rapid Social Change" study and developed further in preparation for the world conference on Church and Society in 1966.

With regard to the second project, an Ecumenical Commission on European Cooperation (later the Committee on the Christian Responsibility for European Cooperation) was formed in 1950 to help the European churches reflect on these issues from an ecumenical perspective. This group of Christian politicians and interested theologians and church leaders from practically every country of Western Europe continued to meet twice a year between 1950 and 1961.

The situation of Christians and churches under communist rule was a particular source of tension in the ecumenical movement from the beginning, constantly threatening to divide the new-found fellowship. The victory of communism in China in 1949, the strong anti-communist movement in the US, the outbreak of war in Korea in 1950, the uprising in Berlin in 1953, the revolt in Hungary in 1956 — all produced a climate of social, political, ideological and military conflict. The WCC struggled to help its member churches to avoid identifying with the Cold War spirit without denying the fundamental theological-ethical issues at stake in the struggle. The Responsible Society encouraged the churches to distance themselves from both ideological extremes. Among the ecumenical consultations between 1949 and 1954 which addressed this issue was one organized by the WCC and several national Christian councils in East Asia in Bangkok in December 1949. Its report drew a distinction between "the social revolution which seeks justice" and "the totalitarian ideology" which perverts it:

> The Christian church must welcome the demand of the people for a fuller participation in the life of society at the level where power is exercised, since this is an expression of human dignity; and the rise of communism is a judgment on the churches for their failure to do so. Nevertheless the struggle for justice frustrates itself if the evil forces inherent in any human situation are not held in check. Because communism lacks a conception of the independence of moral reality over against power, it denies the supremacy of the moral law over power politics and hence in the long run defeats the very purpose of the social revolution. This ideological error in communism, which turns a social revolution for justice into a new oppression, arises out of the self-righteousness of its militant atheism; and at this point the conflict between Christianity and communism is fundamental.

In addition, the Study Department issued papers on the subject, and in 1950 it began publishing a quarterly bulletin, *Background Information on Church and Society*, presenting reports coming to the World Council (especially to the general secretary) about the experience of churches in communist countries. (This was later extended to include information about all churches in situations of social tension and radical social change. Publication of the bulletin continued until 1970.) Moreover, in 1951 the political commission of the World Student Christian Federation (WSCF) produced a study book, *The Christian in the World Struggle* by M.M. Thomas and J.D. McCaughey, which was a notable contribution to the discussion of Responsible Society in relation to the contemporary debates on communism and capitalism.

As to the fourth project, an ecumenical study conference in Lucknow, India, in 1952 offered an opportunity for beginning a systematic study of the problems of the responsible society in East Asia and for the more direct participation of the churches there in ecumenical studies on social questions. The need for "radical reform of land tenure systems" was first identified at this conference as essential to a "positive programme for social justice" in East Asia.

The WCC's second assembly (Evanston 1954) not only reaffirmed the views of Amsterdam on the Responsible Society, but went far beyond them in seeking to relate this idea to actual social problems. Priority in sections III and IV went to social and economic problems in the economically underdeveloped regions. By establishing the Department on Church and Society within the Division of Studies, the assembly delineated organizationally the concern of the World Council for social questions and assured that its own statements on social questions would be systematically followed up.

Evanston affirmed responsibility for Christian peace and justice and urged governments to ban all weapons of mass destruction and abstain from aggression. There were also statements on religious liberty and "intergroup relations", insisting on racial equality. Continuing the Amsterdam discussion, Evanston stressed even more strongly the missionary task of the laity, which "bridges the gulf between the church and the world" and "stands at the very outposts of the kingdom of God".

Post-Evanston discussion of the Responsible Society included a regional study conference on "The Responsible Society in National and International Affairs" in Arnoldshain, Germany, in 1956. Its report outlined five specific aspects of the changing social situation: (1) the problems of a dynamic society; (2) areas of rapid social change in Asia, Africa and Latin America; (3) Christian responsibility in relation to the state and voluntary groups; (4) the worker and modern industrial problems in relation to the church; (5) the farmer and the problem of rural population in a changing society. This conference helped to draw attention to the worldwide nature of social change and to establish the connection between the idea of the responsible society and the Christian attitude to change.

Rapid Social Change, 1955-1960

The purpose and scope of this study were expounded in two statements published in 1955 and 1956, which declared that rapid social change was challenging the churches in four major areas: (1) political independence and nationalism; (2) industrial and urban development; (3) rural and village life; (4) the impact of the West. The study was carried out internationally, regionally and nationally. The WCC staff was directed by a working committee and 25 special consultants who met annually to review progress and planned an international study conference in Thessalonica, Greece, in 1959. For many of the so-called younger churches in Africa, Asia and Latin America, the Rapid Social Change study was their first organizational contact with the World Council of Churches. The tension created by the study between Church and Society and the missionary societies was especially evident at the Thessalonica conference.

Challenging the familiar ecumenical emphasis on reform and gradual social change, enquiries in the new nations pointed to the rapid breakdown of old social systems and traditions and the need for political and economic systems to support rapid development. Although Western Christian thought was deeply concerned about secularization, it still assumed a society greatly influenced by Christian values and institutions. By contrast, Christian social thinkers in the new nations tended to emphasize the Christian contribution to a pluralistic social ethic which would promote human values in a national perspective and objected to the bias in the Western churches' confidence in the traditional structures of world politics and economics. They challenged the assumption of an "international law" developed by the Western powers and imposed on the rest of the world and stressed the creative role of the new nation-states in the work of development and in creating a new sense of human dignity and self-respect.

The report of the Thessalonica conference **(47)** illustrated this challenge to traditional ecumenical social thinking:

> In the earlier years of the ecumenical movement, and particularly at the Oxford conference of 1937, the subject of nationalism was fully discussed. But in view of the circumstances at that time, attention was concentrated almost exclusively on the nationalist movement in Western countries. The specific task in the light of the present situation is to concentrate on a different kind of nationalism in a different phase of history in the areas of rapid social change, especially Asia and Africa... The nationalism of hitherto subject peoples and races gives tangible form to their awakening to a sense of human dignity and their struggle to discover and express their corporate selfhood. This nationalism finds the focus of its unity in the sense of common fate and common fight, that is, in the common determination of peoples to free themselves from alien political domination and racial discrimination (p.55).

Similarly, in the area of economic development Thessalonica pointed to the need for a new understanding of world economic justice and welfare:

> Our ultimate aim should be a situation where there is no unnecessary poverty among nations, and where each nation by the use of its resources and abilities attacks its own conditions of poverty and contributes to the well-being of the whole... Those with greater resources and abilities have the greater obligations. This applies between countries as much as within countries... There is an enormous amount that can and should be done... Above all, the rich countries need to be aware of the impact of what they do on others. In many cases their contribution to economic development in Asia, Africa and Latin America is totally inadequate (p.74).

The churches soon realized that their social thinking was in need of a major re-examination. New problems arising from global political and social change brought new ideas about the task of the church in society. The WCC's third assembly (New Delhi, 1961) was unprepared to cope with the new situation, in part because the meeting was overwhelmed by the Indian venue and by the vast number of newcomers representing many new member churches from the third world, the USSR and other Eastern European countries, as well as the first appearance of observers from the Vatican. In the face of "the accelerating speed, the intensity, the worldwide sweep and the complexity of converging social, political and economic revolutions", it spoke of "*fear*, because so much that is treasured seems to be in danger of destruction; *conservatism* that seeks to preserve and defend as much as possible of the old and familiar structures of society; *passive acceptance* that deplores change, but accepts it as something inevitable that must be endured; *positive acceptance* that welcomes change as an opportunity to promote self-interest; *positive acceptance* that welcomes change as an opportunity to provide a fuller and more satisfying life for mankind" (*The New Delhi Report*, New York, Association Press, 1962, p.94). Thus the assembly could only recognize the new world problems and suggest that further ecumenical analysis and consultation were needed, using the insights of churches and Christians from *every* continent. It was in recognition of the scope and the urgency of this task that the proposal for a world conference on Church and Society arose.

Geneva 1966

Meeting in Paris in 1962, the central committee approved the proposal for this world conference and authorized Church and Society to begin preparations for it. It agreed that the conference should be empowered to speak *to* rather than *for* the churches and the World Council, thus giving it freedom to explore issues and suggest new approaches at a time when the churches saw themselves confronted with a number of new challenges. For example, the civil rights movement in the US had brought to the forefront the question of racism; urbanization was posing enormous problems as well as hopes for the future of humankind; technological developments had not only created devastating weapons but also enabled humankind to see its fragile planet from the new perspective of space and to realize the perils it faced.

The central place the Geneva conference attained in future ecumenical discussion of social issues was partly due to the strong lay representation and the large number of representatives from the non-Western world. Of the 420 participants, about equal numbers came from the third world, North America and Western Europe, making it the first large ecumenical conference in which the participants from the Western countries were not in a majority. Among the laypersons present were 50 political leaders and civil servants, 19 businessmen and industrialists, 28 economists, 36 professional persons and 9 workers or trade union leaders. There were also observers from the specialized agencies of the United Nations.

The eight observers delegated by the Vatican included both lay persons and theologians. Their international outlook and sympathetic understanding of the conference's purposes proved to be a great help in interpreting it to the whole Christian world. Two pre-conference WCC-Roman Catholic consultations on Christian social thought had helped to acquaint each side with what the other was doing in the field of Christian social thinking. The reports of these consultations were published in *Study Encounter* **(200)**.

The papal encyclical *Populorum progressio* in 1967 supported similar goals of world development and opened another door to common Christian action. The WCC and the Roman Catholic Church formed a joint Exploratory Committee on Society, Development and Peace (SODEPAX); and the Pontifical Commission on Justice and

Peace and the WCC sponsored a conference on World Cooperation for Development in Beirut in April 1968, the first major international Christian conference to be so jointly organized and financed. (Roman Catholic social thought is treated further in Chapter XIII.)

During the three years of preparations for the Geneva conference, four volumes of essays on worldwide social and political change were published: *Christian Social Ethics in a Changing World* **(49)**, *Responsible Government in a Revolutionary Age* **(50)**, *Economic Growth in World Perspective* **(51)**, *Man in Community* **(52)**. The basic work of the conference was done in four sections: Economic Development in a World Perspective; The Nature and Function of the State in a Revolutionary Age; Structures of International Cooperation — Living Together in Peace in a Pluralistic World Society; Man and Community in Changing Societies. In addition there were three conference working groups on issues which cut across the concerns of the sections: Theological Issues in Social Ethics; Potentialities of the Contemporary Technological and Scientific Revolution; The Church's Action in Society.

While recognizing the appeal and challenge of some of the revolutionary ideas and social developments in the 1960s, the Geneva conference did not itself endorse general revolutionary action. Nor did it abandon the Oxford-Amsterdam-Evanston theological understanding of the function of the church in society. The unresolved differences and disagreements about revolutionary action by Christians are addressed in the sixth paragraph of the Message, published in the conference report *Christians in the Technical and Social Revolutions of Our Time* **(53)**:

> As Christians we are committed to working for the transformation of society. In the past, we have usually done this through quiet efforts at social renewal, working in and through the established institutions according to their rules. Today, a significant number of those who are dedicated to the service of Christ and their neighbour assume a more radical or revolutionary position. They do not deny the value of tradition nor of social order, but they are searching for a new strategy by which to bring about basic changes in society without too much delay. It is possible that the tension between these two positions will have an important place in the life of the Christian community for some time to come. At the present moment, it is important for us to

recognize that this radical position has a solid foundation in Christian tradition and should have its rightful place in the life of the church and in the ongoing discussion of social responsibility (p.49).

In a statement on "A Theological Understanding of Social Change", the conference echoed Oxford's theological and ethical insights in declaring that, whatever the degree of support for revolutionary action taken by Christians, they cannot escape the judgment of biblical faith on all human action:

> The Christian knows by faith that no structure of society, no system of human power and security is perfectly just, and that every system falls under the judgment of God in so far as it is unable to reform itself in response to the call for justice of those who are under its power. There is no divinely ordained social order, and not every change as such, nor every status quo as such, is necessarily good. There are only relative, secular structures subject to constant revision in the light of new human needs. There is in history a dynamic of evil as well as a dynamic of good. God's action is continually reshaping the order of human power, humiliating the proud and the rich and lifting up the oppressed (p.200).

Yet the reports of both the second and third sections include brief discussions that provide justification for revolution against the established order. Both sections make a distinction between covert and overt violence and argue that revolutionary overt violence may sometimes be a lesser evil than what Section II called "the violence which, though bloodless, condemns whole populations to perennial despair" (p.115). Section III said that the "use by Christians of revolutionary methods — by which is meant violent overthrow of an existing political order — cannot be excluded *a priori*" (p.143). But both sections underscored the limitation of violence. Section III mentioned a consideration that has always been central when anyone in the ecumenical community has given reluctant sanction to the use of violence: "Christians should think of the day after the revolution, when justice must be established by clear minds and in good conscience" (p.143).

In the part of Section I dealing with "World Economic Relations", the need for radical action to meet the moral responsibilities of worldwide economic and social justice is stated in pragmatic rather than ideologically radical terms:

Technological progress gives mankind the possibility of eradicating want and misery from the face of the earth. If it is to do this, growth of power must be matched by growth of responsibility. Increasingly, national economic policies have been geared to growth with social justice. The challenge of our times is to extend this understanding to the world community. All our fine phrases about "human solidarity", "one world", etc. sound hollow in the face of increasing international inequalities. If contemporary economic and social policies are failing to arrest this tendency, they must be radically altered. It is not enough to say that the world cannot continue to live half-developed and half-underdeveloped: this situation must not be allowed to continue. Therefore, all nations, particularly those endowed with great economic power, must move beyond limited self-interest and see their responsibility in a world perspective. The church must say clearly and unequivocally that there is a moral imperative behind international economic cooperation (p.80).

In examining the differences between economic systems, Section I deliberately avoided words like "capitalism" and "socialism". Instead it spoke of "the market economy, the welfare state and the mixed economy, and the centrally planned economy"; and it refused to make a moral judgment in favour of or against any one of them:

All the above systems can, in their various ways, and with varying degrees of success, be employed to support the economic goals [of rapid growth and wide distribution of income]... The role of Christians is to be critical participants in the societies in which they find themselves. All these systems are changing, learning from each other, and apparently converging: they already have more in common than the more enthusiastic supporters of any of them are ready to admit. All must deal with the uncertainties arising from their inability to predict accurately the long-run trends in the fields of population, consumer choices and technology... In all there is some planning. All operate within a framework of government activity; in all, government expenditure absorbs a large part of the national income... Each of the above systems must be challenged by the churches on the way it meets human needs (pp.57f.).

A similar realism and pragmatism marked the section's findings in relation to economic progress and justice in developing countries:

In some countries economic development may demand a profound revolutionary change in the structure of property, income, investment, expenditure, education and political and administrative organization, as well as in the present patterns of international relations. However, there can be no universal prescription for economic development. In an age in which international economic development has become a social and political creed, the special problems of development within each country or region must be understood in terms of both the internal and external forces at play, and must be tackled in their own context and within that of the community of nations. Economic development is a common objective, but it is vain to search for simple formulae to understand it, and a uniform pattern to achieve it (p.66).

Church and Society and Faith and Order jointly sponsored a consultation on "Theological Issues of Church and Society" in March 1968 in Zagorsk, USSR. (A statement from this consultation was published in *Study Encounter*, vol. IV, no. 2, 1968.) It was in substance a follow-up of Geneva 1966, focussing on the meaning of the *humanum* as a criterion in ecumenical social ethics, evaluating the Geneva debate on the "theology of revolution" and opening up a discussion of ecclesiology and ethics.

The statement from Zagorsk distinguished two different methods used in Christian social ethics to find solutions to controversial public problems. Advocates of the *deductive* method start from the biblical tradition and emphasize eternal laws, permanently valid orders and basic principles for social life. The Decalogue, the teachings of Jesus and the like provide indicators of orders — such as the family, the economic order, the dominion of the state — and fundamental principles of social justice. Advocates of the *inductive* method try instead to think through the will of God in the context of concrete experiences and new problems, that is, to relate contemporary experience to biblical-theological ones. The Zagorsk consultation outlined a method of dialectical interaction between these two methods:

Cannot our theological understanding be both confronted with, and transmitted through, the analysis of the human sciences as well as our contemporary experience of human reality? Such a method of dialectical interaction would aim at both obedience to the Word of God and relevance to the concrete problems actually faced by men today. By using the insights of the human sciences, Christian social ethics would remain rational, critical and verifiable. At the same time, the Christian's theological understanding would integrate these findings within a certain framework and direction which is revealed in the biblical witness to God's love manifest in Jesus Christ. Such interdisciplinary dialogue, based on dialectical interaction between Christian theology and the social and behavioural sciences, offers hope for more widespread agreement on the "human" as an ecumenical criterion for Christian social ethics (p.72).

Zagorsk encouraged "combined debate on doctrinal and ecclesiological issues and social ethics" as a means to discover more adequate bases for common social action and to detect where differences of approach to social ethics are rooted not in traditional doctrinal issues, but in even more basic differences in the understanding of the gospel and the role of the church in the world. It listed a spectrum of different emphases more or less rooted in the general view of the mission of the church as follows:

> (a) Even in social action, the "conversion" of all men (i.e. their becoming Christians) remains the ultimate goal; (b) the church being always a minority (i.e. not expecting that "the world will become the church") is to be concerned with justice regardless of conversion; (c) the church empties herself for the sake of her mission, being ready even to be abused or abolished for the sake of those she serves (the church is a priesthood for others and not concerned with self-preservation) (pp.78f.).

Uppsala 1968

Uppsala, the most activist and politically oriented WCC assembly, can be seen as the end of one era in the ecumenical movement and the beginning of another. The assembly faced squarely the conflicts of the world: the growing gap between rich and poor nations, the disastrous effects of white racism, the ambiguity of new scientific discoveries, the tensions between generations and the student revolts. The many articulate youth participants were frequently critical of what went on in the sessions. They had reached the peak of involvement in the vital issues of the ecumenical movement, although the difficulties of living up to their own mandate were soon apparent. For one thing, although laity and youth had been central concerns of the ecumenical movement from the outset, the role of youth within the decision-making processes of the churches was in fact minimal. Moreover, structural changes within the World Council placed the struggles of youth for peace and justice (and later for integrity of creation) predominantly outside the mainstream ecumenical movement of the churches.

Since earlier conferences, including Geneva 1966, did not involve official commitments on behalf of the churches, Uppsala was a major test of the validity of the developing new social thought in the ecumenical movement. The discussion in Geneva about the social and theological meaning of the social revolutions of our time had touched off a vigorous debate in both the churches and the media about what the conference had said and how it was to be interpreted. This debate was still going on at the time of the assembly, and so the warm endorsement given by the delegates in their evaluation of the conference was significant:

> The Conference on Church and Society (1966) has given to the churches and to the World Council of Churches a great stimulus. While it is still impossible to evaluate the full range of this work, the main reaction of the assembly can be only to express gratitude for this comprehensive panorama of socio-ethical thinking... The enquiry has not only deepened the sense of responsibility of Christians and the churches concerning social and political questions but it also reflects the clear view that Christians should be open to the process of change, and that the gospel's call to renewal and repentance compels them continually to re-examine the existing orders, and to enter the struggle for new and better struggles of social justice... *The important point now is for member churches to carry out these findings* (*The Uppsala 68 Report*, ed. Norman Goodall, Geneva, WCC, 1968, p.240).

The issues from the Geneva conference were for the most part taken up at the assembly in Section III on "World Economic and Social Development", with its five sub-sections: (1) The Christian Concern for Development; (2) The Dynamics of Development; (3) Political Conditions of World Development: (4) Some Human Issues of Development; (5) The Task of Christians, Churches and the World Council of Churches.

The report of Section III, somewhat modified by the assembly, placed world economic and social development at the heart of the social policies of the churches; a number of observers called it the most useful of all assembly documents.

In discussing the political conditions for world development, the report said the elimination of world poverty must come about largely through political instruments of development, which cannot be created or activated except through the politics of sovereign nations. Poor or developing countries must reshape their political structures to enable the mass of their people to participate in political and economic life. "The state in a developing nation should be able to enthuse the people to make the sacrifices... necessary for development, by a programme of distributive justice" (*The Uppsala 68 Report*, p.47). This involves revolutionary changes in social structures, but "revolution is not to be identified with violence... The churches have a special contribution towards the development of effective nonviolent strategies of revolution and social change" and "to participate creatively in the building of political institutions to implement the social changes that are desperately needed" (p.48).

A major obstacle to the humanization of development, according to Section III, is white racism. Whites do not have a monopoly on racism, but because white nations largely have a monopoly on wealth, the racism of white people creates a special hindrance to the development of poor nations, whose people are generally dark. "Discrimination against women is another pervasive impediment to personal and community development... The church must actively promote the redistribution of power... so that all men, women and young people may participate in the benefits of development" (p.50).

It was recommended that the churches set aside one percent of their own total income for development aid, help to ensure that all political parties make development a priority in their programmes and influence governments to make the radical structural changes necessary to establish justice. The assembly called on industrialized countries to aid development as desired by the developing countries, give one percent of their gross national product for development, stabilize prices of primary products and give preferential access to their markets for manufactured products of developing countries.

Section IV, "Towards Justice and Peace in International Affairs", was divided in four sub-sections: (1) The Problem of Peace and War; (2) Protection of Individuals and Groups in the Political World; (3) Economic Justice and World Order; (4) International Structures.

The section re-affirmed the declaration by the Amsterdam assembly that "war as a method of settling disputes is incompatible with the teachings and example of our Lord Jesus Christ", declaring nuclear war to be "the gravest affront to the conscience of man". As a matter of human survival, churches should insist that the first duty of governments is to prevent nuclear war. To that end they should halt the arms race and agree never to use and to stop experimenting with weapons of mass human destruction (p.62).

The troubled question of the rights of majorities and minorities gained special urgency in Uppsala because of the Biafra war in Nigeria. While reaffirming the right of self-determination, Section IV recognized that most nations have ethnic, cultural or religious minorities whose right to choose should be respected, although minorities must also recognize that the majority has rights and must restrain their demands in the light of the good of the whole society (p.65). While nationalism can be a constructive and unifying force, particularly in new nations, it is often negative and disruptive. "Today the national unit has become too small, particularly among the weaker nations" (p.69). So the churches should encourage the formation of regional organizations and work for cooperation within the United Nations. The UN itself must be strengthened within its own structure. This is important because "the growing dimensions of the ecumenical movement offer new possibilities for concerted contributions to international relations" (p.70).

Perhaps the most comprehensive statement on world development and economic justice at the assembly was that by Indian economist Samuel Parmar:

> We must move from a welfare state to a welfare world. We are not the first to say this. The United Nations and its specialized agencies, especially the UNCTAD, have been pushing for a global view. But so far this has only been a statement of intent and may soon become a pious platitude...
>
> Rightly understood, development is disorder because it changes existing social and economic relationships, breaks up old institutions to create new, brings about radical alterations in the values and structures of society. If we engage in development through international cooperation we must recognize that basic changes become necessary in developing and developed nations as also in the interna-

tional economy. "Development is the new name for peace." But development is disorder, it is revolution. Can we attempt to understand this apparently paradoxical situation which would imply that disorder and revolution are the new name for peace?

If we believe in progress and development let us not finish at disorder and instability. So often order provides a camouflage for injustice that the very quest for justice generates disorder. But we must live with this dilemma. Our task is to imbue the revolutionary movements of our time with creativity and divest them of their anarchic content. For neither disorder nor revolution is an end in itself. So too development. They are means to human betterment and establishment of a society based on justice (pp.41-43).

In the years following Uppsala several new programmes were added to the WCC: the Programme to Combat Racism, the Commission on the Churches' Participation in Development, the Christian Medical Commission, Dialogue with People of Living Faiths and Ideologies and the subunit on Education. All may be seen as growing out of the assembly's efforts to concretize ecumenical social thought and link it up with experiences of all the people of God.

In his essay on "The Development of Ecumenical Social Thought and Action" **(22)**, written shortly after Uppsala, Paul Abrecht drew the following conclusion from the various trends covered in this chapter:

Despite the achievements in recent years, ecumenical social thinking remains a precarious enterprise. A substantial number of Christians in our churches are probably still very much opposed to the directions it takes or would criticize the World Council and other ecumenical bodies for giving too much attention to social issues. Moreover, as the pressures for rapid change in society increase, the polarization of opinion in our churches on basic social questions will undoubtedly become greater rather than diminish. The continuing division of the churches on basic issues of theology and ecclesiology also weakens the possibility of a more substantial Christian social witness.

Up to the present, the ecumenical consensus on Christian social responsibility has been limited, experimental and provisional, and with relatively slight impact on the action of the churches in society. And no doubt the ecumenical witness will become more difficult in the future. But wherever Christians struggle to maintain the transcendence of the faith to their fellow men, combining the desire for justice with the spirit of compassion, the search for the ecumenical community of ideas and witness will proceed. Possibly the most significant achievement of the ecumenical movement has been its ability to encourage and nourish that dialectic of obedience and unity even in situations where opposing points of view seemed to make real encounter impossible. We can hope for no more and should aspire to no less in the future (p.259).

The concept of ecumenical social thought changed dramatically during the period described in this chapter. The idea of a Responsible Society which formed the framework during the 1950s, had become globalized — as Visser 't Hooft phrased it, a "responsible world society". Everyone had become everyone's neighbour, in the words of Uppsala's message to the churches. The social conflicts between North and South and within nations had thus been revealed to such an extent that refusal to take responsibility for the needy was deemed to be "heresy" (see Visser't Hooft's address to the assembly; *The Uppsala 68 Report*, p.320).

Uppsala attested to the effort of the ecumenical movement to cope with the complexity of the social context in which the human family found itself and to concretize insights that had grown out of long discussion. But the challenges described by Paul Abrecht were formidable. Most of the critical attitude to the change of emphasis arose within the churches that had established the ecumenical movement. Those who had come on the stage between 1961 and 1966 to articulate the cry of anguish and question the power structures would pose a strong challenge to the dominance of the debate on ecclesiology and theology in the ecumenical movement. Moreover, already in these years the complexity of the social structures and their globalization was leading to a tension between the local and the global capacity of perception within the churches. This was in fact the ecumenical context for establishing a WCC subunit on Education, to help the churches to support the process of internationalization and interculturation of Christian social thought.

These challenges remain ecumenically valid today. They can be seen as the constructive tension of the diversity within Christian unity already obtained, which makes the search for adequate witness in today's world an ongoing process.

IV

General Developments since 1968

In the period after Uppsala the WCC's Department (later subunit) on Church and Society was responsible for ecumenical reflection and action on two major topics: the problems raised by worldwide technological change and the question of violence and nonviolence in effecting social justice.

"A proper theological understanding of the churches' responsibility for man's future may most creatively emerge from the encounter of Christian faith and tradition with various ideologies and with insights of the social and natural sciences." This assertion outlined the approach envisaged in 1969 as the starting point of Church and Society's ecumenical enquiry into "The Future of Man and Society in a World of Science-Based Technology". The urgency of the encounter between faith and science became increasingly apparent, a crucial component in defining Christian commitment to social responsibility today and tomorrow. Awareness of the global social and ethical implications of the role of science and technology in shaping human life opened up a broad unexplored area of ecumenical debate.

Such an enquiry was indeed long overdue. The prospectus for the study, presented to the WCC central committee in 1969, noted that "while science-based technology and the ability to predict on the basis of it grow rapidly, the ability to use it for agreed social purposes grows much more slowly and the necessary change in social institutions and structures comes slower still. People lack the basic information as well as the ethical criteria for making responsible choices between the new options which technology makes possible" (cf. *Minutes*, pp.190-98).

In the light of an exploratory conference on "Technology, Faith and the Future" in Geneva in 1970, which included a considerable number of scientists and technologists who were interested in working with the churches in establishing clearer guidelines for the use of science and technology in society, it was decided to focus attention on three themes: Science and Quality of Life; Political and Economic Choices in a Technological Era; Images of the Future. The report was entitled *From Here to Where?* **(57)**.

The strategy was to ensure a wide range of perspectives by addressing the three themes on two levels: through international consultations and working parties on rather specific issues, and through regional meetings relating the total enquiry to the problems of particular regions, especially Africa, Asia and Latin America.

To determine more precisely the focus of the new ecumenical study, an enlarged meeting of the Church and Society working committee was held in Nemi, Italy, in June 1971. Among those present were a number of scientists in the forefront of the new thinking about faith, science and society. There were also some eminent critics of science, and an unusually strong group of theologians. One of the participants was a member of the team of scientists from the Massachusetts Institute of Technology who produced the *Limits to Growth* report, which was published the following year. There was also a keen group of economists, including several from the third world who sharply questioned the thesis of the "limits" study. The debate was fast and furious. Plans were also made here for an enquiry on ethical issues in genetic engineering; and there was the first ecumenical discussion of the deterioration of the human environment.

Among the main issues treated in the succeeding years were:

• *The ethical dilemmas of a scientific era.* There was increasing concern about the consequences of new scientific and technological discoveries for traditional spiritual and ethical values. A consultation on "Genetics and the Quality of Life" at Zurich in 1973 faced the ethical challenges of scientific advances and their inability to prescribe the good (see *Study Encounter*, vol. X, no. 1, 1974).

• *Science as a theological problem.* A working party on the "Critique of Scientific Rationality" was organized to evaluate current theologies as tools for a critical analysis of the assumptions of modern science. A shift was noted from technological triumphalism to technological apocalypticism, the feeling that science-based technology has a momentum that defies any human control or planning and could lead to catastrophe. Doubt was expressed that any existing theological or ethical system has the power to achieve a new understanding of the quality of life and the life-styles which might keep life human (see *Anticipation*, no. 16, March 1974).

• *Cultural values and technologies*. At a West.African regional conference in Accra, Ghana, in 1972, S.A. Aluko of the University of Ife, Nigeria, asserted:

> The majority of Africans believe that Western technology can be imported lock, stock and barrel for the rapid modernization of their economies, and that total cultural imitation of the West or the East is the fastest and surest way to achieve national greatness... This cultural, political and ideological subservience to the West and East creates a barrier to the adoption of distinctive methods and techniques which would lead Africa out of its backwardness, give it a vision of greatness, validate native talents and achievements and provide the strength of a nationalist ideology for continued modernization (*The Ecumenical Review*, vol. 24, no. 3, July 1972, p.314).

• *Global environment, economic growth and social justice*. A 1972 consultation at Cardiff, Wales, affirmed the need for a radical new approach to the technical future:

> In spite of the uncertainty about the position of resource constraints, there is a general consensus that we have entered the transitional period during which decisions must be taken and implemented concerning a major redirection of our technology, particularly that relating to resource consumption. The length of the transition period is uncertain, but the main change of direction ought to be accomplished within the next hundred years. Due to the inevitable delays in technological and social adaptation, the initiation of this process should begin now (see *Anticipation*, no. 13, December 1972, pp.37-40).

The 1974 world conference on Science and Technology for Human Development in Bucharest, Romania, went considerably beyond this outlook in developing the concept of a "sustainable and just society", based on the evident need to see global economic possibilities and material requirements in some kind of equilibrium. It was recognized that this would mean different needs for different parts of the world. For further details on this concept see Chapter V.

Bucharest brought together representatives of two points of view: those who saw the problem of the future only or primarily in terms of achieving greater economic and social justice, and those who saw it only or primarily in terms of human survival because of the foreseeable exhaustion of natural resources and the widespread destruction of the environment by ever-increasing industrialization. Even if these two perspectives are not necessarily mutually exclusive, they have tended to appear in opposition. The opportunity provided in Bucharest for the adherents of the two viewpoints to hear each other out was undoubtedly an important contribution, even if the conflicts were not resolved and substantial differences of opinion and approach remained — which came out most clearly in the examination of the pressures of population and natural limits to growth on human hopes for social justice and material progress (see *Anticipation*, no. 19) **(61)**.

Two further consultations on specific issues in the area of science, technology and faith highlighted important concerns and helped to pave the way for the WCC's world conference on Faith, Science and the Future in 1979. An ecumenical hearing on nuclear energy, held in Sigtuna, Sweden, in 1975, brought together nuclear physicists, engineers, parliamentarians, civic leaders and theologians; and the report of this hearing enabled the WCC to contribute to the growing public debate on nuclear energy. And Church and Society joined with Faith and Order the same year to organize a consultation in Mexico City on science and faith. Taking part were theologians, ethicists, philosophers of science and scientists.

The first grants from the Special Fund of the WCC's Programme to Combat Racism in 1970 turned a spotlight on the question of whether Christians may ever engage — directly or indirectly — in revolutionary violence intended to overthrow a profoundly unjust and oppressive social system. The central committee at its meeting the next year in Addis Ababa asked Church and Society to undertake a two-year programme that would look afresh at violence and nonviolence. The urgency and controversy of the problems became most visible in trying to take account of real contemporary situations in which Christians were agonizing over questions of violence. The final report of the study, *Violence, Nonviolence and the Struggle for Social Justice* **(116)**, presented to the central committee in 1973, gave concrete meaning to the general reflections by describing several specific conflict situations and illustrating the actual experiences and dilemmas of Christians in them. (We shall return to this subject in greater detail in Chapter XIV.)

An international consultation in 1974 on Human Rights and Christian Responsibility, at St Pölten, Austria, sponsored by the Commission of the Churches on International Affairs, brought together the main protagonists of the different views on human rights represented in the ecumenical movement. The meeting agreed on a number of major human rights concerns for the churches, and developed action strategies for their implementation. Four groups were asked to look especially at (a) the right to life and work; (b) the right to equality; (c) the right to national sovereignty, self-determination and international community; and (d) the proliferation of political prisoners and political refugees.

Discussion on ecumenical ethics during this period also took place within Faith and Order, especially in its study on the "Unity of the Church — Unity of Humankind". Particularly at the commission meeting in Louvain in 1974, the quest for unity among the churches was set in the broader perspective of the social and ethical concerns of humanity.

The final report of the *Humanum Studies* **(214)**, a study process that grew out of the concern of Geneva 1966 about the meaning of "humanization", is entitled "The Anguish of Man, the Praise of God and the Repentance of the Church" (pp.81ff.). It begins with a sobering assessment of the expectations of both the Responsible Society and revolution:

> There are no grounds for simplistic hopes either in the advance of justice in the world or in the churches as agents in relation to such advances. Therefore any Christian study of the *humanum* has to ask questions about the expectations with which human cries of anguish and of injustice are to be heard and responded to.

The ecumenical movement in particular should recognize the diverse cultural experiences of people as resources of great richness and encouragement. These resources, evident "in and through the very experiences of human anguish whose cries we hear and whose suffering and anxiety are echoed among us... offer new ways of deepening our understanding of the gospel, just as the gospel offers ways of illuminating, judging and establishing the human significance of these resources".

At the same time, the repentance of the church is necessary if it is to contribute to "the universal search for becoming truly human":

> For the source of humanity and the fulfilment of humanity is the glory of God. The church exists because God made his glory known in Jesus Christ, incarnate and crucified. Therefore, there is the possibility of glory and humanity through anguish, and there is the power to build humanity for glory through all distortions and death. This is the truly humanizing knowledge, judgment and power. So this is that by which the church must live and to which she must bear witness (p.85).

Rather than defending us from reality or distracting us "from either committed action or searching reflection", theology must analyze carefully the social, cultural and historical conditions:

> We must consider not only what we intend to mean when we make theological statements but also how what we say will be understood by those who hear it. In other words, all our theologizing must be characterized by an openness through which we can hear not so much what we say but how we are heard (p.86).

That this leads theological reflection as well as the search for ecumenical social thought into a community of conflicting interests, "which will permit growth towards a mature and realistic love" (p.87), is already foreshadowed in 1974.

Nairobi 1975 to Vancouver 1983

There was a certain measure of expectancy, if not optimism, at the Nairobi assembly in 1975. Within Africa, political independence for Mozambique and Angola, ending decades of racist colonial domination, led naturally to hopes that the process of liberation in the whole of southern Africa would be accelerated. The signing in Helsinki of the Final Act of the Conference on Security and Cooperation in Europe was a remarkable achievement, which gave new hope for disarmament and a general relaxation of East-West tensions. In the context of increased awareness of the injustice in international economic relations, the United Nations' call for a New International Economic Order seemed to be eliciting willingness on the part of at least some of the economically powerful nations of the North to listen to and even negotiate with the weaker nations of the South.

At the same time, these positive indicators were tempered by such negative trends as tensions in the Middle East, the escalation of the arms race, a worsening situation in Latin America and growing awareness of the ecological crisis, all of which received due attention from the assembly.

New emphases were placed on the programmes on faith, science and technology, militarism and disarmament, ecology and human survival and the role of women in church and society. Section V, "Structures of Injustice and Struggles for Liberation", was concerned with human rights, sexism and racism; Section VI, "Human Development, Ambiguities of Power, Technology and Quality of Life", with new dimensions of the quest for development and social responsibility.

The search for a "just, participatory and sustainable society" (JPSS) was proposed as a new programme thrust; and an advisory committee was appointed by the central committee in 1977. Rather than trying to "elaborate and present a blueprint of a Christian model of an ideal society which would be just, participatory and sustainable", it placed its search — which included an intensive build-up of regional networks — in the context of the present historical reality of people's struggles for justice, participation and sustainability. How might churches arrive at a common understanding of this historical reality and become meaningfully involved in this struggle? For the advisory committee, the promise of the messianic kingdom of God provides a purpose and a goal to the present struggles:

> Christian faith understands the present struggles and contradictions as a part and a manifestation of a dynamic in history pressing for eschatological fulfilment, thus defending history against both pretension and discouragement. Christians will always be faced by two temptations: either to escape history by means of a premature eschatology (enthusiasm and illusions, pietism without responsibility, activism without realism); or to eliminate eschatology by way of a self-sufficient history (conservatism without hope for change, cynicism as a caricature of wisdom, self-confidence without self-criticism). The messianic kingdom calls for a present response in human life and action through powerful decision, and at the same time for the

attitude of expectancy, searching for that which cannot be seen, with patience and powerful prayers [quoted in *Perspectives on Political Ethics* **(147)**, pp.178f.].

This attempt at theological interpretation led to a controversial debate at the central committee meeting in Kingston, Jamaica, in 1979. The old discussion on the relationship between the kingdom of God and the purpóse of history, which had been carried on around the Oxford conference, came back with much the same tensions and contradictions. (For further details on JPSS and the discontinuation of the programme, see Chapter V.)

Nairobi's call to the churches and the WCC to "raise consciousness about the dangers of militarism and search for creative ways of educating for peace" was followed up by a consultation on militarism in Glion, Switzerland, in 1977. Its report **(133)** stated that:

Militarization should be understood as the process whereby military values, ideology and patterns of behaviour achieve a dominating influence on the political, social and economic affairs of the state, and as a consequence the structural, ideological and behavioural patterns of both the society and government are militarized. Militarism should be seen as one of the more perturbing results of this process. It must be noted that militarism is multi-dimensional and varies with different manifestations in various circumstances dependent on historical background, national traditions, class structure, social conditions, economic strength, etc.

While militarism is in no way confined to the third world, the major ecumenical concerns have centred on the spread of militarism there. The report identified a number of factors contributing to militarism outside the Western world, including superpower competition and creation of "spheres of influence", the use of the army as the primary agent for modernization and the failure of democratic governments to provide order and justice.

Glion was also the site of conference the next year on disarmament. Its report **(132)** spoke of military doctrines and technology as "idols" which Christians must "unmask and challenge... in the light of the Christian vision of justice and peace". Among the "idols" specified were the doctrine of "nuclear deterrence", which was leading to the development of ever more terrifying weapons; "national security" doctrines used to justify the arms race; and the idea that improved military technology would result in a reduction in arms.

Although the means and resources are available to eradicate world poverty, Nairobi observed, the number of poor people is steadily increasing and opportunities for a more humane life are diminishing. This challenge was the starting point of an action-reflection pro- gramme of the Commission on the Churches' Participation in Development on "The Church and the Poor". The book *Good News to the Poor* **(148)**, published in 1977, dealt with problems of relations with the poor during the early centuries of church life and in the mediaeval period. In a second stage, a study was made of relations between the poor and the churches during the Western colonial expansion and industrial revolution. *Separation without Hope?* **(149)** showed how the poor, although they maintained a foothold in the life of the churches, tended to be relegated to the least important position. The substance of this painstaking study concludes that, as we saw in Chapter I, the churches, with few exceptions, failed during this period to be champions of the poor and exploited.

A workshop organized in Ayia Napa, Cyprus, in 1978, analyzed the challenge that the poor present to the churches and sought new theological perspectives and ways of action allowing Christian com- munities clearly to express their concern for the poor and enabling action in solidarity with them. *Towards a Church of the Poor* **(150)** contains the findings of this workshop.

In 1979 the central committee recommended that the report of the advisory committee on JPSS be followed up by a study of political ethics, that is, "an examination of structures of power, participation and political organization on local, national and international levels". In the foreword to the published report **(147)** of an ecumenical consultation in Cyprus on this subject, WCC general secretary Philip Potter posed three urgent questions:

> First, can Christians and churches go beyond issuing general state- ments to making specific political judgments? If it is agreed that they can, then on what bases may this be done? Second, how do we adequately deal with the qualitatively new situation brought about by modern science and the technological revolution? Technological developments tend to suppress the freedom of people, and the blessings of science are tragically mixed. How do we share in the

benefits they bring without succumbing to their tyranny? Third, how do we evaluate the awakening of people and the organization of people's movements, their determination to struggle against the forces of death and their search for a fuller, richer life? Is the revolutionary option, for a while an inspiration for many, still possible and viable? If it is not, what other options are there?

Questions such as these were being raised increasingly in the 1970s and 1980s by what came to be called contextual or indigenous theologies in various regions of the world. These decades were a flourishing period for the theology of liberation, theology inspired by Marxist analysis, feminist theology, black theology, theology of suffering and hope, which contributed to a vital ecumenical theological debate by pressing for a thorough examination of the situation in which the theologian finds himself or herself, for the sake of a better understanding and living out of the gospel in a particular social situation. Common to most of them is a focus on "reading the signs of the time", the *kairos* experience.

Contextual theologies challenge the assumption that a universally applicable vital and coherent theology is possible. This critical stance has led some to strong resistance against the attempt "at the top" to fit the diverse theological pieces into an "ecumenical" mosaic. Their concern with belief and obedience to Jesus Christ in a particular time and place often gives a strong "movement" character to "doing theology", seeking to root it in the reflection of local communities.

Liberation theologies thrive on giving a consistent interpretation of the dynamism of history, the possibility of the authentically "new" and the relative autonomy of the "created world". Only a new hermeneutical concern — what Clodovis Boff calls an "epistemological break" — which is grounded in a "re-reading" of Scripture and Tradition, can lead into a new direction. Many liberation theologians link the discovery of the authentically new to the process of reflection done between people of similar contextual experiences. This led in 1977 to the formation of the Ecumenical Association of Third World Theologians as a forum for exchanging experiences in the drive for an authentic theology.

What might be termed "contextual liberation ecumenism" and the participatory Christian social ethics of the WCC, based on an overriding concern for the rights of the poor and oppressed and the need to be in solidarity with them, were developed on similar, yet separate, lines. This mirrors the rift in theological and social thinking between what the missionary movement termed "older" and "younger" churches. That has raised several questions, particularly in the theological debates of the older churches. Did the World Council, which never held an international consultation on the birth, growth and impact of liberation theology, simply assume its authenticity and relevance? (It may be noted that Gustavo Gutiérrez, one of the pioneers of liberation theology, was invited to present a major paper on "A Theology of Liberation" which aroused considerable discussion among a formidable group of ecumenical theologians and social ethicists at a SODEPAX consultation on "theology of revolution" in 1971.) Is it because the cross-fertilization of these two social theologies was taken for granted that their mutual contribution to each other was never publicly acknowledged? Is it correct, as has been argued, that theologies of liberation were so caught up in denouncing social injustice and advocating a radical transformation of their national societies that they left it to the official ecumenical movement to develop a doctrine of "the church of the poor"; and that the WCC was so keen to identify key areas of domination and exploitation that it left to liberation movements the problem of determining the precise form and content of appropriate action? Did the World Council not overestimate its own credibility in matters of social and economic justice by incorporating these into large international programmes? Was it not inevitable that the slogan "the church of the poor" would lose plausibility, since the church is still largely made up of middle-class believers while more and more millions of poor live at the level of absolute poverty? Are the notions of "people" and "people's participation" not elusive, even fallacious, since liberation movements themselves are often unable to communicate with each other because each considers its own approach to curing the ills of society and its own particular criteria of theology to be normative?

Such divisive questions as these have made it difficult for the WCC to resolve the conflicts between diverse theological-ethical perspectives and different political-ideological assumptions. Behind this lie two unresolved ecumenical conflicts: the debate on the concept of the "kingdom of God", which preoccupied especially continental and Anglo-Saxon theologians between Stockholm and Oxford; and the unresolved debate on the concept of *missio Dei*, which had not clarified the link between eschatology and ethics. (Chapter XIV will address further the increasing confusion and division among churches on the substance of Christian social ethics that resulted from these unresolved questions.)

Two other important international meetings took place before the Vancouver assembly of 1983. In 1979 the WCC convened a world conference on Faith, Science and the Future at the Massachusetts Institute of Technology in Boston. The preparatory book *Faith, Science and the Future* **(64)** and the two volumes on *Faith and Science in an Unjust World* **(65, 66)**, which came out of the MIT conference, had wide distribution and influenced theological discussions and programmes in many churches. Spin-offs from the conference included further programmes in many parts of the world, and some of the themes discussed were later integral to the WCC discussion of Justice, Peace and the Integrity of Creation.

The issues of nuclear disarmament and the conversion of military technology to socially useful purposes were raised by scientists in particular at the MIT conference. This was followed up in an International Public Hearing on Nuclear Weapons and Disarmament at Amsterdam in 1981. The purpose of the hearing, which listened to testimony from 37 expert witnesses from various fields, different political perspectives and all parts of the world, was to consider the problems posed by the escalation of the nuclear arms race and changing concepts of nuclear war. (The MIT conference and the Amsterdam hearing are further treated in Chapters IX and XIV.)

Vancouver 1983 to Canberra 1991

The Vancouver assembly mandated Church and Society to engage the churches in reflection and action on issues raised by science and technology for faith and witness. The key areas identified for continuing dialogue and work were technology experienced as destructive power; appropriate systems of technological development; automation, micro-electronics and patterns of employment; and the control of science and technology. Issues of particular concern included bio-ethics (especially genetic engineering) and long-term choices about renewable and non-renewable energy supplies.

Central to the work of Church and Society in the post-Vancouver period was a focus on the "integrity of creation", both for its own theological and ethical work and in order to contribute to the Council-wide "Justice, Peace and Integrity of Creation" process. It followed what was described as an "interactive" methodology, in which exist-ing moral and theological insights and the perception of contemporary concrete issues illuminated and deepened one another. To compensate for limited staff resources, Church and Society drew on work being done in several parts of the world by holding small meetings and consultations in different regions. Among issues addressed were the "liberation of life" and animal rights, response to technological disasters (Bhopal and Chernobyl), nuclear testing in the Pacific, toxic waste, nuclear energy, climate change and tropical forest destruction.

Increasingly in these enquiries and discussions the accent fell on the immanence of the divine within the world, rather than on trans-cendence. Mechanistic views of nature and of a remote, deistic God, whose only role was to "set the world going" like a watchmaker, were challenged by more "panentheistic" views that see God present in the world, suffering in the suffering of all creatures and rejoicing in the joy of all creation. Dualistic views separating humanity from nature have been revised by more inclusive and ecologically justifiable views of humanity as within and part of nature. Far from diminishing the value of personal human life created uniquely in the image of God, this gives humanity a responsibility to cooperate with God's purposes in the world (*missio Dei*). This shift also called into question the terminology "church *and* society", as though the church were distinct from society and not part and parcel of it.

The WCC organized three major consultations during this time: in Larnaca, Cyprus (1986), on diakonia, in El Escorial, Spain (1987), on sharing of resources, and in Seoul (1990), on Justice, Peace and the Integrity of Creation; in addition, a world conference on Mission and Evangelism was held in San Antonio, Texas in 1989. A fifth world conference on Faith and Order was postponed until 1993. There was considerable criticism of holding so many world gatherings in such a short period.

The Larnaca meeting said that inter-church aid should be seen in terms of "preventive and prophetic diakonia" in support of people's struggles for justice, peace and authentic self-determination. It called on the WCC's Commission on Inter-Church Aid, Refugee and World Service to work as much as possible through representative regional groups who could "direct appropriate diakonia for their own communities". The El Escorial gathering, which concluded a study of ecumenical sharing of resources that had its roots in the Nairobi assembly, insisted that making resources available to victims of injustice is not enough: "the power to decide on their use is part of the sharing".

In his report to the 1990 central committee meeting, WCC general secretary Emilio Castro noted that, although "the specific search for models of society" had been left to one side by the ecumenical movement, "in the contemporary historical situation we are challenged to define images of society which can help those who have to take urgent existential decisions". This requires "studies and practical activities which show how within history we may come close to the coming kingdom". In reflecting on the future role of Church and Society, the central committee report to the Canberra assembly (*Vancouver to Canberra, 1983-1990*) expanded on Castro's remark, calling for renewal of

> the long tradition of work on issues of ecumenical social ethics, as they relate to the full range of questions arising in societies about the values, the vision and practice which can contribute to the shaping of our common future. This must enable a creative exploration of the possible economic, political, social and ecological structures which can respond to the prayer to be expressed by the seventh assembly: "Giver of Life — Sustain Your Creation!". Many have said that the world is entering a "post-modern" age, when the values which have shaped contemporary societies, in East and West, North and South, will need to be refashioned if the world is to have a future where life can be sustained (p.130).

This statement sums up the basic challenge to all theological reflection in the ecumenical movement. Its consequences and implications remain unanswered; indeed, it is as much an historical ecumenical problem as a problem of the future.

The Basis of the WCC, last revised in 1961, reads: "The World Council of Churches is a fellowship of churches which confess the Lord Jesus Christ as God and Saviour according to the scriptures and therefore seek to fulfil together their common calling to the glory of the one God, Father, Son and Holy Spirit." This is too short and too general to serve as a concise definition of the role of the church in the world. Similarly, the Toronto statement of 1950 on "The Church, the Churches and the World Council of Churches: The Ecclesiological Significance of the World Council of Churches" has never been revised. Any new formulation of these foundational texts would have to be undertaken in the light of the churches' being together for nearly a half century and of convergence and growing consensus on issues which are at the root theological: baptism, eucharist and ministry; mission in Christ's way; justice, peace and the integrity of creation.

Nor has much attention been given to revising and updating programmes of the Council. Basically, these go back to 1971. To be sure, a new four-unit programme structure, developed to facilitate the overall work of the Council, was put in place in 1992. The tasks of the four units — Unity and Renewal; Churches in Mission — Health, Education, Witness; Justice, Peace and Creation; Sharing and Service — have been outlined in some detail, but the absence of precisely formulated aims and functions seems to suggest that it is taken for granted that the earlier formulations somehow remain in the new structure, even though the central committee in 1991 made explicit reference to the need for "space to enable renewal and to give flexibility".

All this points to the discrepancy that is still prevalent between the Council understood as a growing "conciliar fellowship" and the Council interpreted as progressively engaged in the "conciliar process of justice, peace and the integrity of creation". Ecumenical social ethics is clearly one of the important elements, but is it considered a vital and indispensable part of the WCC by its member churches?

Several questions have not been addressed. One is whether the right approach to ecumenical ecclesiology leads to the right approach to ecumenical social ethics, or whether ecumenical social ethics plays a liberating role in achieving a full church fellowship. This is of course an old issue on the ecumenical agenda; as we noted earlier, in connection with the Stockholm conference in 1925, the conviction of the Life and Work movement that "doctrine divides, service unites" was nevertheless confronted by "a profound theological difference which made full agreement on social responsibility impossible".

Equally unanswered is the question of why the Council is not solely engaged in mission and unity but is also involved in the affairs of the world. Is the "common calling" referred to in the Basis seen as being primarily for the sake of humanity or for the sake of the churches? If the former, then what is precisely the raison d'être of the Council and what is its bearing on the search for unity? This is in fact the unfinished agenda of the Faith and Order study process on the Unity of the Church and the Unity of Humankind, initiated in 1968 and reformulated in 1975 into the Unity of the Church and the Renewal of Humankind.

In the realm of Church and Society other questions must be raised. We saw in Chapter III that the Department on Church and Society became in 1954 a sub-unit of the Division of Studies. But *The Evanston Report* (London, SCM Press, 1955) notes that

> there was considerable discussion of the question whether all studies of the Division of Studies might be carried out in relation to a general theme and whether this general theme should be "The Mission of the Church into the World", emphasis to be put on its christological interpretation and an ecumenical biblical approach. This general theme was not meant as a separate topic for study but rather as an indication of the direction in which the various study projects should be undertaken. The Committee was unable to come to a clear decision as to the advisability of such a general theme, the main objection being that a general theme might restrict the flexibility of departmental studies (pp.221f.).

From 1968 on, as this chapter has shown, Church and Society continued to function as it had in previous decades — mainly as an entity of interdisciplinary studies and an international forum for dialogue with experienced and qualified scientists, technologists, industrialists, politicians and sociologists. At the same time, however, several "offsprings" of Church and Society in what was then Unit II (Justice and Service) were born, taking "action-reflection" as their model (often with more emphasis on action than on reflection) and advocacy as their approach. This was clearly an outcome of the widening "community" in the ecumenical family as more and more churches in the South voiced their commitment and their understanding of the gospel on the basis of their experience with human anguish.

The whole approach became more conflictual; the world was seen as divided between oppressors and oppressed. Dealing with the North-South cleavage became more intricate than addressing the problem of the humanization of society in the West. In the words of the final report of the *Humanum Studies* **(214)**:

> We may find ourselves freed to break community or unity in the search for truth, justice and the mutual correction and confrontation which will permit growth towards a mature and realistic love... We may well discover that Jesus Christ unites us in the confession of his name and so in the praise of God, Father, Son and Holy Spirit, and in the freedom to repent, but that on that basis we are liberated into all sorts of conflict, confrontation and anguish (p.87).

Thus a dual approach to social ethics increasingly marked the ecumenical movement. On the one hand, the ecumenical study tradition, with its emphasis on dialogue between opposing opinions, continued to analyze and evaluate the world's political tensions and social conflicts. A good example is the Church and Society study on violence and nonviolence **(116)** mentioned above, which showed the ecumenical value of an independent examination of the ethical assumptions of militant action programmes and the trap of a too-easy acceptance of violence in the struggle for justice.

On the other hand, the superiority of the socialist liberation perspective over against the older liberal capitalist approach was widely affirmed. The liberation alternative was clearly considered the valid model for all the developing countries — with inescapable consequences for the entire world. A vivid expression of this was the report *Towards a Church of the Poor* **(150)**, also mentioned earlier in this chapter. Nowhere did it admit that representative democracies of advanced capitalism, despite their highly imperfect state forms, are still superior to anything yet fashioned to compete with them.

These differences in emphasis not only impede the effectiveness of ecumenical social ethics, but also have implications for the entire outlook of the whole ecumenical movement. For example, perhaps the reason that the long and laborious Faith and Order study on the Unity of the Church and the Renewal of Human Community has remained inconclusive is that in fact it ought to have been focused on the *renewal* of the church — suiting its action to its words — and the potential *unity* of humanity.

Doctrinal reflection is not sufficient to remove the obstacles to church unity; *costly action* is required to overcome its divisions and conflicts. When the actual unity of the church is not unconditionally linked to the quality of a new human community in Christ, the church only manifests a pseudo-unity, and its social activity is consequently ambiguous.

Chapter XIV will seek to show that a new analysis of the world political and economic situation will be possible only if the ecumenical movement overcomes the split between reflection and action. If the search for new and creative solutions in the areas of social justice, true freedom and lasting peace is to progress, it will demand from the World Council of Churches new efforts of study, enquiry and dialogue. To match insight and resourcefulness with involvement and action requires great wisdom, patience and grace. What is necessary is to scrutinize again the justification for the existence of the ecumenical movement, as was done faithfully in the past.

V

Three Ecumenical Concepts of Society

Since 1948 three concepts have been successively developed to offer an overarching framework for ecumenical reflection on the shape of society which could command the commitment of churches and Christians and offer a point of integration and coherence for the work of the World Council of Churches. All three are rooted in the worldwide experience of strife and injustice, domination and exploitation, conflict and violence, and have served to overcome the chasm between, on the one hand, a Christian conservatism based on a neutral or anti-political attitude and undue pessimism and, on the other hand, a Christian optimism which tends to identify itself with the utopian illusions of secular society. Each concept provided a basis for relevant common study and action and helped to struggle against traditional divisions between the churches which impede joint responsible engagement.

The concept of the Responsible Society, proposed at the WCC's first assembly in Amsterdam in 1948, proved to be the key phrase in nearly two decades of ecumenical social thinking. In the 1970s the concept of the "just, participatory and sustainable society" was elaborated, but already by the end of that decade it was being criticized for trying to offer a "blueprint" of society. At the Vancouver assembly in 1983 a third concept — that of a conciliar process of mutual commitment (covenant) to "justice, peace and the integrity of creation" — emerged as a priority for the WCC's programmes and activities.

The Responsible Society

Already before the Amsterdam assembly several ecumenical pioneers discussed what term would best express the responsibility of the church in society. Various phrases were suggested — "free society", "open society", "free and responsible society". J.H. Oldham suggested "humane society", but Visser 't Hooft objected that translating "humane" into French and German would cause considerable misunderstanding. In the end, the term "responsible society", also coined by Oldham, was adopted and widely used in subsequent years. Of the three concepts dealt with in this chapter, this was the most Eurocentric — a point made already at the Amsterdam assembly. Earlier we mentioned Visser 't Hooft's correction of the term at the Uppsala assembly: "responsible *world* society".

Section III in Amsterdam, "The Church and the Disorder of Society" **(31)**, surveyed the contemporary world situation as a consequence of the "industrial revolution with its vast concentrations of power", manifest on a large scale "not only in the greed, pride and cruelty of persons and groups, but also in the momentum or inertia of huge organizations of men, which diminishes their ability to act as moral and accountable beings". The task was therefore "to find ways of realizing personal responsibility for collective action in the large aggregations of power in modern society" (p.75).

Man is created and called to be a free being, responsible to God and his neighbour. Any tendencies in state and society depriving man of the possibility of acting responsibly are a denial of God's intention for man and his work of salvation. Man must never be made a mere means for political or economic ends. Man is not made for the state, but the state for man. Man is not made for production, but production for man (p.77).

The report defined a "responsible society" as

one where freedom is the freedom of men who acknowledge responsibility to justice and public order, and where those who hold political authority or economic power are responsible for its exercise to God and the people whose welfare is affected by it.

For a society to be responsible under modern conditions, it is required that the people have freedom to control, to criticize and to change their governments, that power be made responsible by law and tradition, and be distributed as widely as possible through the whole community. It is required that economic justice and provision of equality of opportunity be established for all the members of society.

On this basis, the report condemned

> any attempt to limit the freedom of the church to witness to its Lord
> and his design for mankind and any attempt to impair the freedom of
> men to obey God and to act according to conscience..., freedoms
> implied in man's responsibility before God; any denial to man of an
> opportunity to participate in the shaping of society, a duty implied in
> man's responsibility towards his neighbour; any attempt to prevent
> man from learning and spreading the truth (p.78).

But the churches are far from being only victims of oppressive
governments:

> They themselves have contributed to the very evils which they are
> tempted to blame wholly on the secularization of society. While they
> have raised up many Christians who have taken the lead in move-
> ments of reform, and while many of them have come to see in a fresh
> way the relevance of faith to the problems of society, and the
> obligations thus laid upon them, they share responsibility for the
> contemporary disorder.
>   Our churches have often given religious sanction to the special
> privileges of the dominant classes, races and political groups, and so
> they have been obstacles to changes necessary in the interests of
> social justice and political freedom. They have often concentrated on
> a purely other-worldly or individualistic interpretation of their mes-
> sage and their responsibility. They have often failed to understand the
> forces which shaped society around them, and so... have been
> unprepared to deal creatively with new problems as they have arisen
> in technical civilization.

The report stressed that "coherent and purposeful ordering of
society has now become a major necessity. Here governments have
responsibilities which they must not shirk" — as do the churches.
"There is no inescapable necessity for society to submit to undirected
developments of technology, and the Christian church has urgent
responsibility today to help men achieve fuller personal lives within
technical society" (p.77).

Pursuing this line, the report scrutinized the different types of
social order, including mainly communism and capitalism. Its judgment with reference to both was clear:

Christian churches should reject the ideologies of both communism and *laissez-faire* capitalism, and should seek to draw men away from the false assumption that these extremes are the only alternatives. Each has made promises it could not redeem. Communist ideology puts the emphasis upon economic justice, and promises that freedom will come automatically after the completion of the revolution. Capitalism puts the emphasis upon freedom, and promises that justice will follow as a by-product of free enterprise; but that, too, is an ideology which has proved false. It is the responsibility of Christians to seek new, creative solutions which never allow either justice or freedom to destroy each other (p.80).

One reason the concept of the Responsible Society proved to be durable was that its relatively mild language had considerable strength and provided flexible guidance. Speaking to both the East and the West, it clearly opposed all totalitarianism, but not in the strongly ideological tones heard from governments and the press. In exposing various social evils, it offered a basis from which to approach the major secular faiths of scientism and materialism.

Nevertheless, there were criticisms of the Section III report in the West, in particular from the United States, the leading capitalist country of the world. Having supported the economies of the free nations in two world wars, and now in 1948 standing as their hope in the desolate aftermath of the second, many people in the US thought that the system which made it possible for their nation to do this at least deserved an appreciative reference to its virtues. They argued that capitalism of the kind described by the report belonged to the past — which the assembly had indeed recognized by adding the modifier "*laissez-faire*" before the word "capitalism".

At its first meeting in 1949, the study commission on Christian Action in Society elaborated on the political and economic implications of the Responsible Society. Its report, entitled *The Responsible Society* **(33)**, responded to the debate in various circles concerning the Amsterdam critique of both communism and *laissez-faire* capitalism and further clarified the vital connection between freedom and justice:

> The Responsible Society calls not only for a new combination of economic and political procedures (new in contrast to both a consistent capitalism and a consistent socialism or communism), but also for a new spirit, a new sense of the values that are important. There is

hope for the development of a Responsible Society where two convictions are held with equal force: "that freedom lacks substance unless it is combined with economic justice and, second, that the quest for economic justice leads to new forms of oppression unless it is united with an insistent concern for political and spiritual freedom" (p.7).

The Evanston assembly in 1954 broadened the term Responsible Society and further clarified its meaning as a guide for action:

> Responsible society is not an alternative social political system, but a criterion by which we judge all existing social orders and at the same time a standard to guide us in the specific choices we have to make. Christians are called to live responsibly, to live in response to God's act of redemption in Christ, in any society, even within the most unfavourable social structures.

The second assembly pointed to the great changes in economic and social policy which had come about in many countries in the post-war years:

> These developments suggest that disputes about "capitalism" and "socialism" disguise more important issues in the field of economic and social policy. Each word is applied to many different social forms and economic systems. It is not the case that we have merely a choice between two easily distinguishable types of economic organization... The concrete issues in all countries concern the newly evolving forms of economic organization, and the relative roles of the state, organized groups and private enterprises.

What the churches had said at Oxford and Amsterdam about the points of opposition between the Christian faith and Marxist ideology and totalitarian practice was reaffirmed:

> (1) The communist promise of what amounts to a complete redemption of man in history; (2) the belief that a particular class by virtue of its role as the bearer of a new order is free from the sins and ambiguities that Christians believe characteristic of all human existence; (3) the materialistic and deterministic teachings, however they may be qualified, that are incompatible with belief in God and with the Christian view of man as a person, made in God's image and responsible to him; (4) the ruthless methods of communists in dealing with their opponents; (5) the demand of the party on its members for

an exclusive and unqualified loyalty which belongs only to God, and the coercive policies of communist dictatorship in controlling every aspect of life (*The Evanston Report*, London, SCM Press, 1955, pp.113, 120f.).

In the most comprehensive work on this concept, *Foundations of the Responsible Society* **(32)**, Walter G. Muelder traced the development of the idea from Stockholm to Evanston, concentrating on aspects of responsibility about which competent scholars have had persistent theoretical and practical differences. Various chapters deal with the responsible family, economic aspects of the responsible society, Christian criticisms of the welfare state, responsible agricultural policy, work and social responsibility, responsible management, responsible consumption and responsible world community.

In an essay on ecumenical social thought from Oxford to Vancouver **(24)**, Paul Abrecht addresses the question of whether the idea of the responsible society and the programme that developed from it reflected a Western bias:

> I believe the evidence shows that the concept evolved as it was applied to the problems arising in the changing world situation of these years. Thus it was able to express the preoccupations of the changing constituency of the WCC and contributed to making the political and social witness of the ecumenical movement a force for justice and peace in these years.
>
> Nevertheless, by the late fifties the world political and economic situation had greatly changed... The Western countries also faced demands for radical social change, emanating especially from youth dissatisfied with life in societies organized and dominated by a technological and exploitative approach to life and indeed to all of nature... Under these circumstances it became clear that there was need for a review of ecumenical social thought and its applicability to the new social situation. This was the basis for the 1962 proposal... for a world conference on Church and Society (pp.153f.).

A Just, Participatory and Sustainable Society

The need to assess the adequacy of the Christian response to rapid social change which lay behind the Geneva conference of 1966 took on new relevance in the 1970s, when the "oil crisis" sharpened awareness, particularly in the industrialized countries, of the "limits to growth" and highlighted demands for a new paradigm for human development. This was reinforced by a growing recognition that the ecological imbalance created under the old paradigm was leading to a "threat to survival".

"Science and Technology for Human Development", the report of the 1974 world conference in Bucharest **(61)**, introduced "a long-term concept of a sustainable and just society":

> The goal must be a robust, sustainable society, where each individual can feel secure that his/her life will be maintained or improved. We can already delineate some necessary characteristics of this enduring society. First, social stability cannot be obtained without an equitable distribution of what is in scarce supply or without common opportunity to participate in social decisions. Second, a robust global society will not be sustainable unless the need for food is at any time well below the global capacity to supply it, and unless the emissions of pollutants are well below the capacity of the ecosystem to absorb them. Third, the new social organization will be sustainable only as long as the rate of use of non-renewable resources does not outrun the increase in resources made available through technological innovation. Finally, a sustainable society requires a level of human activity which is not adversely influenced by the never-ending, large and frequent variation in global climate.

The report's idea of "a world where (1) the security of the individual, (2) the redistribution of material wealth and (3) the implementation of a maximum consumption level are affected by a transnational social security system dividing the responsibility for the fate of the individual among all people" (p.12) was debated in 1975 at the Nairobi assembly; and in 1977 the central committee mandated an advisory group to stimulate further theological and ethical reflection through a new ecumenical programme theme: "A Just, Participatory and Sustainable Society" (JPSS).

The focal point of JPSS was *justice*; participation and sustainability were seen as necessary dimensions of the contemporary struggle for justice. From the perspective of the kingdom of God, justice is neither a principle nor an ideal value that will never be fully realized, but the historical embodiment of love, indicating a quality of relationships in community and a criterion for evaluating and changing social structures.

The biblical root of the idea of *participation* is fellowship (*koinonia*). Christians can and must work together in the realization that their faith is not a mere private affair between the individual and God. But how can participation be organized and guaranteed? How can people be freed from being at the mercy of the "experts" and given greater control over the direction of developments in science and technology? How can human relationships and community be maintained in the struggle against impersonal structures of nationalism and internationalism?

The concept of *sustainability* brings to the fore the critical problem that to a large extent the "developed countries" have achieved their high levels of consumption by exploiting the rest of the world. A further dilemma is raised by the need to attain ecologically sustainable material growth. Can an acceptable life be achieved in the short run while avoiding long-term setbacks? Will permanent global solidarity require a drastic elimination of differentials in income, wealth and power in the industrialized nations? If economic development in less industrialized nations is to be sustainable, does it first require a redistribution of wealth?

In his article "How Ecumenical Must the Ecumenical Movement Be?" **(198)** Preman Niles compares the concept of the responsible society with the search for a just, participatory and sustainable society:

> What happens when "the most unfavourable social structures" are not amenable to change and are so oppressive that they are perceived to be "systems of injustice"? This is the issue that confronted the "search for a just, participatory and sustainable society"... The advisory group placed at the centre of its search the concern for social justice, rather than the issue of safeguarding democracy (the central concern of the responsible society), and focused on the struggles of the people (the poor) for liberation from oppressive political power structures. In this context, the responsible society concept seemed to engender political pessimism with its emphasis on Christian realism in the midst of the ambiguities of history.
>
> In contrast, the JPSS model advocated revolutionary action. Underlying this position was a more positive reading of the ambiguities of history... JPSS presented the conviction that the kingdom of God is already operative in human history as an alternative reality

of hope pressing towards fulfilment and that the struggles of the oppressed, in spite of their ambiguities, are pointers to this truth...

To give prominence to the JPSS model is not to reject the concerns of the responsible society, but rather to modify and subordinate them to the emphasis of the former. Christian realism cannot be discarded; we live in an imperfect world and have to envision proximate goals which will be achieved through less than perfect means. However, it is necessary to move beyond the political pessimism engendered by the concept of the responsible society by using the kingdom perspective inherent in the JPSS model (p.454).

Another redefinition of the "responsible society" was proposed by Ronald H. Preston in "Breakthrough in Ecumenical Social Ethics" **(222)**:

One of the reassessments of the concept certainly is embedded in the realization of the worldwide scope of responsibility. In the absence of a world government there are people, groups, organizations, governments, inter-governmental groupings, which wield power and have a deep influence on other people and nations. But there is no formal accountability or specific responsibility entrusted to the powerful and mighty, there is only moral responsibility. In other aspects also the Amsterdam assembly formulation, at least implicitly, does not suffice. "Responsibility to justice and public order" is not very appealing to those who are caught in a life-and-death struggle *between* justice and public order. There was and is "public order" in many historical settings without justice (pp.53f.).

As noted in the previous chapter, the WCC central committee decided in 1979 not to accept the findings of the JPSS advisory committee. Old and unresolved debates on the relationship between the kingdom of God and history resurfaced, and the focus of the study was shifted to a search for ecumenical political ethics. According to the 1979 central committee minutes:

Taken together, the reactions to and the comments on the JPSS report were varied, diverse and in some cases even contradictory. Where criticisms, reservations or hesitations were expressed, the following reasons were given: the distinction between the human and the divine, history and eschatology was not made clearly enough; there was a tendency at times towards an unexamined messianism; the elements of "sin", "humility", "repentance", "sacrificial servant", etc. were not given sufficient consideration; the use of biblical materials should be more carefully treated; a great deal more work needs to be done in order to move from theological categories to political categories.

Where approval, excitement and enthusiasm were expressed, the following reasons were given: the basic orientation of the JPSS report perceived history and eschatology from the perspective of the poor and the oppressed for whom the struggle for justice, participation and sustainability (in many situations, even mere existence) was a matter of life and death; the basic concerns embodied in the report were consonant with the guidelines of Unit II's work. It was generally agreed that the report had considerably advanced the WCC reflection on the JPSS emphasis; yet, more clarity and fuller articulation were needed, especially regarding the sustainability aspect (pp.17f.).

Justice, Peace and Integrity of Creation

In deciding that a priority for future WCC programmes should be engaging the churches "in a conciliar process of mutual commitment (covenant) to justice, peace and the integrity of creation" (JPIC), the Vancouver assembly was responding to a situation whose perceived gravity is clearly expressed in its statement on peace and justice:

Humanity is now living in the dark shadow of an arms race more intense, and of systems of injustice more widespread, more dangerous and more costly than the world has ever known. Never before has the human race been as close as it is now to total self-destruction. Never before have so many lived in the grip of deprivation and oppression...

The churches today are called to confess anew their faith, and to repent for the times when Christians have remained silent in the face of injustice or threats to peace. The biblical vision of peace with justice for all, of wholeness, of unity for all God's people is not one of several options for the followers of Christ. It is an imperative in our time...

The foundation of this emphasis should be confessing Christ as the life of the world and Christian resistance to the powers of death in racism, sexism, caste oppression, economic exploitation, militarism, violations of human rights, and the misuse of science and technology (*Gathered for Life*, ed. David Gill, Geneva, WCC, 1983, pp.131f.).

In thus presenting the confession of Christ as the life of the world and Christian resistance to the powers of death as one and the same activity, Vancouver shifted from the view that Christian involvement in world affairs is largely the concern of Christian ethics: translating the values of the kingdom into achievable social goals (the middle axioms of the responsible society). The new emphasis on confessing the faith called for a new understanding of the missionary task of the church. To realize this intention, the assembly envisaged bringing churches together to take common stands on urgent issues concerning the survival of humankind. This is the meaning of the phrase "conciliar process of mutual commitment". The expected outcome of the process is a council that could take the churches to a new stage in the covenant relationship into which they had entered at the inaugural assembly at Amsterdam in 1948.

But the parenthetical term "covenant" did more to confuse than to clarify the meaning of "mutual commitment". At least four difficulties were encountered: (1) "covenant" is often used for pacts and alliances between human partners, and it is not clear what more is meant when it is used as a theological term in conjunction with "mutual commitment"; (2) the Bible mentions several types of covenant, each with its own character and emphasis, so that a common biblical understanding of the term cannot be assumed; (3) the fact that "covenant" has ecclesiological significance in some church traditions but not in others makes it unsuitable as a way of stating the mutual commitment of all churches to JPIC; (4) many churches understand God's covenant to have been accomplished "once for all" in Jesus Christ; what then does it mean theologically to speak of covenanting?

The Vancouver call did elicit a process to which many local groups as well as national, regional and confessional organizations around the world contributed. There were regional conferences or assemblies on JPIC in the Pacific, Europe and Latin America. Other contributions came from specific theological perspectives: Orthodox (consultations in Sofia 1987 and Minsk 1989), Roman Catholic (response from the Pontifical Council on Justice and Peace, 1989) and the World Alliance of Reformed Churches (general council meeting, 1989).

The WCC's world convocation in Seoul, Korea, in March 1990 agreed on ten short affirmations in the areas of justice, peace and creation: (1) all exercise of power is accountable to God; (2) God's option for the poor, (3) the equal value of all races and peoples; (4) male and female are created in the image of God; (5) truth as the foundation of a community of free people; (6) the peace of Jesus Christ; (7) the creation as beloved of God; (8) the earth is the Lord's; (9) the dignity and commitment of the younger generation; (10) human rights are given by God. In addition, the participants entered into an "act of covenanting" on four concrete issues:

1) a just economic order and liberation from foreign-debt bondage;
2) the true security of all nations and peoples and a culture of non-violence;
3) building a culture that can live in harmony with creation's integrity and preserving the gift of the earth's atmosphere to nurture and sustain the world's life;
4) the eradication of racism and discrimination on all levels and the dismantling of patterns of behaviour that perpetuate the sin of racism.

The report of the Seoul convocation **(40)** acknowledges that deep and divisive differences among the participants had been evident:

> During the earlier stages of the convocation, when it tried to reach an agreement on a common analysis of the threats to life in our time and a common response of the churches, there was a clear tension between local/regional perceptions and a global analysis. Equally evident were the differences in preparation for and expectation of the convocation. The term "conciliar process", used in the Vancouver call, had to be abandoned for theological reasons. In spite of all the attempts made, there were still some unresolved differences in the understanding of "covenant". Also, due to a lack of time, some items on the agenda could not be finished (pp.3f.).

In the article cited earlier in this chapter **(198)**, Preman Niles argues that

> the JPIC emphasis on commitment to action, to resist the threats to life as an indispensable part of confessing our faith, has once again surfaced the conflict between two models for Christian social and political responsibility and action that have co-existed somewhat uneasily in the ecumenical movement. One is the model of the

responsible society and the other is the model of the just, participatory and sustainable society (JPSS)... One of the main complicating factors in this conflict is that the model of the responsible society has been viewed largely as a Western proposal for Christian social and political responsibilité with an emphasis on Christian realism, while the model of the just, participatory and sustainable society is seen as the one most favoured by third-world people concerned with revolutionary political action for realizing social justice.

In evaluating these two models, it is important to remember that ecumenical social thought does not have an accepted system of ethical propositions. It has responded to changing historical situations, so that an appeal to authority or precedent is not convincing in ecumenical discussions. The real issue is: which is the most helpful ethical model or combination of models for responding to the present situation? (p.453).

Preparations for the Seoul convocation had been intensive, and the results of the various regional, confessional and theological preparatory meetings had created high expectations for its outcome. Despite the failure to fulfil the plans with which the convocation began, it can be argued that Seoul made a significant contribution to the ecumenical *debate* on social ethics and created a new awareness of the diversity in approaches due to the differences of conceptual frameworks within the ecumenical movement. This ongoing discussion raises some central questions for the ecumenical family; and it may be useful to highlight some of the positions and arguments that have come to the fore in the aftermath of Seoul.

For one group in the discussion, the expectation was that the JPIC process would come up with answers to the unresolved questions stemming from Oxford. Thus several experts in ecumenical social ethics have argued that the Seoul convocation was a one-sided ecclesiastical gathering and that JPIC is not able to offer a viable new model for interpreting contemporary reality in such a way as to provide meaning and open horizons for humanity today.

Seoul's weakness, it has been said, is that it used biblical quotations as a theological stick to hit the secular world. Moreover, it had a tendency to offer a running commentary on every point of the world's agenda, thereby opening the floodgates to church activism while (unlike the 1966 Geneva conference) lacking adequate input from sociology, economics and politics. Others contend that it should have been evident that an international ecumenical conference in the 1990s had even less chance than one in the 1960s of speaking properly on behalf of the churches. Seoul ought instead to have spoken *to* the churches and advised them on the Christian response to the challenges of contemporary radical changes. Only in this way could the right balance between church leaders, theologians and different types of lay specialists have been assured. The recommendation for a "conciliar process" was premature and unhelpful for promoting dialogue between church representatives and those with expert knowledge in the various historical and sociological disciplines.

Others argued, by contrast, that the very concept of expertise for this convocation was completely different from the one at Geneva 1966. Experts are to be found where people experience human anguish and the difficulties of participating in the struggle for justice, peace and the integrity of creation. The "conciliar process" had succeeded in bringing concerned Christians from all over the globe into a vital discussion on the role and function of faith confronted with the everyday "threats to survival". The ecumenical movement had rediscovered the "movements" as part of its search for relevant ecclesiology.

As to whether such a convocation could "speak for the churches", it was argued that this in turn poses the question of who actually is the church. In fact, one outcome of the discussion around JPIC was to re-open the rather dormant ecumenical discussion of the role and function of the "laity" in the church. Thus, it was said, in order to develop the ethical foundations for a "Theology of Life", not only must traditional academic "experts" relate with each other, but also "people-experts", who live amidst the threats to life, must make their contribution.

How to integrate these two broad groups of respondents to Seoul requires a new approach in the search for ecumenical social ethics and surely adds to the growing uncertainty in the search for the *one* ecumenical answer to today's problems. Hopes were voiced that Faith and Order would also take up this challenge, so that the debate would include a cross-fertilization of theology and ethics as we approach the third millennium.

The WCC central committee meeting immediately after the Seoul convocation resolved that JPIC should continue to be a primary emphasis in the Council's work. This can be seen as the result of two insights: (1) The churches have genuinely tried to listen to the cries of anger, disillusionment and suffering in many parts of the world, so that continuing the search in the midst of all this for adequate Christian praxis is warranted. (2) The concept and approach seem to be valid in the sense that they stimulate broad participation in the search for relevant ecumenical social thought and solid theological foundations. This will continue to demand from the WCC — and in particular its member churches — profound, professionally informed analysis and evaluation, as well as methodologies of participatory research in which movements — that is, all the people of God — can contribute to the results. In all this it is urgent for the WCC to bridge the gulf between prophetic denunciation and sensible policy-making so that people and nations may find effective ways to incarnate at least some approximations of the social ideals proposed by ecumenical ethics. The credibility of the churches' advice and encouragement is at stake here.

Charles C. West, in his article "Ecumenical Social Ethic beyond Socialism and Capitalism" **(210)**, analyzes the theological shortcomings of the Seoul convocation and thus points to a number of key issues still open in the discussion of ecumenical social thought. He writes:

(a) The term "integrity of creation" is never defined, and it begs a basic question: how should God's non-human creation interact with the history of God's dealing with his covenant people? On this question the report of Section II from the MIT conference in 1979, "Humanity, Nature and God", is far more profound and helpful. It has, however, been ignored.

(b) Such analysis of social powers and trends as there is in this document is unrealistic and undialectical. A black-and-white, good/evil schema seems to dominate the whole. The tone is exhortative and idealistic, and therefore not very helpful to faithful witness in the real world.

(c) The theology of the document, despite some good statements, is vague, sometimes contradictory, sometimes lacking. The term "covenant" is over-used and ill-defined. Forgiveness and grace are missing, nor is anything said about sharing in the redemptive suffering of Christ. There is no theology of the powers or of the church. In short, one senses that once again, in a break with ecumenical tradition, theological reflection is not taken seriously.

(d) The document lacks an evangelical witness to the saving work of God in human society. God is present as creator, sustainer, and opter for the poor, but the rest is left to human struggle as defined in a long list of possible actions. There is too much ill-digested law here and not enough convincing gospel (pp.337f.).

In the light of West's first remark, it is worthwhile to take a brief look at ecology, environment and the preservation of the balance of creation on the agenda of ecumenical social thought. During the 1970s the WCC served as an international forum where churches and nations could deliberate on the destructive consequences around the world of technology, irresponsible industrial expansion for the sake of profit and the plunder of nature. By and large, the churches did not begin to address the problem of ecology until after the so-called limits-to-growth debate made itself fully felt in the ecumenical movement.

The report of the 1974 world conference on science and technology in Bucharest **(61)** conceived of the sustainable society as one

with a stable population and a fixed material wealth per person, a society actively pursuing quality of life in basically non-material dimensions such as leisure, service, arts, education and sport. In the sustainable state, problems will appear at a more manageable rate than today. People will be able to afford the luxury of delaying the use of new technology to increase human options... until after the unavoidable side effects are unearthed and publicized and after the decision to implement is agreed upon (p.12).

From Bucharest a document on threats to survival and the destructiveness of capitalism was forwarded to the 1974 central committee meeting in Berlin, which also received a finding of the Commission of the Churches on International Affairs on "The Economic Threat to Peace — Crisis and a New International Economic Order". The former in particular was influential in triggering the ecumenical debate on creation which continues today.

The report of the 1979 world conference on Faith, Science and the Future **(66)** included two carefully drafted sections on "Humanity,

Nature and God" and "Technology, Resources, Environment and Population". According to the former,

> as Christians we speak of humanity and nature in the context of the work of God as Creator and his goal for creation. By the term "creation" we mean the entire universe in relation to God. It includes therefore both humanity and nature and the disciplines which study them, whether the natural or social sciences or the humanities. God remains free in relation to his creation. In his faithfulness he grants it continuity and permanence. He is always at work in creation, enters it in Jesus Christ and purposes to complete and perfect his communion with it. This cannot be deduced from a scientific view of nature but only from our knowledge of God in the history of Israel and through Jesus Christ. But it gives the work of science and technology a basis, meaning and direction (pp.32f.).

The section on technology and resources made a number of specific recommendations in several areas and, although acknowledging that no general criteria could be established, insisted that "we *can* say that God values *all* of his creation and that human redemption involves the redemption of the whole cosmos from 'its bondage to decay'" (p.70).

To prepare the Seoul convocation in 1990, an international consultation on "The Integrity of Creation" was held in Granvollen, Norway, in 1988. Recognizing that this formulation was a new one, the report **(41)** identified a number of possible mistakes in approach and attitude to creation theology:

> (a) *reductionism in theology*, reducing the gospel to personal salvation, with emphasis on the eternal destiny of the human soul, and ignoring God's work in the world;
>
> (b) *scientific-technological hybris*, persuading us that the ecological crisis is a technical problem to be solved by purely technical methods;
>
> (c) a *romantic response*, reflected in the "back-to-nature" approach, nostalgic for a return to a pre-technological way of life, ignoring the God-given dynamism of science and technology as a force to be brought under control rather than to be escaped from;
>
> (d) a *neo-apocalyptic approach*, which sees the ecological crisis as harbinger of the end of the world, rather than as a judgment of God calling us to repentance and the mending of our ways;

(e) the *utopian response*, which seeks unrealistic, naive and fanciful pictures of a perfect and problemless world in history, failing to recognize the structures of sin which will continue to menace us even without the ecological crisis (pp.15f.).

The 1990 Seoul convocation and the WCC assembly in Canberra the next year made it clear that a sound theology of ecology still has to be elaborated in the ecumenical movement. Sometimes the argument for ecology is based on a theme related to the doctrine of creation, sometimes on Christology or the gospel, including the doctrine of redemption, sometimes on eschatology. Affirmations 7 and 8 from Seoul — "The creation as beloved of God" and "The earth is the Lord's" — are too brief to be very helpful to this end, and the explanatory statements attached to them do not add more clarity. In a sub-section on "The Church: Covenanting for the Life of All Creation", the Canberra assembly could go no further than to state that "a critical examination of the church's faith, polity and structures may be necessary if the spiritual and organizational resources of the church should meet human and ecological needs. This implies a redirection of church policies, priorities and programmes" (*Signs of the Spirit: Official Report Seventh Assembly*, ed. M. Kinnamon, Geneva, WCC, 1991, p.67).

Canberra was clear about the inseparability of the present worldwide crises in social justice and in ecology and the environment:

> Social justice cannot happen apart from a healthy environment, and a sustainable and sustaining environment will not come about without greater social justice. Justice is truly indivisible, not only as a matter of theological conviction but in practice. The biblical concept of justice recognizes the need for healthy relationships in creation as a whole. This way of viewing justice helps us understand the linkage between poverty, powerlessness, social conflict and environmental degradation (p.55).

New ecumenical insights into the theology of creation have come from the inclusive trinitarian approach of Orthodoxy. The point of departure for speaking of the integrity of creation must be the confession of the Nicene Creed: God is the Creator of all things, Christ is the one through whom all things were made, the Holy Spirit is the Lord, the Giver of Life. It is not human beings who integrate creation; its integration is prior to their concern, prior to their participation. The integrity of creation is the work of the one who creates, redeems and sanctifies it. In addition, it may be that a certain revitalization of the recent discussion on the cosmic Christ could contribute to a broader understanding of ecological theology, without the elements of triumphalism sometimes entailed in the concept earlier.

* * *

This brief survey of some criticisms of recent ecumenical models of society inevitably raises the question of whether the ecumenical movement at this juncture is equipped to develop a new concept of a world society in such a dialogical way as to attract people and institutions that have not yet been part of Christian ecumenical deliberations. Can the ecumenical movement show the obvious limitations of its insights and convictions as much as it can communicate the central thrust of the gospel that all members of the human race are called into mutual dependence on one another, despite all their differences, because God is unceasingly and undiscriminatingly involved in the history of his precious planet? Only when such questions are honestly faced will the ecumenical concept of society gain relevance.

Equally crucial is the problem to which Konrad Raiser refers in the last chapter of *Ecumenism in Transition* (Geneva, WCC, 1991): the relation between the ecclesiological significance of the World Council of Churches and the Council's aim to grow through a conciliar process for justice, peace and the integrity of creation into a truly conciliar fellowship:

> It is not surprising that the initial attempt to link the conciliar process for justice, peace and the integrity of creation directly with steps towards the unity of the church in conciliar fellowship had very early to be given up: it led only to increased reservations on the part of the Roman Catholic Church and the Orthodox churches. What still remains of the original vision is not able to inspire much enthusiasm...
>
> The conciliar process needs to be directed towards formulating "touchstones", guiding markers in face of the challenges of justice,

peace and the integrity of creation. But such touchstones and criteria for the churches' witness and service are then not the product of superior conciliar authority and certainly not the result of conclusive deductions of general statements of faith. They are rather the results of insights gained in striving for truth. They remain provisional, revisable, and depend on being received in the fellowship of believers in Christ and on their truth being constantly tested (pp.118-20).

We will see the relevance of these pertinent contemporary observations at the end of Chapter XIV.

VI

International Affairs

Christian concern for peace and justice was expressed in the earlier ecumenical movement not only at the Stockholm (1925) and Oxford (1937) conferences of the Universal Christian Council for Life and Work, but also by the Tambaram conference of the International Missionary Council (1938). However, although these conferences delineated areas of concern for Christian witness, they provided no specialized structure or secretariat for continuing work.

The Commission of the Churches on International Affairs

A conference of church leaders in Cambridge, England, in 1946, organized by a joint committee of the International Missionary Council and the World Council of Churches in process of formation, proposed that the two ecumenical bodies set up a joint Commission of the Churches on International Affairs (CCIA) in order to serve their worldwide constituency as a "source of stimulus and knowledge in their approach to international problems, as a medium of common counsel and action and as their organ in formulating the Christian mind on world issues and in bringing that mind effectively to bear upon such issues".

The Cambridge conference defined the objectives of the Commission: alerting churches to international problems, stimulating the formation of Christian agencies on international affairs, distributing educational material and organizing international study and church conferences. It also outlined several areas of concern to guide CCIA in representations to international bodies, including the United Nations and related agencies: the development and codification of international law and effective international institutions, respect for and observance of human rights, in particular religious liberty, international regulation of armaments, furtherance of international economic cooperation, advocacy for dependent peoples and their advance to self-government and the promotion of international social, cultural, educational and humanitarian enterprises.

CCIA was established as a commission of the WCC at the Amsterdam assembly in 1948. Its principal aim, as revised by the central committee in 1985 reads:

> It shall be the task of the Commission to witness to the lordship of Christ over human beings and history by serving people in the field of international relations and promoting reconciliation and oneness of human beings by creation; to God's gracious and redemptive action in history; and to the assurance of the coming kingdom of God in Jesus Christ. This service is demanded by the church's participation in the continuing ministry of Christ in the world of priestly intercession, prophetic judgment, the arousing of hope and conscience and pastoral care. This task necessitates engagement in immediate and concrete issues as well as the formulation of general Christian aims and purposes (*Minutes*, p.119).

The Amsterdam assembly expressed the important contribution the church has to make to international relations through its own life and work:

> The establishment of the World Council of Churches can be made of great moment for the life of the nations. It is a living expression of... fellowship, transcending race and nation, class and culture, knit together in faith, service and understanding. Its aim will be to hasten international reconciliation through its own members and through the cooperation of all Christian churches and all men of goodwill. It will strive to see international differences in the light of God's design, remembering that normally there are Christians on both sides of every frontier. It should not weary in the effort to state the Christian understanding of the will of God and to promote its application to national and international policy (*Man's Disorder and God's Design*, vol. IV, London, SCM Press, 1949, p.223).

From the beginning CCIA has maintained formal relations with the United Nations Economic and Social Council and its Commissions, the Food and Agriculture Organization (FAO) and UNESCO.

There were also informal contacts with the Trusteeship Council, the Technical Assistance Board and Administration, the office of the High Commissioner for Refugees (UNHCR), the International Labour Office (ILO), the World Health Organization (WHO), the UN Korean Reconstruction Agency, the UN Relief and Works Agency for Palestine Refugees (UNRWA), the UN Children's Fund (UNICEF), the Inter-Governmental Committee for European Migration and the Council of Europe.

More recently, in its work within the UN system, CCIA has maintained close liaison on behalf of the WCC with several other UN bodies, notably the Centre for Disarmament, the Department of Political and Security Council Affairs, the Committee of 24 (Decolonization), the Centre against Apartheid and its committee, the Division of (now Centre for) Human Rights and others. It has long had direct contacts at the highest levels of the UN, participating regularly in meetings of the Human Rights Commission and sponsoring delegations to meetings of the UN General Assembly, the FAO and special events related to disarmament, women, racism and the like.

The CCIA has submitted documents on a great variety of subjects related to international tensions and conflicts and has made verbal interventions at many UN meetings. It has taken a leadership role in the community of non-governmental organizations (NGOs). Often it renders technical assistance to churches and regional ecumenical bodies in furthering their participation in intergovernmental bodies. Its commissioners hold positions in churches, education, government and other walks of public life. National commissions of the churches have cooperated with CCIA, their impact on their own governments varying in accordance with national circumstances.

At the Evanston assembly (1954) and in CCIA's subsequent work, efforts were made to expand the concept of a "responsible society" to the concept of a "responsible international society". Earlier the term had largely been used for domestic political and economic arrangements; now guidelines were also provided for responsible international behaviour. In its statement on an international ethos, Evanston tentatively listed some principles or "middle axioms" for nations:

(a) All power carries responsibility and all nations are trustees of power, which should be used for the common good.

(b) All nations are subject to moral law, and should strive to abide by the accepted principles of international law, to develop this law and to enforce it through common actions.

(c) All nations should honour their pledged word and international agreements into which they have entered.

(d) No nation in an international dispute has the right to be the sole judge in its own cause or to resort to war to advance its policies, but should seek to settle disputes by direct negotiation or by submitting them to conciliation, arbitration or judicial settlement.

(e) All nations have a moral obligation to ensure universal security and to this end should support measures designed to deny victory to a declared aggressor.

(f) All nations should recognize and safeguard the inherent dignity, worth and essential rights of the human person, without distinction as to race, sex, language or religion.

(g) Each nation should recognize the rights of every other nation which observes such standards to live by and proclaim its own political and social beliefs, provided that it does not seek by coercion, threat, infiltration or deception to impose these on other nations.

(h) All nations should recognize an obligation to share their scientific and technical skills with peoples in less developed regions, and to help the victims of disaster in other lands.

(i) All nations should strive to develop cordial relations with their neighbours, encourage friendly cultural and commercial dealings and join in creative international efforts for human welfare (*The Evanston Report*, London, SCM Press, 1955, p.142).

International order and the United Nations

There are considerable differences between national and international law. In almost all states national law is part of a constitutional and legal order, with authority attributed to legislative, judicial and executive branches of government and institutions existing to enact and to enforce the law. By contrast, the international community of nations has no central institutions vested with such authority. The international law that governs relations between nations derives its authority primarily from acceptance and consent on the part of the nations, rather than from institutions created to enact and enforce it.

A distinction must be made between international law of coexistence and international law of cooperation. Characteristic of the former, which aims at keeping states "peacefully" apart rather than working fruitfully together, are the principles of sovereign equality, self-determination and non-intervention. The latter requires positive and effective measures on the basis of the interdependence of peoples and nations. An international order which upholds the values inherent in peace, justice and the integrity of nature can be shaped only through collective efforts in international organizations. It is in this context that the activities of the United Nations and its special agencies are of crucial importance. They give impetus to the development of the international law of cooperation.

The overall position of the WCC on the role and function of international law has changed from a theoretical and ethical approach to a more contextual and pragmatic stand. In more recent statements the Council has made few references to the role of international law as such, but has frequently appealed for respect for existing international agreements or for new agreements to be concluded. Awareness of ever newly emerging crises in international relations has led to a shift of emphasis from participating in the reform of order to supporting those struggling for liberation and justice. An international order based on maintaining existing political, economic and financial structures has increasingly been perceived as the main obstacle to the true well-being of all nations. The ecumenical task is seen in terms of building an "oikoumene of solidarity" rather than an "oikoumene of domination".

Yet it is clear that if the United Nations is to become a truly effective international order the need to develop an international ethos in breadth and depth is as real as ever. The UN's objectives and directions are set and altered by the operation of its political process, in which the clash and consensus of the aims of member states determine the choices made. Consequently, what is important is not believing in the UN as a sacred cause, but recognizing it as an agency subject to manipulation by states for their own purposes.

The United Nations can at best facilitate the balancing of power against power and mobilize the resources of political adjustment. In the long run it may transform the working of the multi-state system; in the short run it is inevitably more affected by the circumstances of international relations than it is effective in altering them. From this it follows that the realization of the ideals of the UN Charter depends on how responsibly the sovereign states exercise their membership. In practice they use the UN for a variety of ends, some of which do not figure in the Charter and in fact militate against it.

Commemorating the fortieth anniversary of the founding of the United Nations, the WCC central committee meeting at Buenos Aires in 1985 stated:

> The world is witnessing a crisis of confidence in international institutions, a growing breakdown in multi-lateralism and a gradual erosion in the authority of the UN. This threatens to sweep away the foundations of world peace and a stable international order. As the UN Secretary-General has said: "We are perilously near to a new international anarchy"...
>
> Over the past four decades, the United Nations has lived through an unprecedented period of turbulent change: the rapid transformation of society by science and technology as well as the aspirations of the people to equality, participation and dignity; the doubling of the world's population; the tripling of its membership as over 700 million people emerged from colonial rule; the threat of global nuclear destruction; and the widening disparities between affluence and poverty among and within nations. Sitting in the vortex, the UN has demonstrated itself to be indispensable, unique in its hopes, achievements and potential (*Minutes*, pp.23, 106).

Public statements

It is often difficult to decide when the World Council of Churches should take up a clear position and when it should be intentionally silent. Both in the context of the UN and in the context of relations between nations and their governments, the problem of issuing public statements and commending them to the churches — when to speak and when not to speak — has regularly been discussed in the ecumenical movement.

The Amsterdam assembly recognized the importance of public Christian statements:

> With respect to public pronouncements, the Council regards it as an essential part of its responsibility to address its own constituent members as occasion may arise, on matters which might require united attention in the realm of thought or action. Further important issues may arise which radically affect the church and society. While it is certainly undesirable that the Council should issue such pro-

nouncements often and on many subjects, there will certainly be a clear obligation for the Council to speak out when vital issues concerning all churches and the whole world are at stake.

According to the rules adopted for the WCC:

> While... statements may have great significance and influence as the expression of the judgment or concern of so widely representative a Christian body, yet their authority will consist only in the weight which they carry by their own truth and wisdom, and the publishing of such statements shall not be held to imply that the World Council as such has, or can have, any constitutional authority over the constituent churches or right to speak for them (*The First Assembly of the World Council of Churches, Amsterdam 1948*, London, SCM Press, 1949, pp.128,210).

The rules also provide for statements to be made by the executive committee, the officers of the central committee and the general secretary.

Particularly at the level of an assembly, it is difficult to decide how to select a limited number of "vital issues" on which to speak. The Vancouver and Canberra assemblies (1983 and 1991) gave a clear example of that quandary; and they were accused by some of having said too much on too many issues and by others of having said too little and on too few concerns.

In 1976, the central committee tried to make explicit the criteria that help the Council to select the issues on which it makes statements. It listed: (1) areas and issues in which the WCC has had direct involvement and long-standing commitment; (2) emerging issues of international concern to which the attention of the churches should be called for action; (3) critical and developing political situations which demand the WCC to make known its judgment and lend its spiritual and moral voice; (4) expectations from the member churches that the WCC should speak; (5) the need to set a policy mandate for the WCC secretariat. But this list is not exhaustive nor a set of hard and fast rules. Sensitive to the special nature of a situation and taking into account other forms of action available, the assembly, central or executive committee or general secretary, assisted by CCIA, decides whether a public statement would be appropriate.

Several decades of experience in an interdependent but conflictive world have shown not only the elusiveness of ultimate political, social or economic solutions, but also the ease with which Christians may lose their way in this area. It is in this perspective that public ecumenical statements must be seen. They are often ignored, and their impact is often limited. But sometimes governments, other bodies and political movements do pay attention to Christian pronouncements and even seek advice or assistance. Sometimes they seriously overestimate the capacity of the Council, but they do look upon it as a trusted partner in dialogue, not so much because they perceive the WCC as having a strictly humanitarian or neutral position, but because they see in it signs of hope that go beyond apparent historical possibilities and a willingness to listen to and understand their positions and dilemmas. Significantly, among those who seek the Council's mediation are many who are not Christian and many from sectors of world society with whom the WCC has had little contact.

Ronald Preston has summarized the value of those ecumenical pronouncements which "do not unchurch those who disagree", but "put the onus on them to produce cogent reasons for disagreeing". He suggests in an essay entitled "A Breakthrough in Ecumenical Social Ethics?" **(222)** that there are six reasons why such statements may be useful:

> (1) as a help to the individual Christian in his own decisions;
>
> (2) as a link between those of different confessions;
>
> (3) as a potential link between Christians and those of other faiths and none;
>
> (4) as a dissolver of the division between the parson and the layman, for the experience of both is needed to formulate them;
>
> (5) as a stimulus to creating a bad conscience when society, and perhaps the church as a whole, is complacent;
>
> (6) in helping the church to achieve some purchase over events and not lag behind them (pp.36f.).

Challenges in the post-Cold War world

Recent dramatic and unexpectedly radical changes in the world have deeply affected the whole of humanity. Although the uncontrollability, irrationality and inhumanity of concentrated political, economic, technological and military power have created an intricate global problem for some time, there was at least some kind of "balance" between two superpowers during the Cold War. The collapse of totalitarian Marxist systems in Eastern Europe and the critical changes in the former USSR have left a single military superpower which threatens to dominate the whole of world affairs. Some have suggested that the former balance of terror was preferable to today's situation.

This "new world order" can also be described in terms of the increasing prerogative of a few affluent nations to dictate the terms of international "cooperation":

> Humankind is experiencing one of the most momentous shifts in modern history as a group of powerful nations has, through the internal collapse of Eastern Europe, been given the opportunity to put an economic and political gridlock over most of the world. It could mean a further exacerbation of the North-South divide in power, wealth, political influence, education and technological proficiency, a deeper marginalization and impoverishment of third world societies with all its attendant evils and a virtual replay of the old colonialism in subtle but far more lethal forms. Psychologically and politically, such a situation could encourage a new racism of the peoples of the North against those of the South as the latter press upon the borders of the former (*Utopia and Liberation — Towards a Human World*, Geneva, WCC, 1992, p.58).

The need to impose limits on geo-political and economic power in the interests of justice and freedom is increasingly dramatic in the present violent and explosive world. A democratic tradition in international politics, founded on a complex balance and division of powers and the accountability of all powers, political and economic, takes on new importance in ecumenical social ethics. The responsibility and accountability of the United Nations and its agencies are of particular concern.

But a rash adventurism seemed to contaminate the United Nations, and even some NGOs, immediately after the Cold War. Although "democracy" has become a catchword in the 1990s, the United Nations has seemed to move away from two fundamental principles of democracy: separation of powers and decentralization of power. The maintenance of peace has been entrusted to political instruments, the Security Council and to a lesser degree the General Assembly, and development to specialized institutions and organisms. The present tendency is to entrust increasingly more importance to the UN's political organs. Among the negative consequences of this separation of the functions are the transformation of the role of the Security Council from "maintaining" peace into "establishing" peace and the imposition of more and more political (rather than social and economic) conditions on nations receiving development aid.

Two tendencies in the definition of democracy are matters of serious concern. The first is the minimalist tendency to identify it exclusively with a pluralistic system and free and impartial elections. Such a definition guarantees neither wide participation in national affairs nor the right usage of political power. The second is the equating of democracy and development with the transition to a market economy — a definition which many countries in the South reject as itself non-democratic. To speak of an equal access of unequal partners to the market economy is a contradiction in terms. In the zeal to promote the free market, the specific recognition by the UN Charter that there are several ways to tackle the question of development and the economy is ignored.

The accomplishments of the UN in the humanitarian, educational and cultural fields are undeniable. Its agencies have contributed substantially to alleviating human suffering and laying the foundations for the independence of many nations. The problem is that the UN is manipulated by a few powerful countries which exercise absolute authority over the international infrastructure. The Gulf War of 1991 pushed the UN Security Council even further into the powerful sphere of influence of the United States.

But how to expose the ways in which this concentration of power hinders life-enhancing developments is not evident. The status of NGOs at the UN is a consultative one, and it is difficult for them and other institutions to concentrate international attention on concrete issues which are clearly global — arms production, world trade, the environment-development link, eradication of Northern agricultural subsidies and the reduction or abolition of third world debt. For the ecumenical movement this would require a sustained focus on the problems of every continent which neither churches nor regional ecumenical bodies have yet found it possible to undertake together.

There is, moreover, more divergence than convergence within the churches themselves with regard to various international relations (see Chapters IX and XIII). There is not a single recent joint statement on a burning world issue by the Roman Catholic Church and the World Council of Churches. For many years the National Council of the Churches of Christ in the USA has been faulted for what is seen in some quarters as making unfair criticisms of the US government and taking positions on international affairs which are contrary to the national interest. The Christian Conference of Asia was forced to move out of Singapore for what were called by the government subversive activities.

In post-communist Central and Eastern Europe, will the Orthodox churches and other Christian communities, particularly in the new Russian Federation, support and strengthen the present experiments with democracy or will they rally to the defence of traditional nationalist aspirations for a political and social system quite distinct from other countries in Europe? To what extent will churches be able to contribute to the renewal of society by helping their faithful to engage the complicated issues of social ethics and political theology which arise incessantly? The answers to such questions are not yet clear. Moreover, it must be remembered that there is a perception in some parts of these churches that the ecumenical movement did not help them sufficiently to grapple with their predicament in the past, so that communication between them and the World Council of Churches is still impaired and mutual understanding has yet to be achieved.

In all their hard and complex realities, international affairs seem to be the locus of the greatest denial of God's promise of his coming reign over peoples and nations. The wealthy countries, monopolizing scientific, technological and military power, will continue to resort to any possible strategy to sabotage efforts to challenge their dominance. And yet at the root of Christian faith and ecumenical engagement there is not the slightest doubt that, despite all opposition, God will achieve his purpose of unlimited peace and the well-being of the whole of humanity.

VII

Human Rights and Religious Liberty

From 1948 onwards the engagement of the ecumenical movement on behalf of justice has been concerned with promoting human freedom and dignity and combating violations of human rights, including religious liberty. The WCC has come to discern new dimensions in human rights, both qualitatively and quantitatively. The list of human rights has been considerably extended, and the inter-relation between the violation of human rights and evil structures of society has come to the forefront.

Historical developments

The first director of the CCIA, O. Frederick Nolde, participated alongside governmental representatives in drafting the Universal Declaration of Human Rights, serving especially as a consultant on religious liberty and freedom of conscience. In the years following its adoption in December 1948, the CCIA was constantly present to advise and lobby the UN on human rights matters and to promote the elaboration of the international covenants on human rights, as well as other human rights instruments.

In 1948 there was a tendency to regard individual rights as a prerequisite to the rights of the whole society and collective rights as an accumulation of individual rights. The "Declaration of Religious Liberty" adopted by the Amsterdam assembly reflected this position. But continued exposure to the experience of churches under diverse social systems and suffering from a large variety of human rights abuses has taught the ecumenical movement that the individual is naturally and inevitably linked to and part of a community, so that corporate rights, people's rights and national rights must have a place in any comprehensive understanding of human rights.

In the WCC understanding it is not appropriate to arrange rights in a hierarchy of importance. The report **(98)** of an international consultation at St Pölten, Austria, sponsored by CCIA in 1974, put it this way: "Individual and collective rights... are related. It should be the aim of the community to secure the welfare of all its members, the aim of the individual to serve the general good. In both instances rights involve responsibilities" (p.60). Political structures have often become instrumental in dehumanizing large sectors of the population. Human rights violations have become widespread and even institutionalized in many countries. It is important to challenge any society which, for the sake of what it calls national security or the common good, violates human rights, including religious liberty.

After the Nairobi assembly (1975) CCIA worked closely with member churches, regional ecumenical bodies and national councils of churches in analyzing key issues arising from the struggle for human rights, initiating actions to help victims of human rights violations and tackling the root causes of such violations. A number of Christian communities have taken up the difficult task of conscientiously carrying out a prophetic and pastoral role in the face of the prevalent abuses of power.

But many churches, supporting the status quo, still tacitly accept discrimination and inequality, particularly against women, children, minorities and people of other races. Churches are also tempted to judge other societies more harshly than their own and to see problems elsewhere through the eyes of their own histories, theologies and worldviews. Furthermore, ecclesiastical structures on the whole do not permit participation and action at the levels of decision-making and power politics.

In the report of Section III, "Structures of International Cooperation: Living Together in Peace in a Pluralistic World Society" **(53)**, the world conference on Church and Society (Geneva 1966) explicitly urged Christians everywhere to encourage ratification and enforcement by their governments of the various international human rights covenants, in part in order to stimulate "the evolution of an international moral ethos":

The church... must strive to be faithful to its spiritual heritage and teaching... The pulpit shares with the classroom the important task of giving instruction in the gospel and its meaning for full brotherhood without discrimination. It must press for adoption of educational curricula that stress the oneness of humanity instead of its differences, and inculcate appreciation and respect for the cultures of other peoples. It must take positive initiatives to ensure such teaching especially within the church itself (pp.136f.).

In the report of Section IV, "Towards Justice and Peace in International Affairs", the Uppsala assembly (1968) addressed the protection of individuals and groups in the political world:

Human rights cannot be safeguarded in a world of glaring inequalities and social conflict. Even slavery has not yet been totally abolished in every country. A deep change in human attitude is now required. Christians and Christian churches should in their own relations set an example of respect for human dignity, equality and the free expression of thought... The active engagement of people of all ages in development, reconciliation and social work is to be encouraged and supported as an expression of worldwide solidarity. The churches must assist in channelling this engagement. Governments should recognize and support such services as ranking at least as national service...

Violations of human rights in one place may be quickly communicated to all, spreading an evil and destructive influence abroad. Nations should recognize that the protection of fundamental human rights and freedoms has now become a common concern of the whole international community, and should therefore not regard international concern for the implementation of these rights as an unwarranted interference...

All peoples have the right to self-determination. This is a basic essential of human dignity and of a genuine family of nations. But nations are seldom altogether one homogeneous people. Most nations have ethnic, cultural or religious minorities... The churches must defend minorities when they are oppressed or threatened. They must at times urge restraint upon minorities in the pursuit of their ambitions. But also they must help majorities to respond creatively to the impatience of minorities in their struggle for justice (*The Uppsala Report 1968*, ed. Norman Goodall, Geneva, WCC, 1968, pp.64f.).

The statement on human rights by the Vancouver assembly (1983) recalled the categories of human rights listed by the Nairobi assembly in 1975: to basic guarantees of life; to self-determination, cultural identity and the rights of minorities; to participate in decision-making within the community; to dissent; to personal dignity; to religious freedom:

Following Nairobi, the churches have seen the need to broaden their understanding of human rights to include the right to peace, the right to protection of the environment, the right to development and the right to know one's rights and to struggle for them. We have also come to appreciate more clearly the complexity and inter-relatedness of human rights. In this regard we recognize the need to set individual rights and their violation in the context of society and its social structures.

We are increasingly aware of the fact that human rights cannot be dealt with in isolation from the larger issues of peace, justice, militarism, disarmament and development. The fuller the rights that every person enjoys in society, the more stable that society is likely to be; the fuller the implementation of human rights globally, the more stable international relations are likely to be. Injustice in a society, including the corruption of public officials, may contribute to domestic economic and political disorder, which in turn may lead to the deterioration in relations among nations. We have moved beyond mere reflection to concrete engagement in human rights struggles. In doing so, however, we have discovered how difficult and painful it is to cope with human rights and their violations. We have found that in promoting the rights of women, youth, children and disabled persons, for example, the churches need to examine and often alter their own structures and methods of operation. In struggling for justice many Christians are experiencing the way of the cross...

Considerable thought needs to be given to the development of new initiatives in order to improve the churches' record of implementation. Among the possible initiatives that might be undertaken are the announcement of an international day of prayer for human rights, the creation of a world action week for the education of church members and the promotion of human rights, and the establishment of a series of regional and global review conferences to evaluate the work done by the churches in the field of human rights (*Gathered for Life*, ed. David Gill, Geneva, WCC, 1983, pp.140-43).

An assessment

It should be noted that Vancouver's assessment of the modesty of the church's record in this field came after a decade and a half which had seen intensive and high-profile ecumenical engagement in human rights issues, through such steps as the creation of the Programme to Combat Racism after the Uppsala assembly in 1968, the concerted effort to reach a consensus on an ecumenical understanding of human rights at the Nairobi assembly in 1975, the setting up of a WCC Human Rights Resources Office for Latin America following a number of military coups in the mid-1970s, the establishment of a Human Rights Advisory Group within CCIA in 1978 and creation of numerous regional ecumenical human rights programmes.

Is there an ecumenical theological basis for human rights? The St Pölten consultation attempted to make a theological statement on human rights **(98)**:

> The emphasis of the gospel is on the value of all human beings in the sight of God, on the atoning and redeeming work of Christ that gives to man his true dignity, on love as the motive for action and on love for one's neighbour as the practical expression of an active faith in Christ. We are all members of one another, and when one suffers, all are hurt. This is a Christian interpretation of "human solidarity" (p.59).

But in the entry on "Human Rights" in the *Dictionary of the Ecumenical Movement* (Geneva, WCC, 1991) Erich Weingärtner warns against giving the churches too much credit in this area:

> In light of official church opposition to human rights, viewed for much of their history as the product of humanistic philosophy, the claim of a "theological basis of human rights" might be considered somewhat presumptuous. It is only after the second world war that serious theological work related to human rights has surfaced, and even then much of it concentrated solely on the right to religious liberty. In the Roman Catholic Church, human rights received official sanction through Pope John XXIII's encyclical *Pacem in terris* of 1963 and in the Second Vatican Council's pastoral constitution *Gaudium et spes*, 1965. Ecumenically, the WCC co-ordinated an interconfessional study project on theology and human rights begin-ning in 1979, in which Anglican, Lutheran, Reformed, Baptist and

Methodist world bodies as well as the preparatory committee of the pan-Orthodox council and the holy see's Pontifical Commission Justice and Peace participated.

Institutional efforts which for the most part try to derive human rights systematically from traditional theological concepts such as natural law, covenant, grace, Christology or redemption have been criticized for functionalizing theology in order to regain the churches' credibility or to justify Christian engagement in human rights activities. Such an approach differs radically from that adopted by Christians and theologians who are themselves engaged at the fore-front of human rights struggles, impelled by their Christian faith, but without an articulated prior justification. Theological literature emanating from Christian reflection on concrete life-and-death experiences is growing rapidly, especially in regions where the violation of human rights is most severe. Much of this discussion evades or resists systematic classification according to traditional theological categories and is therefore open to controversy, as for example Latin American liberation theology, Korean minjung theology or the Kairos document by South African theologians. The free development of such unorthodox theological approaches has itself become a human rights claim and raises the question as to whether the limits imposed by church hierarchies on theological or ecumenical dialogue are themselves an infringement of human rights (pp.486f.).

The promotion of religious liberty has also become more complicated and demanding. For some decades, the WCC has played an active role in promoting dialogue among people of different faiths as a way to prevent Christians from disfiguring the image of their neighbours of different faiths. This presupposes mutual respect and trust in the integrity of each participant. But inter-faith dialogue has been easier in an international context than at the national level, where religious groups, including churches, have often never engaged in serious conversations with each other. Rather, each religious community stresses its own legitimate existence and the unique authenticity of its faith.

In a recent book, *Religious Freedom in a Changing World* (Geneva, WCC, 1992), Ninan Koshy observes:

Promoting religious harmony is one important way to contribute to peace. Today, one major threat to peace comes from violations of religious liberty and intolerance on the basis of religion and belief. Hence the urgency of giving more attention to religious liberty. Fundamental to humanity is an inescapable quest for meaning and belonging, for making sense of life and finding community. This urge to find meaning is as precious as life itself. It finds expression in ultimate beliefs. Religious liberty is the freedom to uphold such beliefs free from any coercion. Its basis is the God-given and inviolable dignity of the human being. It is intertwined with freedom of conscience. The right to religious liberty in its essence is inalienable and non-negotiable. The affirmation of religious liberty is inseparable from Christian witness. The defence of religious liberty is thus integral to the mission of the church (p.115).

This brief overview of the involvement of the ecumenical movement in defining and defending human rights reveals that the churches can claim no special initiatives in championing the human rights of millions of human beings; and they should not present themselves as a kind of an avant-garde in spelling out and protecting human rights. Too often they share with society as a whole an impotence and a vulnerability to hypocrisy on this point. In fact the struggle for human rights requires no theological justification as such. It arises as part of the human struggle and it is authentic and authenticated as such. Churches should not seek proprietary rights over this struggle, as though it is up to Christians to validate its legitimacy. This is David Jenkins' position in "Some Questions, Hypotheses and Theses for a Theological Inquiry Concerning Human Rights", included in the St Pölten report **(98)**:

Men and women are committed to this struggle because of what they are, because of what is happening to them and because of what they long and hope to be. As Christians we know that all this is a reflection of the reality that men and women are made in the image of God and made for self-fulfilment in the glory of God. But this is a faithful and theological reflection on a human reality established and to be taken absolutely seriously in its own right. Theology and faith are to respond to this human reality. No other justification than the reality and the nature of the struggle is required either for the existence of the struggle or for the demand that we respond to it and are part of it (p.30).

VIII

Ideology and Ideologies

From the 1930s to the 1960s the term "ideology" was exclusively used in a pejorative sense in the ecumenical movement. Ideologies, particularly those of Marxist origin, were regarded as total systems competing for the spiritual allegiance of humankind. Utterly godless, growing out of distorted perspectives on society and utopian expectations, they must be rejected unequivocally. The report of the 1937 Oxford conference, *The Churches Survey Their Task* **(3)**, insisted that "every tendency to identify the kingdom of God with a particular structure of society or economic mechanism must result in moral confusion for those who maintain the system and in disillusionment for those who suffer from its limitations" (p.96).

In his encyclical letter *Divini redemptoris* (New York, Paulist Press, 1937), Pope Pius XI issued the strongest condemnation of communist ideology of any 20th-century church document. Quoting Leo XIII, who defined communism as a "fatal plague which insinuates itself into the very marrow of human society only to bring about its ruin", Pius warned that "communism is intrinsically wrong, and no one who would save Christian civilization may collaborate with it in any undertaking whatsoever" (pp.4, 26).

Ideology as negative

The first two WCC assemblies at Amsterdam (1948) and Evanston (1954) carried the argument in a new direction. The dramatic debate at Amsterdam between conservative US Presbyterian layman and diplomat John Foster Dulles, over-confident in his defence of the "free world", and Czech theologian Josef Hromádka, little sophisticated in his defense of communism, helped the delegates to sense the need to find a way between these opposing perspectives. The concept of the Responsible Society was accepted as the criterion for determining Christian thought and action in the conflict between these competing ideologies. Christians should "reject the ideologies both of communism and laissez-faire capitalism", the assembly report **(31)** stated, "and should seek to draw people away from the false assumption that these extremes are the only alternatives... It is the responsibility of Christians to seek new, creative solutions which never allow either justice or freedom to destroy the other" (p.50).

Evanston, reflecting the cold war experience, reiterated the main points made by Amsterdam on the conflict between Christian faith, Marxist ideology and totalitarian practice. As a "criterion by which we judge all existing social orders" and a guide for specific choices, the responsible society was seen as "a symbol of the social arrangement maintaining in dynamic equilibrium freedom and order, liberty and justice, while barring the road to tyranny and anarchy". The assembly called disputes about "capitalism" and "socialism" misleading, because the terms are used for so many different social forms and economic systems:

> It is not the case that we have merely a choice between two easily distinguishable types of economic organization. Private enterprise takes many shapes in different countries at different stages... and is profoundly affected by the forms of government regulation... In some countries the "welfare state" or the "mixed economy" suggests a new pattern of economic life; others may be regarded as "capitalist", but the capitalism of today is very different from the capitalism of even twenty or thirty years ago. The concrete issues in all countries concern the newly-evolving forms of economic organization, and the relative roles of the state, organized groups and private enterprises (*The Evanston Report*, London, SCM Press, 1955, p.113-17).

While Evanston for the first time mentioned the unfortunate effects of "sterile anti-communism" in many Western societies, the idea that Christians must say a clear No to the communist state before they can begin to recognize positive aspects of the Marxist achievement remained current until 1966. The churches must work to enlarge the area of human freedom through "gradual and slow" reforms. After Amsterdam and Evanston no later WCC assembly included ideology and ideologies on its agenda or dealt explicitly with the subject.

Towards a new understanding

At the world conference on Church and Society (Geneva 1966), the theme of ideology was approached for the first time from a largely non-Western perspective. The conference report **(53)** defines ideology in a non-pejorative sense:

> By ideology we mean a process quite different from a total system of ideas which is closed to correction and new insight. Ideology as we use it here is the theoretical and analytical structure of thought which undergirds successful action to realize revolutionary change in society or to undergird and justify its status quo. Its usefulness is proved in the success of its practice. Its validity is that it expresses the self-understanding, the hopes and values of the social group that holds it, and guides the practice of that group (p.202).

This new, more positive understanding of ideology reflected the concern for opening Christian thought to new ideological developments arising in the liberation struggles in Africa, Asia, Latin America and the Middle East. Geneva admitted that "theology reflects not only action but interaction between God's revelation and human beings' ideological understanding of their own condition and desires. Christians, like all other human beings, are affected by ideological perspectives" (p.202). The report of a Church and Society exploratory conference on "Technology and the Future of Man and Society" **(114)** went on to say that "the relation of faith to ideology remains a question to be worked out in concrete situations" (p.76).

In a report entitled "Images of the Future" **(58)** the working committee on Church and Society, meeting in Nemi, Italy, in 1971, listed seven current ideologies — liberal ideology, Marxist ideology, social democratic ideology, "technocratism", nationalism, reactive ideologies and cultural traditionalism. To its description of each it added a few sentences of critical evaluation and a healing vision of their future. But despite the apparently objective method of sociological analysis followed, this classification of current ideologies did little to offer inspiration and challenge for specific political actions in actual power conflicts and social struggles.

To facilitate deeper analysis and to locate the issue of ideology within the World Council's programme structure, the central committee decided at Addis Ababa in 1971 to add the two words "and

Ideologies" to the name of the sub-unit on Dialogue with Men of Other Faiths. By doing so it indicated that the outreach of dialogue should include the proponents of both religious and ideological views. But it made no recommendations on how to work out a combined dialogue between religions and ideologies or even a bilateral Christian-Marxist dialogue. While there are legitimate grounds for not totally separating ideologies and religions, especially since all religions tend to deny forcefully any ideological infiltration or bias within their own systems of faith, the follow-up of this 1971 mandate was not a success.

On the one hand, a small Christian-Marxist consultation, sponsored by Church and Society in 1968, remained a single and isolated event. Only a few Marxists from Eastern Europe and communists from the third world were willing to participate in a meaningful dialogue. Also old questions were raised about the purpose of such a dialogue, the specific issues to be discussed and the methodology to be followed. On the other hand, despite a more positive view of ideology in some ecumenical quarters, it remained true, as the Geneva conference **(53)** had put it, that "there is no agreement among Christians themselves on the degree to which analysis and action in Christian ethics itself must wrestle with ideological bias" (p.206). Thus the WCC continued to face the task of defining the term ideology more precisely for its own use and of undertaking some conclusive studies of the ideological presuppositions and perspectives implicit in the formulation and implementation of a number of its own programmes and activities. The urgency of this task became increasingly obvious in the context of the disintegration of the socialist movement following the 1968 Warsaw Pact intervention in Czechoslovakia.

In 1974 the WCC central committee in Berlin approved recommendations to seek an alternative terminology that would avoid the ambiguity of "ideology", which refers both "to a constructive vision for social change and to an idolatrous system", to ask "how far ideological presuppositions may be contributing to the unity or disunity of the church" and to find "appropriate ways to support Christians for whom ideologies represent a threat rather than a positive challenge" (*Minutes*, pp.31f.). This mandate was followed up by an ecumenical consultation on faith and ideologies at Cartigny, near Geneva, in 1975. The memorandum issued by this exploratory meeting **(110)** was a general and defensive document, unrelated to the actual ideological struggles and clashes in all parts of the world. By adopting a neutral usage of "ideology" as "an expression — systematic or not — of human views of social reality which reflect the basic conditions of the life of social groups" (p.2), the consultation in fact reversed the process of dealing concretely with ideologies.

The main concern of the Cartigny meeting was "to see how Christians of different ideological commitments can live together in the 'space for confrontation in Christ' without turning diversity into hostility". The participants were satisfied to raise the questions of the effect on the unity of the church of the diverse ideological commitments of Christians in different parts of the world and the limits beyond which diversity may break the fellowship of the church. The centre of the debate was not the theoretical and analytical structure of the ideological reflection that undergirds successful action for social change but the integrity and continuity of the worldwide Christian community. Only a few were concerned that the common task is not to prove that the ecumenical fellowship can comprehend various ideologies, but to emphasize that the creation of a new conscious and critical infrastructure of society is a matter of Christian discipleship and obedience. A concrete ideological commitment need not be interpreted as a total religious commitment but always remains a provisional undertaking.

The Nairobi assembly (1975) was not able to carry the debate further. Participants in the third sub-section of Section III on "Seeking Community: The Common Search of People of Various Faiths, Cultures and Ideologies" frankly admitted that they were not prepared to discuss such a complicated topic. Much time was spent on the questions of whether socialism (in contrast to communism) is an "ideology" or a movement and whether ideological co-existence is possible.

In 1981 the WCC sub-unit on Dialogue with People of Living Faiths and Ideologies (DFI) sponsored a special consultation on ideology and ideologies in Geneva. The theme was not churches and Christians *against* ideologies but *among* ideologies. Using the working definition of ideology of the Church and Society conference of 1966, the report of the consultation **(109)** added:

The given definition needs one qualification. There are, on the one hand, comprehensive blueprints for the structure of society. On the other hand, there are to be found ideological elements or factors that might not be part of a well-thought out system but are nevertheless of great influence on the behaviour of human beings, perhaps without their conscious knowledge (p.3).

The report goes on to discuss WCC structures and ideological presuppositions, ideologies and ideological convictions in the WCC as consciously expressed and as perceived by others, the need for similar self-examination in the member churches and a recommendation to engage in a positive encounter with people of other ideologies.

Receiving the report, the 1982 central committee meeting recommended that DFI develop additional programmes focusing on the so-called ideological captivity of the churches, the ideological elements in interfaith dialogue and direct dialogue "between and among Christians and persons for whom ideological convictions alone give meaning to their lives" (*Minutes*, p.59). Two years later the central committee, for reasons that are not entirely clear, completely reversed its position, relieving DFI of programmatic responsibility in the area of ideology and shifting it to the Programme Unit on Justice and Service (*Minutes*, p.42).

Meeting in Hanover in 1988, the central committee "noted with great interest the developments in many Marxist-led societies which have profound and positive implications for the life and witness of the churches in these societies and the ecumenical community". The committee asked the Unit on Justice and Service, in collaboration with other units, to give special attention to the study and examination of "the economic and political changes, the fresh approaches to ideological and philosophical issues and the contribution of the churches towards the restructuring of the society" (*Minutes*, p.93).

The unresolved problem

The World Council of Churches has not been able to spell out concretely and in detail a contemporary communitarian ethics regarding private and state production, maximum and minimum wages, equal employment, control of over-consumption, participation in development aid, protection of the environment, irresponsible technological advance, disarmament, the debt crisis, social welfare, the role of labour unions, public transportation and so on. Despite the difficulties, which caution against simplistic expectations of the advance of justice in the world and the churches' role in this, the analysis and evaluation of all the structures of society is a crucial ecumenical enterprise. It can advance only if powerful and powerless, believers and unbelievers, liberal democrats, social democrats, socialists and others spell out *together* how more favourable human social, political and economic conditions can be obtained.

Three essays on "Ecumenical Social Thought in the Post-Cold War Period" **(210)** document the uncertainty, disorientation and indifference that characterize the present situation, which Charles C. West summarizes as follows:

(1) In a world where major ideologies are breaking down and religious-cultural nationalisms are rising, the time is past when we can coerce each other's consciences with moral absolutes. Past also is the time when we can dismiss each other's theology or social analysis with a hermeneutic of suspicion. In their place we need to confront one another's faith and morals in the context of the work of God who judges and redeems us all. This does not mean that the struggle for justice and liberation should be less intense or that bad theology should go unchallenged. It means rather that this struggle and this challenge become truly serious, because it does not come from the hopes and desires of the challenger but from the calling and command of God who corrects and directs us all...

(2) We need a more subtle, a more differentiated analysis than now of the powers at work in the modern world and their relation to the justifying and reconciling power of God. There is more human power abroad in the world today than ever before in history. Its distribution is drastically unequal, yet there is little clarity about where the centres of power, and therefore of responsibility, lie. In this condition conspiracy theories, whether Marxist or right reactionary, do more harm than good. The ecumenical task of the church is to discern and serve the justice of God, realizing itself among the powers of this world, calling them to responsibility and service to their neighbours, resisting their claims to self-sufficiency and their oppressions in the process. This is the context in which new thinking about the relation of government to economic power is called for. Neither capitalism nor socialism provides the answer...

(3) In a world where plural centres of religion, culture and social self-identity are thrown more into dependence on one another than ever before, the church needs to ask with new intensity about the character of human community in the light of the promise of God. The liberal answer, which idealizes pluralism within the context of a few government controls, breaks down every time. The radical assumption that oppressed peoples of all kinds everywhere are in solidarity with one another is an illusion that breaks down with every revolutionary success. Both are based upon a humanist anthropology that is less than human. The central message of the Christian gospel is that human beings are called into mutual dependence, in their differences, on one another, just as they are given their humanity by the calling and the covenant of God. The first human reality is not independence but the claims of the other — first God, then our neighbour — upon us. In this context, and only in the love which informs it, does human freedom have meaning...

(4) In a post-ideological world the Christian community becomes in a new way the custodian of human hope. We know that the human economy will not expand indefinitely through human enterprise in a free market. We know that the revolutionary victory of the poor and oppressed will not change selfish human nature and create a new ideal community. We have learned from experience what biblical teaching has always known, that we cannot save ourselves by human projects and movements. For what then can we hope? Christian eschatology needs continually to be re-thought at this point. The final judgment of God relativizes and inspires every human hope... To infect the world with this kind of hope may be our greatest contribution (pp.338-40).

Julio de Santa Ana offers down-to-earth insights into the futility of competing ideologies and the way out of the current, totally unexpected impasse:

The worst thing that can happen when we become aware of the failure of both projects is to fall into the trap of "realism". In the case of the "free market society", the "wealth of nations" is merely the wealth of the few, and in the case of the socialist societies, freedom has not been built up, only suffocated in most cases. If we give way to "realism", the bewitchment created by the feeling of powerlessness, we lose our energies. We close ourselves against the force of the

Spirit and we surrender to the powers that be. This means acquiescing in injustice and oppression. For Christians, this is serious; it indicates that God's design is turned into mockery. In that sense it is blasphemy...

Utopian reason is not looking for effectiveness, for it is moved by ultimate goals. In this sense the transcendent dimension of life (which instrumental reason does not take into account) is affirmed. Utopian reason seeks peace, the humanization of the market, the end of racism and sexism, the recognition of human rights, a world where dialogic communication among people and cultures could prevail, sustainability of personal, social and natural life. It is part of the movement of freedom, a sign of messianic energy. It is, because of all this, an inclusive rationality (p.371).

In his article, Paul Abrecht asks about the next steps to be taken in the reconstruction of ecumenical social thought:

What kind of economic order and justice should Christians work for in the post-Cold War era? To some it will seem like a defeat to give up the heroic revolutionary struggle for a "new world economic order"; they cannot accept the failure of the "socialist" vision and a return to the idea of the responsible society. Such an approach does not look "prophetic" as that term has been used in recent years to proclaim the liberation of the oppressed within history. However, there is no disguising the fact that the present approach to ecumenical social thought lacks credibility and needs to be substantially reformulated. It has caused the churches to lose credibility with their own members and with society at large. It is therefore important for the churches to take stock of the new political and social situation. In the past the churches worked for years, in study, discussion and consultation together, before they could arrive at a measure of agreement on the critical social issues...

The process of theological and ethical reconstruction will this time be especially difficult because the spirit of dialogue and the discipline of cooperative "study" of socio-ethical issues by the churches, involving different points of view, has been neglected and has to be recovered. The present confusion about the relation of study to action and about the contribution of the social and physical sciences to Christian social thought is a further grave hindrance to new thinking. But it is impossible to believe that the ecumenical movement has lost the capacity for renewal and for the self-criticism which such renewal implies. After all, that is what its faith is all about (p.327).

Surprisingly, debates on the relevance of religion and militant atheism have suddenly faded into the background. Earlier comparisons of Christian and Marxist conceptions of transcendence and eschatological hope now seem to be outmoded. Churches in Central and Eastern Europe should seize the chance of giving an account of their difficult but promising existence within an atheist environment during more than forty years. And churches in the West should comprehend anew that empirical and practical atheism remains a challenge to the complacent religiosity and religious indifference promoted by a sophisticated consumer society.

This points to the need to continue Christian-Marxist dialogue — or whatever it is now called — in a new context, with new insights and with new vigour. Opting for a moderate capitalism, a market economy "with a human face", controlled by labour unions and a responsible government, as today also newly advocated in many church circles, is clearly insufficient. So-called intermediary forces are hardly capable of correcting the international capitalist market and financial mechanisms, which function in and by themselves and are accountable to no national and international authority. Calling for the integral human development of the peoples of the third world — more than two-thirds of the world population — without taking into account their demographic problems and cultural conditions is utopian. It must also be acknowledged that a change in the monopoly of the West (and Japan) on scientific and technological progress is hardly likely to take place in the near future, though correcting this imbalance is decisive for the well-being of the whole of humanity.

Mark Ellingsen has observed **(227)** that in the ecumenical movement

> societies heavily dependent on science and technology were seen to be in serious predicaments. Thus more critical evaluation of the aims and methods of technology are now thought to be necessary. An important consequence of this line of thinking is that for the first time it opened the ecumenical movement and the churches to reflect systematically on the depletion of physical resources and environmental pollution by an unrestrained, voracious technology. The result

was that the way was opened to a preoccupation with ecology, a fact given testimony by the large amount of church statements issued on ecology since the... WCC Bucharest conference. The data certainly seem to verify the contention that the modern church's failure until recent years to take the ecological mandate seriously was related to its uncritical confidence in modern technology. Only after the churches had begun to take a critical perspective towards technology did they seem able to reappropriate the previously overlooked ecological emphases of the biblical tradition (p.42).

Secularists and believers adopting a partisan socialist position today must clarify how far the social, economic and ecological aspects of peoples' lives can be engineered without destroying the very elements that make them human. If they take seriously the fact that individual self-interest and the collective selfishness of nations always corrupt efforts for human liberation and economic justice, they may be able to choose the right direction in their social and political battles. That the concern for a socialist society has been and will be betrayed by many people and institutions does not count against its transforming power. There is a dire need for effective challenge to the excesses of capitalism and neo-colonialism and for public instrumentalities that put that challenge into practice.

In the substance of its claim socialism remains an unmistakable sign of eschatological hope. It can therefore contribute to solving at least some human, political and economic problems in an unjust, violent and broken world. That world is now also more thoroughly secularized than ever before, despite the resurgent attraction of many religions. The significance of resuming dialogue between believers and secularists is conditioned by this fact.

IX

Peace and Disarmament

In their unceasing search for solutions to the problem of armed conflict and the suffering and injustice it creates, churches have become increasingly aware of the complexities of these issues, the reality of oppressive power and the great difficulty of finding effective ways of being involved in conciliatory processes.

No other issue has been discussed more widely and intensively in the ecumenical movement from its very beginning and in the World Council of Churches since 1948 than peace and disarmament. Every major ecumenical gathering dealing with social issues has placed the establishment of peace on its agenda. All WCC assemblies have debated the threatening situation of conflict and violence of their time.

It is not easy to say where peace ends and war begins. If nations continue on hostile terms for years, building up their armed forces, steadily succumbing to the ideology of militarism and seeking allies, but do not declare war on each other, it is debatable whether they can really be said to be at peace. It was Europe, the cradle of Christianity, where the two most disastrous and destructive wars in this century were fought, but some 150 violent local conflicts have taken place since 1945 and it is estimated that more lives have been lost in these local wars than during the second world war. There seems to be no end to the brutal killing and massive destruction.

There is no definition of peace which is generally accepted as sound and valid. A situation that qualifies as peace according to international law may be at the same time a situation of the most sinister oppression. If peace is understood only as the absence of war it may be synonymous with a state of deepest misery or total wrong. Peace conditioned by nuclear deterrence is threatened peace and does not deserve the name. Nor are definitions of peace in terms of the absence of violence, oppression, fear, servitude and distress satisfactory.

The Hebrew *shalom* designates not only the absence of conflict but righteousness, wholeness, justice, liberation, salvation. In sum, it denotes things as they should be and shall be in the divine purpose for humanity. This *shalom*, fulfilled in the work of Jesus Christ, is what the apostles called good news. "Peace on earth" was promised by the angels in Luke 2:14. The promise of Jesus was that the inauguration of God's rule is at hand. The seventh beatitude calls peacemakers God's children. According to Ephesians 2:14, Christ is "our peace", because by reconciling Jew and Gentile he has created "one new humanity".

Effective reconciliation is a real experience in the believing community, and its extension to the ends of the earth is a concrete social project. Yet there is neither a comprehensive theology of peace nor an elaborated theology of justice. So real are the worldwide absence of peace and prevalence of grave injustice that biblical and theological approaches to them can have only a provisional character, even more so in the eschatological perspective of the kingdom. This explains why ecumenical statements on peace and disarmament have not been refined theological treatises.

Some appropriate and unpretentious sentences on maintaining world peace were written by Alan Booth, a secretary of the Commission of the Churches on International Affairs, in 1967, in *Not Only Peace: Christian Realism and the Conflicts of the Twentieth Century* **(120)**:

> All our solutions are partial, contingent and temporary, a balance of advantages carefully struck and constantly reviewed. None, in the Christian view, can represent the final meaning of our lives on earth. Indeed the greatest threat to human life in history perceived in the Jewish-Christian tradition is that involved in the attempt to find ultimate meaning in our political and social structures. This is the idolatry which in the end demands human sacrifice, the liquidation of men on the altar of ideology. We know this all too well in the twentieth century.
>
> But if there is no political and social structure which can contain the meaning of our lives, there are certainly some which can betray and distort that meaning... and some which can create conditions in

which our understanding of life's meaning can be enriched and enlarged. It is therefore one of the great functions of true religion in the political realm to present at every point a determined challenge to all absolutizing of political philosophies and programmes, to expose the relative and provisional character of all political choices and at the same time, with equal and even greater vigour, to provide the stimulus and conviction for men to pursue what is good in what is partial, temporary and always incomplete (p.140).

Major pronouncements and statements

During the earlier period of the ecumenical movement, until the late 1960s, many general and diplomatic statements were made on peace and disarmament. The armaments race was acknowledged, but it was analyzed superficially and the frightening escalation in arms production and the distribution of arms was not anticipated. The economic havoc caused by the first world in the third world was gravely underestimated, and it was not seen clearly that the under-developed nations could not achieve political autonomy and national self-reliance without impartial and generous assistance from the developed nations — assistance that was seriously hampered by the staggering amount of money spent on the production of sophisticated weapons.

Regarding the relation of the church to war, the report of the Oxford conference in 1937 **(3)** made several observations which remain valid today:

Multitudes are oppressed by the actual menace of war. While we seek to influence nations which may avert the immediate danger, our main task is to probe the underlying sources of the evil and point to the ultimate remedy.

Wars, the occasions of war and all situations which conceal the fact of conflict under the guise of outward peace are marks of a world to which the church is charged to proclaim the gospel of redemption. War involves compulsory enmity, diabolical outrage against human personality and a wanton distortion of the truth. War is a particular demonstration of the power of sin in this world and a defiance of the righteousness of God as revealed in Jesus Christ and him crucified. No justification of war must be allowed to conceal or minimize this fact.

Oxford wrestled with the conflict between an "essential principle (the 'just war' principle) to defend the victims of wanton aggression or to secure freedom for the oppressed" and the pacifist principle that "individuals may be called directly by God to refuse categorically to take part in any war, and so to draw attention to the perverted nature of a world in which wars are possible". This discussion still continues in the churches. They would be wise to listen again to the advice of the Oxford conference:

> We do not affirm that any of these positions can be held to represent the only Christian attitude. The church must insist that the perplexity itself is a sign of the sin in which its members are implicated. It cannot rest in permanent acquiescence in the continuance of these differences, but should do all that is possible to promote the study of the problem by people of different views meeting together to learn from one another as they seek to understand the purpose of God as revealed in Jesus Christ... It should call them to repent and to seek together that deliverance from the entangling evil which can be found in Christ alone. (pp.178-82).

The Amsterdam assembly in 1948 elaborated on Oxford's insights and recommendations by insisting that (1) war is contrary to the will of God; (2) peace requires an attack on the causes of conflict between the powers; (3) the nations of the world must acknowledge the rule of law; (4) the observance of human rights and fundamental freedoms should be encouraged by domestic and international action; (5) the churches and all Christian people have obligations in the face of international disorder.

Regarding the causes of conflict between the political powers Amsterdam said:

> The greatest threat to peace today comes from the division of the world into mutually suspicious and antagonistic blocs. This threat is all the greater because national tensions are confused by the clash of economic and political systems. Christianity cannot be equated with any of these... A positive attempt must be made to ensure that competing economic systems such as communism, socialism or free enterprise may co-exist without leading to war. No nation has the moral right to determine its own economic policy without consideration for the economic needs of other nations and without recourse to

international consultation... We resist all endeavours to spread a system of thought or of economics by unscrupulous intolerance, suppression or persecution (*The First Assembly of the World Council of Churches held at Amsterdam, 1948*, ed. W.A. Visser 't Hooft, London, SCM, 1949, p.91).

In the midst of the Cold War the second assembly (Evanston 1954) made the following theological statement on peace:

This troubled world, disfigured and distorted as it is, is still God's world. He rules and overrules its tangled history. In praying, "Thy will be done on earth as it is in heaven", we commit ourselves to seek earthly justice, freedom and peace for all men. Here as everywhere Christ is our hope. Our confidence lies not in our own reason or strength, but in the power that comes from God. Impelled by this faith, all our actions will be humble, grateful and obedient acknowledgment that he has redeemed the world. The fruit of our efforts rests in his hands. We can therefore live and work as those who know that God reigns, undaunted by all the arrogant pretensions of evil, ready to face situations that seem hopeless and yet act in them as men whose hope is indestructible...

Christians must face the fact that... peace will not be easily or quickly attained. We live in a world in which from generation to generation ignorance of God and rebellion against him have resulted in greed and an insatiable lust for power. War and its evils are the consequences. Basically the problem is a spiritual one, and economic and political measures alone will not solve it. Men's hearts must be changed. This is always the supreme evangelistic challenge of the church, although we must confess that our response has been tragically casual and feeble (*The Evanston Assembly, 1954*, New York, Harper, 1955, pp.131f.).

The third assembly (New Delhi 1961), faced the issue of the elimination of nuclear weapons and total disarmament as a goal. It emphasized that the approach to disarmament must be equally global as local. Much of the assembly discussion was based on a study completed in 1958, *Christians and the Prevention of War in an Atomic Age* **(121)**, which emphasized the restraints governments must accept and essential positive steps in avoiding a nuclear holocaust.

In the report of the committee on the CCIA to the New Delhi assembly the following was outlined:

Since war is an offence against God, the task of the Christian is to do all in his power to prevent, and even to eliminate, war. Nevertheless, the elimination of war, though especially in the context of nuclear power essential to the future survival of mankind, would not by itself solve all outstanding problems. Nor is it a question only of a possible nuclear war. There are many areas of the world where so-called "limited" wars have been raging for years. But the evils which they have brought in their train — subversion, terrorism, counter-terrorism, corruption of police and public values, concentration camps, refugees, even genocide — have been no less horrible or evil... As no universally acceptable definition of general and comprehensive disarmament exists, it is suggested that the CCIA should take this matter under consideration and see if it is not possible for them to reach a definition of the goal towards which all should be striving (*The New Delhi Report, 1961*, London, SCM, 1962, pp.264-66).

In his 1963 encyclical letter *Pacem in terris* **(192)**, John XXIII quoted the words of his predecessor Pius XII: "The calamity of a world war, with the economic and social ruin and the moral excesses and dissolution that accompany it, must not be permitted to envelop the human race for a third time", adding:

All must realize that there is no hope of putting an end to the building up of armaments, nor of reducing the present stocks, nor, still less, of abolishing them altogether, unless the process is complete and thorough and unless it proceeds from inner conviction: unless, that is, everyone sincerely cooperates to banish the fear and anxious expectation of war with which men are oppressed (p.28).

In his 1967 encyclical *Populorum progressio* **(196)**, Paul VI summoned the Catholic faithful and all persons of good will to greater responsibility in the face of the widening gap between rich and poor nations. "Peace, today, means development... Only worldwide collaboration... will succeed in overcoming vain rivalries and in establishing a fruitful and peaceful exchange between peoples" (pp.37f.).

Section IV of the Uppsala assembly (1968), "Towards Justice and Peace in International Affairs", saw in "the growing dimensions of the ecumenical movement... new possibilities for concerted contributions to international relations... Even if differences in historical ecclesiastical structures, cultural backgrounds, political systems and styles of action present substantial obstacles to cooperation, these possibilities must be fully explored" (*The Uppsala Report 1968*, Geneva, WCC, 1968, pp.70f.). The Nairobi assembly (1975) called justice "a way of relating both to God and to other people. Its consequences are seen first in the poor, the humiliated, the exploited and the oppressed. The search for a more just world and more just relations between nations, peoples and generations brings us together as a uniting force" (*Breaking Barriers*, London, SPCK, 1976, p.121).

Almost every issue group at the sixth assembly (Vancouver 1983) dealt with problems of peace; and the message of the assembly said explicitly:

> We renew our commitment to justice and peace. Since Jesus Christ healed and challenged the whole of life, so we are called to serve the life of all. We see God's good gift battered by the powers of death. Injustice denies God's gifts of unity, sharing and responsibility. When nations, groups and systems hold the power of deciding other people's lives, they love that power. God's way is to share power, to give it to every person. Injustice corrupts the powerful and disfigures the powerless. Poverty, continual and hopeless, is the fate of millions; stolen land is a cause of bitterness and war; the diversity of race becomes the evil imprisonment of racism. We urgently need a new international economic order in which power is shared, not grasped...
>
> The arms race everywhere consumes great resources that are desperately needed to support human life. Those who threaten with military might are dealing in the politics of death. It is a time of crisis for us all. We stand in solidarity across the world to call persistently, in every forum, for a halt to the arms race. The life which is God's good gift must be guarded when national security becomes the excuse for arrogant militarism. The tree of peace has justice for its roots (*Gathered for Life*, ed. David Gill, Geneva, WCC, 1983, p.3).

As we have seen, Vancouver also urged the WCC "to engage member churches in a conciliar process of mutual commitment (covenant) to justice, peace and the integrity of all creation".

Militarism and militarization

Nairobi called on the churches and the WCC "to raise consciousness about the dangers of militarism and search for creative ways of educating for peace". To follow this up, the WCC held a consultation on militarism in Glion, Switzerland, in 1977. Its report **(133)** noted that:

Although most of the major faiths stand for peace, religious justifications are put forward to justify the threat of militarism. Attempts are made to equate the defence of a particular economic and social system with that of "Western-Christian civilization". Certain repressive governments define themselves as "Christian" and profess to be defending "Christian values". This poses both a serious threat and a serious challenge to the Christian churches in many nations. Furthermore, this and similar claims on behalf of other religious faiths and ideologies make it imperative for the churches to join in a dialogue with men and women of other religions and ideological convictions and to cooperate with them in the struggle against militarism.

A WCC consultation on disarmament in Glion the following year **(132)** made the following statement about the "exposure of idols":

It is the prophetic duty of Christians to unmask and challenge idols of military doctrine and technology in the light of the Christian vision of justice and peace. Such idols include: (1) the doctrine of "deterrence" which holds millions hostage to the threat of nuclear war terror but which has led to the development of still more terrifying weapons of mass destruction; (2) any doctrine of national security that is used to justify militarism and the arms race; (3) the doctrine that "qualitative improvements" in military technology will result in a reduction in arms. In fact, the arms race has escalated as the risks of nuclear war have vastly increased.

The report on "The Programme on Militarism and the Armaments Race" presented to the 1979 central committee meeting recalled the Nairobi assembly's "alarm at the qualitatively new developments in the arms race, which, coupled with spiralling arms production and sales, pose to a degree hitherto unimagined the threat of global destruction". However, it went on to cite the words of one of the participants in the Glion conference on disarmament: "The churches can no longer urge the governments to place disarmament at the top of their agendas so long as they themselves give it such a low priority on their own" (*Minutes*, p.164).

The Vancouver assembly underlined the links between militarism and economic injustice:

We believe that the present military build-up and arms race are integrally related to the practices of an unjust world economic order. The worldwide trend towards militarization is not a mere confrontation and tension between the major powers, but also an expression of the desire to repress those emerging forces which seek a more just world order. It is this latter which poses a fundamental threat to peace. Whereas people's aspirations for and expectations of a more just order have been supported as legitimate, the big powers still use military might to buttress the unjust order in order to protect their own interests. The defence of these interests can often be disguised as appeals for national security, the upholding of law and order, the defence of democracy, the protection of the "free world", the need to maintain spheres of influence and sometimes even the cause of peace.

Among the factors promoting militarism one can identify: technological advances enhancing the effectiveness and power of military and police forces; growing integration of military and civilian sectors; a conscious promotion of psychological insecurity to justify the further acquisition of arms; a growing worldwide military trade network; alarming increase in the number of foreign military bases; unhealthy competition between the USA and the USSR to achieve military and technological superiority; creation and maintenance of spheres of influence by major developed nations and some of the two-thirds world nations; the egomania and prestige-seeking of certain political leaders; religious fanaticism (*Gathered for Life*, pp.74f.).

With regard to the increasing threat of nuclear war and the spectre of an arms race totally out of control, Vancouver said:

Nuclear deterrence can never provide the foundation of genuine peace. It is the antithesis of an ultimate faith in that love which casts out fear. It escalates the arms race in a vain pursuit of stability. It ignores the economic, social and psychological dimensions of security, and frustrates justice by maintaining the status quo in world politics. It destroys the reality of self-determination for most nations in matters of their own safety and survival, and diverts resources from basic human needs. It is the contradiction of disarmament because it exalts the threat of force, rationalizes the development of new

weapons of mass destruction, and acts as a spur to nuclear proliferation by persistently breaking the "good faith" pledge of disarmament
in the Non-Proliferation Treaty, thus tempting other governments to
become nuclear-weapon states. It is increasingly discredited by first-
strike and war-fighting strategies which betray the doubts about its
reliability (p.76).

Various statements by the WCC and the Holy See on militarism
and the arms race are collected in *The Security Trap: Arms Race,
Militarism and Disarmament — A Concern for Christians* **(134)**.

The continuing split in world Christianity

It would seem evident that the arms race, which frustrates
humanity's aspirations for justice and peace, has no part in God's
design for the world; that it is a demonic force which demands a
response of uncategorical rejection from all Christian communities. In
fact, not all churches have been ready to portray the arms race in such
unambiguous terms. In a less than perfect world, it is argued, the
tensions between the ideal and the realizable are genuine; and the
churches have frequently been tempted to defend compromises
between what justice demands and what is possible at the time. On the
other hand, the story of the churches offers dramatic evidence that
there are limits to compromise — points at which prophetic voices rise
above the ambiguities that are the stock-in-trade of compromisers and
clearly and simply demand righteousness.

Before It's Too Late **(118)**, the report of a WCC public hearing on
nuclear weapons and disarmament in Amsterdam in 1981, makes clear
the divisions within the churches on the establishment of true and
lasting peace:

> War, any war, is an undoubted evil. There is a stark contradiction
> between the way of love and suffering, which is Christ's way, and the
> deliberate infliction of suffering and death on others. Yet most
> Christians in most ages have believed that there are circumstances in
> which fighting can be the lesser of the two evils. All the theologians
> who gave evidence to the hearing were in their different ways caught
> in this dilemma, and none presumed any hope that theology could
> provide easy answers. The questions posed by nuclear weapons are
> new. There has been little world discussion from a theological
> perspective of the issues involved and there is no consensus. Each

spoke against a different political background, and illustrated the extent to which theological and ethical judgments have to be related to the circumstances in which they are formed, and to the practical details of the subject in hand (p.28).

To be sure, all churches favour the prevention of atomic war, a mutual and verifiable halt to the testing, production and deployment of nuclear weapons as a necessary step towards disarmament, a new international order based on justice for and within all nations and the establishment of nuclear-free zones in various parts of the world. Many churches have acknowledged the urgent need for study, reflection and education on the possibilities of nonviolent resistance and nonviolent civil disobedience. There is an insistence on establishing a theology and ministry of peace-making.

Yet despite these serious intentions and proposals, deep divisions between the two main sub-traditions of Christian ethical thought — pacifism and just war doctrine — were heightened by the discussion of nuclear deterrence. The just war theory became part of Christianity 1500 years ago as a consequence of the Constantinian settlement of the roles of church and state and to some extent remains, in the more structured and institutional Christian communities like the Roman Catholic, Anglican, Lutheran and Reformed churches, the predominant approach to questions of war and peace.

The reality of sin in human hearts and in human institutions has made the use of coercive force at certain moments in history to seem morally justifiable as a lesser evil. The conviction that war may be ethically justifiable, even necessary, in the name of justice remains intact. To be sure, the first use of nuclear weapons and indiscriminate retaliatory action taking countless innocent lives are generally condemned. But the legitimacy of deterrence on strict conditions as a temporary expedient leading to progressive disarmament has still been widely accepted in many Christian quarters. A clear expression of this view came from Pope John Paul II at the second UN special session on disarmament in 1982: "In current conditions 'deterrence' based on balance, certainly not as an end in itself but as a step towards progressive disarmament, may still be judged morally acceptable."

On the other hand, voices are heard which take a more or less pacifist position in rejecting the idea of nuclear deterrence, although on the question of a defensive war fought exclusively with conventional weapons, their position differs from that of the historic peace churches such as Mennonites or Quakers. On this view, any preparation for nuclear war is morally wrong, whatever the political circumstances. By supporting, even timidly and reluctantly, the present irrational arms race Christians are guilty of sin and disobedience, and invite God's judgment upon humanity. The attitude of the Christian towards all weapons of mass destruction should be solely determined by the Christian faith; it is a question of affirming or denying the liberation of the gospel itself.

An intensive debate which raged during the WCC's Canberra assembly in 1991 laid bare the persistent differences among Christian positions on war and peace. An amendment was proposed to the public statement on the Gulf War which would have added the following sentence: "We call upon [the churches] to give up any theological or moral justification of the use of military power, be it in war or through other forms of oppressive security systems, and to become public advocates of a just peace" (*Signs of the Spirit*, ed. Michael Kinnamon, Geneva, WCC, 1991, p.203). The amendment was finally defeated because of objections to what was seen as its inherent pacifism (now often called "active pacifism").

Since the Canberra discussion was so long, heated and painful, many have questioned the credibility of the statement as finally adopted (with some opposition), arguing that it did not express the "truth and common wisdom" which are the only foundations for the authority of ecumenical statements. Others would respond that it does no harm to such a widely representative body as the WCC to admit in a given situation that it does not have a common voice. Honesty in such a case is not necessarily a sign of incompetence. If the Council seeks to occupy a high moral ground far removed from this wicked and destructive world, it only betrays its own weakness. Thus the debate continues.

The ecumenical movement has revealed that cooperating and competing confessions, imprisoned in their bureaucracies, cannot mobilize the energies and shared commitments demanded by the vision of restored wholeness, of *shalom*. A realistic analysis of the world's predicament shows that both the continuation of the status quo of the arms race and unilateral disarmament increase the risk of war. It will take considerable time and effort to find a new way which aims at total disarmament without threatening national security, while seeking an alternative to military defence which prevents war on a mass scale.

In the last several years ethnic conflicts and civil wars have become ever more widespread, bloody and destructive. Not only are the responses of national governments hypocritical, belated and ineffective and the interventions of the United Nations impotent, but also the statements of ecumenical organizations and churches are ignored or misinterpreted. Merely speaking about the need to build bridges of reconciliation and to overcome breakdowns in communication contributes little to the reduction of violence. The service of peace — whether in Bosnia-Herzegovina, Rwanda, Azerbaijan and Armenia or anywhere else — involves more than unanimously condemning the appalling carnage. Despite its scope, the aid which thousands of refugees receive from the international community, including international church organizations, is often trifling. Accustomed to bringing church leaders together for public statements, the ecumenical movement is humbly learning that the role of grassroots action by Christians and others to create a more just and peaceful society is indispensable.

X

Development

As with racism (see Chapter XI), the ecumenical address to the issue of development can be divided into two distinct stages: before and after 1968, the year of the WCC's fourth assembly in Uppsala.

Well into the 1960s, the simplistic conviction prevailed, also in the churches, that once poor people in the third world obtained a minimum of technology and began to profit from "the benefits of more machine-production", the process of development would be moving in the right direction and the living standards of a large part of the population would be raised. The typical image of development was of the unfolding of a flower from a bud, a natural process of painless transformation from a situation of poverty into a society of well-being. It was assumed that the results and advantages of economic growth would penetrate automatically to the materially disadvantaged classes. The successful experience of the Marshall Plan after the second world war — an effective European recovery programme in grants and loans — nourished the optimistic idea that similar large-scale programmes could be designed for the benefit of the third world.

A section of the report on "Reshaping the Pattern of Missionary Activity" at the International Missionary Council assembly in Willingen in 1952 was devoted to "Technical Assistance and Welfare Services". It stated:

> Believing that the extreme inequalities of wealth between different areas constitute a challenge to the Christian conscience, we consider that it is a duty of Christians everywhere to encourage and to assist the governments concerned in programmes for raising the standard of living of the hungry and under-privileged areas of the world... We therefore urge governments and other agencies offering technical

assistance: (1) to recognize the fundamental rights and the cultural heritage of the peoples served; (2) to give attention, in selecting technical experts, not only to professional qualifications, but also to the moral and spiritual requirements of the work they do; (3) to co-operate with nationals already engaged in working for technical and welfare services, and to foster their training and development; (4) to concentrate effort upon those fundamental improvements which will enable the people to help themselves (*Minutes of the Enlarged Meeting of the Committee of the International Missionary Council, Willingen, Germany, July 5-21, 1952*, London, IMC, 1952, pp.83f.).

The WCC's study on Common Christian Responsibility towards Areas of Rapid Social Change arrived at similar conclusions and similar recommendations, warning paternalistically at a conference in Thessalonica in 1959 that:

(1) Men do not necessarily know how to consume responsibly; (2) men become absorbed in the means and techniques that make for an affluent society; (3) when men get richer they worship riches and forget God; (4) society may become marked by new forms of social stratification, conspicious consumption and status seeking, as people look for marks and symbols of personal prestige and success; (5) men may become slaves of the production machine and victims of the vast and elaborate apparatus upon which they have come to depend for material abundance.

It is impossible to foresee an ideal pattern of development without difficult problems. Some costs in human hardship and misery are inevitable. It will often be necessary to work out proximate goals and least-harmful measures. Christians must accept the hard facts of economic life and be ready to make the necessary choices and to run the unavoidable risks (*Dilemmas and Opportunities: Report of an International Ecumenical Study Conference, Thessalonica, Greece, July 25-August 2, 1959*, Geneva, WCC, 1959, pp.67, 89).

Christian responsibility for economic and social development

It was the world conference on Church and Society at Geneva in 1966 that put the issues of world economic development and develop-ment aid on the agenda of the churches in a major way. The conference report on these themes set forth a new and comprehensive understanding of the hopes and concerns of developing countries, the contributions needed from the "richer" nations and the changes in world economic and political structures required for global economic development. Taking the practical steps recommended by the report would demand new commitments by the churches to world economic and social justice.

Stimulated by the Geneva conference and the conference on world co-operation for development co-sponsored by the WCC and the Vatican in Beirut in April 1968, the Uppsala assembly focused major attention on development issues, urging the churches to go beyond the charitable understanding of "rich" nations helping "poor" nations to advocacy and action for fundamental changes based on a new and urgent concern for social justice in a world perspective:

> Effective world development requires radical changes in institutions and structures at three levels: within developing countries, within developed countries and in the international economy. Precisely because such structural changes have not been promoted, we find that as a community of nations we are unable to do the good we would and efforts for international co-operation tend to be paralyzed. At all three levels it is necessary to instill social and economic processes with a new dynamic of human solidarity and justice (**154**, p.46).

This statement undoubtedly reflected the address to the assembly by Samuel Parmar of India, who had declared:

> Modern technology in the West operates in terms of planned obsolescence, that is, quick replacement of things and techniques. This is necessary, we are told, on grounds of efficiency and high effective demand. High-consumption societies operate on the basis of institutionalized waste. Purely in national terms this could be understandable. But the moment we look at the whole world together, the planned obsolescence of the rich alongside the planned austerity of the poor nations becomes an anachronism... Even assuming that developing nations clubbed together (which is highly improbable), they cannot muster enough economic or political power to make an international class-conflict successful. From all accounts the economic and military power of developed nations will be greater in the year 2000 than it is now. We are also beginning to realize that if the West and the East come together, as they seem to be doing, they could maintain their economic prosperity, technologi-

cal superiority and military strength completely independently of the third world (pp.41f.).

Thus the ecumenical discussion of world development, treated for more than two decades almost exclusively in terms of expanding aid and trade, merged with the discussion of revolutionary social change. An awareness grew that interdependence between partners with power and those without power leads to dominance and dependency rather than mutually beneficial relations. As long as the Western churches retained their confidence in traditional political and economic structures, they could not hear the challenge coming from Christian communities in the South of the validity of an "international law and order" developed by the Western powers and imposed on the rest of the world. Already the New Delhi assembly (1961) had been unable to cope with the rapidly changing situation through a thorough re-examination of the world's predicament. And even the conferences sponsored by SODEPAX from 1968 to 1971 were optimistic that the prosperity so far enjoyed by a minority would eventually be shared by the majority of the human race.

Radical change

From the Uppsala assembly onwards the conviction grew that justice should be the focus of the churches' participation in development. Only the political will to bring about distributive justice within and among nations will enable the poor majorities of people to have a fair share of the benefits of development and better participation in directing the process. Development is therefore first of all a political problem. But it is also a human problem. People should not become *objects* of development. The acknowledgment of cultural plurality, the distribution of power and equal opportunities are important parts of development. Responsibility for the poor, the weak and the oppressed is an integral part of the Christian faith.

These new insights led to various changes in the approach to Christian social ethics. First, a new methodology came into prominence. Alongside analytical studies of conflict situations much emphasis was laid on common action. Action-reflection models were developed. As will be seen in the next chapter, the Programme to Combat Racism, created in 1969, followed this pattern. Second, there was a shift from a global to a contextual approach. With the failure of the first development decade (1960-70), the universality of traditional Western theology (a theology of the victors) was less and less accepted. Theology must be contextual and related to concrete action. Third, the importance of development education was stressed. If economic structures and behaviour within and among nations are to be changed, public opinion needs to be built up towards increasing the political will of the people. In this respect, churches have a unique role to play in promoting local and national educational campaigns.

To determine how to carry out the mandate of the Uppsala assembly to assist churches in participating effectively in the development process, the WCC called a world consultation at Montreux in 1970. The consultation report **(143)** spoke of development as aimed at three inter-related objectives: justice, self-reliance and economic growth. The churches' task was seen primarily as participating with the poor and the oppressed in their struggle for development and seeking to change the socio-economic and political structures which continue to enslave, impoverish and dehumanize the poor population.

The mandate of the Commission on the Churches' Participation in Development (CCPD), which came into being after the Montreux consultation, gave it responsibility "for proposing strategy and policy for ecumenical assistance to development programmes and projects; promoting development studies and educational programmes; administration of the Ecumenical Development Fund and coordination of the activities of the World Council of Churches in the field of development".

Recognizing that if the churches' participation in development is to be effective, they must opt in favour of the aspirations of the poor and oppressed, the Commission defined the following programme priorities following the Nairobi asssembly (1975):
— to assist churches and their constituencies to manifest, in their theological outlook, styles of life and organizational structures, their solidarity with the struggle of the poor and oppressed;
— to assist development agencies of the churches to evaluate and redirect their efforts in line with the criteria proposed by the assembly;
— to assist churches to provide support to organizations of the poor and oppressed;

— to assist churches to make their contribution towards the search for a just, participatory and sustainable society.

This option in favour of the poor and the oppressed created tensions, because it questioned the structures not only of society but also of many churches.

Theological perspectives on development

Section VI of the Nairobi assembly, "Human Development: Ambiguities of Power, Technology and Quality of Life", acknowledged the difficulty of articulating a common understanding of development:

> In the past few years there have been many conscious efforts to give human development a conceptual clarity that it lacked, but the relation between concept and reality seems to become more diffused and more evasive. The uncertainties and ambiguities resulting from this situation are made more pronounced because of the few certainties that cannot be evaded: that after two decades of efforts to remove poverty and reduce inequality there are today more people in the grip of dire poverty and the gap between the rich and the poor has widened; that in a world with tremendous technological possibilities, there is a persisting threat of famine; that in the spaceship earth the expenditure on armaments is steadily mounting; that in numbers mankind is continuing to grow at an unprecedented rate. In the quest for development, thus, we find ourselves caught in a pensive mood, raising many questions and finding few answers (*Breaking Barriers*, ed. David Paton, London, SPCK, 1976, p.122).

To confront the churches with these perplexing realities, CCPD started an action-reflection programme on the theme "The Church and the Poor". *Good News to the Poor* **(148)**, published in 1977, dealt with problems of relations with the poor during the early centuries of church life and in the mediaeval period.

In the next stage, a study was made of relations between the poor and the churches in the crucial period of Western colonial expansion and the industrial revolution. *Separation without Hope?* **(149)** showed how in the life of the established churches the poor tended to be relegated to the least important position. With a few exceptions, the churches failed during this period to be the champions of the poor (see also Chapter I).

In recent times, churches have become more aware of the challenge that the millions of poor present to them. A workshop in Ayia Napa, Cyprus, in 1978, analyzed this challenge, and sought to work towards new theological perspectives and new ways of action which would allow the churches to express clearly their concern for the poor and enable them to act in solidarity with them. *Towards a Church of the Poor* **(150)** contained the findings of the workshop.

In 1976 CCPD decided to add "the search for a just, participatory and sustainable society" (JPSS) to its programme emphases. It collaborated in the WCC programme on militarism and disarmament and in the preparatory reflections for the world conference on Faith, Science and the Future (see Chapters IV and V). The commitment of CCPD to JPSS was also manifested through the Programme on Transnational Corporations (TNCs) as well as through a study on political ethics. In 1978 CCPD organized an Advisory Group on Economic Matters (AGEM) to assist the WCC and its member churches on issues related to the international development debate. Building on the insights gained by CCPD through the action-reflection process on "The Church and the Poor", AGEM sought to give economic substance to the vision of a just, participatory and sustainable society. Its work developed the concept of "new economics", presenting a set of various alternative assumptions to prevailing economic patterns. Among these are the following:

— modernization (in the form of rationalization, maximization and centralization of technical and economic power) usually leads to increasing domination and not automatically to justice and participation;
— in the present system economic growth generally leads to injustice;
— at present, technological advance tends to enhance the power of the powerful;
— all these threaten, in their present forms, the life of future generations and the preservation of God's creation.

People's participation and people's technologies

The concern for people's participation in the search for a just, participatory and sustainable society has been central to the understanding of development as it evolved in the WCC. An action-reflection process involving CCPD partners and churches in the

Philippines, Nicaragua and Tanzania identified people's participation as a social phenomenon in history which poses challenges to the structures of society and to the church. Closely related to this concern is the issue of people's technologies. CCPD's technical services to churches and related groups participating in development led to an emphasis on "appropriate technology", one which fits the people's values and cultures and can be appropriated by them.

The emphasis on people's participation and people's technology is part of a shift observed by Ellingsen in *The Cutting Edge* **(227)**. Earlier church statements on development models advocated "transfer of technology..., enhancing the position of the rich and already powerful in the underdeveloped nations". The "newer model", which first asks about the needs, culture and environment of a society, is that

> development is not to be measured solely in terms of economic growth. Rather, development must also be assessed in relation to the quality of life that is engendered... As a result of this model's correlation of development and human development, it is not surprising to see that proponents of newer models include many of the best human values under the rubric of development. For example, the WCC Nairobi assembly claimed that development must include seeking justice. More recently the WCC Sub-Unit on Church and Society has related development to ecology. At least in the organized ecumenical movement the predominance of this approach to development has been quite apparent in the last two decades (p.29).

In no way do these emphases on people's participation and appropriate technology warrant ignoring larger questions about the responsibilities of churches and Christians in economic life and the interaction between theology and economic theory and practice. The Vancouver assembly issue group on "Struggling for Justice and Human Dignity" underscored this in its critical assessment of the injustice of the prevailing international economic order:

> It has institutionalized domination by Northern economies of trade, finance, manufacturing, food processing and knowledge. Handled mainly through transnational corporations, this economic order subordinates and renders dependent the Southern economies... Power elites concentrate wealth for the control of political and economic instruments and institutions... The machine of the prevailing eco-

nomic order starves millions of people and increases the number of unemployed every year... We interpret this development as idolatry, stemming from human sin, a product of satanic forces. We are in a situation where we must go beyond the normal prophetic and intercessory actions of the churches... The church is thus challenged not only in what it does, but in its very faith and being... In confessing Jesus Christ, churches must also confess their sins; they should recognize their complicity in, or their tolerance of, the processes of death and be prepared to confront the dangers inherent in exorcising such evils (*Gathered for Life*, ed. David Gill, Geneva, WCC, 1983, pp.84-87).

Is the concern for world development tenable?

Few serious consequences have been drawn by the churches from their insight into God's preferential love for the poor and exploited. The enthusiasm displayed by representatives of WCC member churches at the Uppsala assembly for setting aside at least 2 percent, if not more, of their income for development aid soon ebbed away. Only a handful of Christian communities accepted and practised the 2 percent appeal for development aid as an action model. Meanwhile, only in Norway, Sweden and the Netherlands have governments spent around 1 percent of their annual gross national product on development aid. Foreign assistance remains controversial. Its critics either charge that it is badly administered, severely reducing its ability to promote development and tackle poverty, or believe that it is harmful in principle, prolonging dependency, poverty and underdevelopment after centuries of colonialism.

According to the report of a WCC workshop in 1982, the 2 percent appeal in 1982 was conceived as an action model to integrate all the elements of participation in development. But the response was limited. It was originally envisioned that the appeal would generate about US$10 million a year for development programmes, but the income of the Ecumenical Development Fund during the entire decade of the 1970s was only $22.3 million.

The difficulties of promoting development were further underlined by the WCC Canberra assembly in 1991, which drew out the distinction between growth and development:

While advocating "sustainable development" many people and groups in fact often have found themselves promoting "growth".

Growth for growth's sake — the continued addition to what already is present — is the strategy of the cancer cell. Growth for growth's sake is increase in size without control, without limit, in disregard for the system that sustains it. It ultimately results in degradation and death. Development on the other hand — like the strategy of the embryo — is getting the right things in the right places in the right amounts at the right times with the right relationships. Development, while supported both by growth and *reduction* of its parts, results in a self-sustaining whole. Development of the earth by human beings, if accomplished in a manner similar to development of the human body, maintains a balance among all parts of the whole. What is "just" and "right", then, must be found in social, biological and physical relationships involving humanity and earth. True development, as opposed to simple growth, focuses on the eco-system level (*Signs of the Spirit*, ed. Michael Kinnamon, Geneva, WCC, 1991, pp.63f.).

Unless there is a much deeper awareness among the churches in the affluent nations about the economic disparities in the world and the reason for their existence, their opportunities to change the structures of their own existence and contribute to establishing a new international economic order will remain unused. Engagement in development education at the grassroots is surely necessary. But for an effective corporate engagement the whole church, including its leadership, needs to become aware that it lives in a totally different world from that of fifty years ago, giving new meaning to the confession that God in Christ divested himself of all power, taking the nature of a slave, accepting suffering to the point of death on a cross. It is possible to denounce injustice and exploitation and announce liberation in Christ through a corporate message, deeds and life-styles. Christian ignorance and complacency can be turned into daring consciousness and contagious commitment.

Conceiving development in terms of liberation is based on the understanding that developing countries are at the mercy of the developed countries and that underdevelopment in the South is a direct consequence of overdevelopment and domination in the North. In order to end this tyranny the South should disconnect itself from the North and enforce its mutual cooperation. Liberation is, of course, a central biblical concept based on the exodus of the people of Israel from slavery in Egypt. But is this idea of the liberation of the South and the pooling together of its minimal forces anything more than utopia? That question is posed by the report of a WCC seminar in Berlin in November 1991:

> The principal life-force of the new global reality is the free market economic system, which has now gained the allegiance of its former detractors, the former leaders and peoples of the old socialist societies. The free market system "allows no alternatives" and has shown itself to be unhesitating in sacrificing everything for the sake of profit. In the absence of a competing superpower to check its hegemonic ambitions, it could easily strengthen systemic structures of injustice, pay no heed to the misery and suffering of the poor and powerless and wreak havoc upon the environment. Centre-periphery relations would be far more pronounced in practically every aspect of life, particularly in general education, cultural relations and technological development. In fine, the South could lead a life of virtual slavery to the North (*Utopia and Liberation: Towards a Human World*, ed. Israel Batista, Geneva, WCC, 1992, p.58).

In 1988 the WCC central committee asked CCPD to start a process which would lead to an ecumenical statement on economic life. Between 1989 and 1991, an international and interconfessional group of economists, social scientists and theologians met three times, supported by a global process of feeding regional contributions and experiences into their work. After discussion by the central committee in 1991 a revised text, *Christian Faith and the World Economy Today*, (Geneva, WCC, 1992), was received by the committee in 1992 and commended to the churches for study and action. The document deals in four chapters with why economics and Christian faith should be taken together, major issues of concern in the world economy today, criteria for economic policy-making and possibilities for action by Christians.

The document contains a pertinent paragraph on scarcity in the midst of abundant life:

> The production of goods can be a blessing, as the word *good* in fact suggests. But to claim and possess more and more goods does not mean that we achieve abundant life, neither in its biblical meaning nor in the secular sense of the word. Ever-increasing production can,

paradoxically, lead to scarcity rather than abundance. Goods like clean air, clean water, stillness and time become more and more scarce. Unpriced scarcity of so-called non-economic goods is on the increase and while it seems that, through increased production, we have been moving from scarcity to abundance, we seem to be moving in the opposite direction... The emergence of generalized scarcity is due to the reality that human needs and desires have increased faster than we have been able to meet them. When this occurs, and when we assume that human needs are virtually limitless, then scarcity increases, regardless of the current level of material prosperity. Many seem to have lost the perception of *enough*. However, one cannot be aware of abundance without having an awareness of enough because abundance is more than enough. There are both material as well as spiritual limits to economic growth (pp.30f.).

Although some have suggested that this study document does not sufficiently reflect the differences of opinion among professional economists regarding economic mechanisms and that a shorter and simpler document would have been more accessible to a wider Christian constituency, it is undoubtedly an honest effort to wrestle with the complicated issues at stake and to relate the world economic situation to the specific responsibilities of the ecumenical movement.

Particularly helpful are these paragraphs from the last chapter:

Appropriate actions will usually be modest, growing out of a double awareness: on the one hand, that our actions as Christians have often failed to confirm what we have said — we have more often been part of the problem than of the solutions; and on the other that our action in this world is not for our own sake, but for that of God's kingdom. Therefore we do well to seek partnership with people of other backgrounds who share our concern for more fully human features of the common life and for a caring relation with the creation as a whole. It is abundant life for all that God promises in Christ, and which we are called to seek.

At the same time, we are not to be so modest as to fail to act; again, Christians, especially in the middle-class churches, have too often been silent in the face of injustice, with an acquiescence which is itself a counter-witness to the Christ who stood up to the powers. And in face of the global threats we have been discussing, it will be important to act in ways that seem right for our particular context, while also bringing out the links with other levels of reality. "Think globally, act locally" is a useful motif (p.43).

This survey of development as it has been considered in ecumenical social thought raises a question posed by Ellingsen **(227)**: whether the ecumenical consensus that context plays a determinative role in shaping one's theology and ethics does not deserve critical reconsideration. Moreover, Ellingsen asks,

> What are the implications of the fact that many ethical disagreements among the churches are not related to doctrinal differences for the concern that disagreement on social ethics might divide the churches? Might there be implications for church unity in the fact that theological differences do not necessarily entail disagreements in praxis? (p.34).

These questions hark back to an old ecumenical issue. Already in preparation for the 1937 Faith and Order conference in Edinburgh the "non-theological factors of unity" were a distinctive element of discussion (cf. H. Richard Niebuhr, *The Social Sources of Denominationalism*) **(219)**.

XI

Racism

Historically, ecumenical attention to worldwide racism falls into two parts: before and after 1968. The two periods differ considerably in outlook, approach and participation. Earlier, Christians tended to speak of "race prejudice" and "racial discrimination", and their declarations and documents on the subject dealt with problems of inter-racial relations mainly from an observing and exhorting point of view, even when overt racism was manifested, as it was at the 1937 Faith and Order conference in Edinburgh, where an African-American bishop was prevented on racial grounds from entering his hotel.

Around the time of the WCC's fourth assembly in Uppsala in 1968, terms such as "change of racist structures of society" and "combat against racism" (particularly "white racism") began to be heard for the first time in ecumenical circles. Not only did ecumenical statements become more and more passionate and concrete, but there was also a general consensus that words had to be matched by actions.

The race problem was already on the agenda of the first Life and Work conference in Stockholm in 1925. The report introduced and discussed was marked by a naive optimism. The churches and their faithful believed that the preaching of the "brotherhood of man" and the spread of modern education would soon eliminate race prejudice. Little if any attention was given to the non-rational character of overt and covert racism, much less to the implications of the fact that churches and related organizations at that time were overwhelmingly white in their leadership. The development of autonomous churches outside the Western hemisphere was still in the future.

The International Missionary Council meeting in Jerusalem in 1928 adopted a statement demanding "worldwide inter-racial unity".

Two years earlier, J.H. Oldham had published his seminal volume on *Christianity and the Race Problem* **(162)**. This pioneer of the ecumenical movement was far ahead of his time in stressing the fundamental unity of humanity, the responsibility of the white race and the obligation of the church to be in the mainstream of the life of the world. In his characteristically clear and penetrating style, Oldham analyzed and described the situation of his day on the basis of firm theological convictions, issuing the following challenge to Christians:

> Christianity is not primarily a philosophy but a crusade. As Christ was sent by the Father, so he sends his disciples to set up in the world the kingdom of God. His coming was a declaration of war — a war to the death against the powers of darkness. He was manifested to destroy the works of the devil. Hence when Christians find in the world a state of things that is not in accord with the truth which they have learned from Christ, their concern is not that it should be explained but that it should be ended. In that temper we must approach everything in the relations between races that cannot be reconciled with the Christian ideal (p.26).

The second universal Life and Work conference (Oxford 1937) included in its report on "The Church and Community" **(3)** a section on "The Church and Race" which set forth some basic concepts of Christian race relations for subsequent ecumenical gatherings. Human sin was seen as asserting itself in "racial pride, racial hatreds and persecutions and the exploitation of other races. Against this sin in all its forms the church is called by God to set its face implacably and to utter its word unequivocally, both within and without its own borders" (p.72). Oldham was decisive in formulating these sentences.

From the middle of the 1930s the dominant issue came to be National Socialist racism in Germany and specifically anti-semitism. For Christianity the Jewish problem was not a primarily racial but a deeply religious issue (Rom. 9-11). But since the Nazi government persecuted the Jews on racial grounds, the churches had to face the racial issue also. The first frontline was that of the membership of people of Jewish ancestry in the Christian community. With great conviction the universality of the church as the people of God, embracing men, women and children of all races, was strongly proclaimed.

As to the fate of the Jewish people, the record is ambiguous. It is true that leaders of the ecumenical movement protested against the persecution of the Jews and tried to help Jews to escape. But only too late was it realized that the most ghastly crime in human history was being carried out in the name of racial purity: the systematic murder of six million Jews. During this period other important problems of racial conflict received scarcely any attention. It was too easily assumed that the defeat of the crude racism of National Socialism would mean the defeat of racism per se. Christians were unable to see that unavowed racism can be equally pernicious.

Apartheid the central issue

After the second world war, various WCC statements urged churches to eliminate racist practices in their own ranks, recognize their involvement in racial and ethnic tensions in the world and denounce the violation of human rights through discrimination on grounds of race, colour and culture.

The Amsterdam assembly in 1948 suggested that

> if the church can overcome national and social barriers which now divide it, it can help society to overcome those barriers. This is especially clear in the case of racial distinction. It is here that the church has failed most lamentably, where it has reflected and then by its example sanctified the racial prejudice that is rampant in the world. And yet it is here that today its guidance concerning what God wills for it is especially clear. It knows that it must call society away from prejudice based upon race or colour and from the practices of discrimination and segregation as denials of justice and human dignity, but it cannot say a convincing word to society unless it takes steps to eliminate these practices from the Christian community, because they contradict all that it believes about God's love for all his children (cited in **156**, p.21).

The second assembly at Evanston (1954) engaged in an even more severe self-criticism:

> All churches and Christians are involved, whether they recognize it or not, in the racial and ethnic tensions of the world. But it is in communities where segregation prevails that they face the plainest difficulties and the most challenging opportunities; for such segrega-

tion denies to those who are segregated their just and equal rights and results in deep injuries to the human spirit, suffered by offender and victim alike. The great majority of Christian churches affiliated with the World Council have declared that physical separation within the church on grounds of race is a denial of spiritual unity, and of the brotherhood of man. Yet such separations persist within these very churches, and we often seek to justify them on other grounds than race, because in our own hearts we know that separation solely on the grounds of race is abhorrent in the eyes of God (cited in **156**, p.22).

The first years of the World Council coincided with the birth of the policy of apartheid in South Africa, and this soon became a central issue. At almost every meeting of the central committee from 1949 on, the appropriate action to be taken was debated. But the declarations made by WCC officers or committees made little impression in South Africa. During these years, moreover, the acuteness of racial problems was overlooked, and the churches simply trusted too much in the immediate impact of ecumenical assemblies and conference statements. In spite of several brave resolutions, the churches and the ecumenical movement did not respond effectively to the challenges. Only in 1960 was a secretariat on racial and ethnic relations set up within the WCC Department on Church and Society.

In the same year a multiracial delegation of the WCC and its South African member churches participated in a consultation on race at Cottesloe in Johannesburg. Its final statement emphasized black people's rights to own land, to equal work opportunities and education and "no objection in principle to the direct representation of coloured people in parliament". The Cottesloe Declaration was adopted with more than 80 percent of the votes of the South African delegates. But not only did the white Dutch Reformed churches, under strong political pressure, subsequently reject the report; they also left the WCC. From the perspective of a generation later, the Cottesloe Declaration now appears as a well-intentioned but too timid document. It emphasized the need to struggle against apartheid rather than the struggle for a new society with true justice and truly equal social and economic development. Yet even that was too much for the white Dutch Reformed churches in South Africa; and the WCC's growing engagement in the struggle against apartheid in the succeeding years would elicit considerable controversy and opposition from outside the country as well.

From 1964 to 1975

More than fifty theologians and lay leaders from churches in four southern African countries, including many who were active in the growing movements for liberation from white colonial domination and minority rule, took part in a consultation in Kitwe, Zambia, in May 1964. Three of the presentations at the conference made a noteworthy contribution to ecumenical social thought and action: Z.K. Matthews' paper on the "Road from Non-Violence to Violence in the Struggle for Racial Justice in Southern Africa"; the address of Eduardo Mondlane, leader of FRELIMO, on the aspirations of the people of Mozambique for freedom from Portuguese colonialism; and W.A. Visser 't Hooft's theological study of "The Christian's Role in the Transforming of Society".

The Kitwe consultation marked a turning point in the ecumenical understanding of and approach to the struggle for racial and social justice in South Africa. Shortly thereafter, the WCC executive committee recommended that the report of the meeting be distributed to member churches. Its publication in South Africa provoked a remarkable theological, political and legal tumult. It was thus the beginning of a new WCC commitment to the campaign for racial justice in southern Africa and a clearer recognition of the relation between the spiritual and political realities of the struggle for racial justice. It was also an important contribution to the ecumenical debate on "revolutionary social change" which would emerge at the Geneva conference two years later.

The world conference on Church and Society in Geneva in 1966 stressed that "in dealing with racial and ethnic problems, Christian churches must be fully aware of the political and economic structures of society and see the problems in their context". Especially in the face of the explosive situation which had surfaced in South Africa and the racial unrest in the United States, which had prevented the scheduled preacher of the conference, Martin Luther King Jr, from appearing in person, the Geneva report **(53)** urged Christians and churches everywhere:

(1) to oppose, openly and actively, the perpetuation of the myth of racial superiority as it finds expression in social conditions and human behaviour as well as in laws and social structures;

(2) to engage in the common task of changing the structure of society through legislation, social planning and corporate action, and to mobilize all its resources to ensure the full and equal participation of all racial and ethnic groups in the corporate life of a pluralistic society; ...

(3) to make organized efforts to eradicate from the church and Christian community all forms of discrimination based on race, colour or ethnic origin in the selection of persons for church leadership, admission to the membership of congregations, and in adapting social and cultural values and traditions to the present;

(4) to use the powers inherent in its administrative structure, such as those that come from the investment of its resources or from the influence of its means of communication, to correct racial malpractice in society as well as within the church itself (pp.175f.).

Addressing theological issues in racial and ethnic relations, the statement insisted:

It is not enough for churches and groups to condemn the sin of racial arrogance and oppression. The struggle for radical change in structures will inevitably bring suffering and will demand costly and bitter engagement. For Christians to stand aloof from this struggle is to be disobedient to the call of God in history. The meaning of the cross for our time can be nothing less than this (p.205).

The assassination of Martin Luther King four months before he was to address the WCC's Uppsala assembly in 1968 gave the issue of racism an even more urgent focus there than at the Geneva conference two years earlier. The assembly urged the World Council to "embark on a vigorous campaign against racism" and to undertake a "crash programme to guide the Council and member churches in the matter of racism". With regard to the linkage of racism with economic and political exploitation the assembly said:

The churches must be actively concerned for the economic and political well-being of exploited groups so that their statements and actions may be relevant. In order that victims of racism may regain a sense of their own worth and be enabled to determine their own future, the churches must make economic and educational resources available to underprivileged groups for their development to full participation in the social and economic life of their communities. They should also withdraw investments from institutions that perpetuate racism. They must also urge that similar assistance be given from both the public and private sectors. Such economic help is an essential compensatory measure to counteract and overcome the present systematic exclusion of victims of racism from the mainstream of economic life. The churches must also work for the change of those political processes which prevent the victims of racism from participating fully in the civic and governmental structures of their countries (*The Uppsala Report 1968*, ed. Norman Goodall, Geneva, WCC, 1968, p.66).

Still more pressure came in 1969 from a WCC-sponsored world consultation on racism held at Notting Hill, London. In an emotional and often confrontational gathering, representatives of the racially oppressed demanded, among other things, a boycott of all institutions supporting racism, a fund for the payment of "reparations" for the injustices suffered over the centuries and support for the armed struggle of oppressed blacks in situations where all other means of liberation had failed. Though these demands were not met, they undoubtedly influenced the recommendations of the WCC central committee meeting a few months later in Canterbury, England, which set up the Programme to Combat Racism.

The central committee described the historical context as follows:

We have sadly to recognize that in spite of the battle that has been fought against racism by churches, mission agencies and councils of churches... racism is now a worse menace than ever. We have also sadly to confess that churches have participated in racial discrimination. Many religious institutions of the white northern world have benefited from racially exploitative economic systems. Lacking information about the possibility of developing sophisticated strategies to secure racial justice, Christians often engage in irrelevant and timid efforts to improve race relations — too little and too late (cited in **156**, pp.272f.).

Theologically, the committee made an even more prophetic statement:

Our struggle is not against flesh and blood. It is against the prin-
cipalities, against the powers of evil, against the deeply entrenched
demonic forces of racial prejudice and hatred that we must battle.
Ours is a task of exorcism. The demons operate through our social,
economic and political structures. But the root of the problem is as
deep as human sin, and only God's love and man's dedicated
response can eradicate it. The World Council's programme is but part
of that response. It is God's love and not the hatred of man that must
ultimately triumph. By God's love, by the power of his Spirit, some
day, soon, we shall overcome (p.277).

On the same theological grounds the report of a consultation
organized in 1975 by Faith and Order and the Programme to Combat
Racism **(164)** spoke of the gospel of forgiveness and the confession of
collective sin:

The demonic pervasiveness of racism compels us to speak of collective sin. "None is righteous, no not one" (Rom. 3:10). We are thrown
together in the solidarity of sin. We are not free to dissociate
ourselves self-righteously from this evil... Repentance action will not
be unambiguous nor safe from misinterpretation. We could wish it
were otherwise but the sad fact is that all our actions will inevitably
bear the mark of histories and structures in which we live and will
therefore still sometimes have racist elements. There will always be a
risk of making ourselves vulnerable on all sides (pp.7f.).

Official texts, including a 1970 statement from the WCC executive committee outlining the criteria of the Special Fund to Combat
Racism and approving the first grants to liberation movements, as well
as many subsequent declarations, have revealed a growing ecumenical
consensus on the evil of racism. Among these convictions are that
white racism is by far the most dangerous source of present racial
conflicts; that institutional racism, reflected in social, economic and
political structures, must be radically challenged; that combatting
racism entails a redistribution of political, economic and cultural
power from the powerful to the powerless; that no single strategy to
combat racism is universally appropriate.

PCR has provided many opportunities for contact, consultation
and dialogue with the leaders of the racially oppressed. Besides the
Special Fund, programmes and projects have been developed to

support local, national and regional churches and groups in solidarity with the racially oppressed. Research has been done and analytical documents have been published which have espoused the cause of marginal groups and made public the investments of churches, banks and multinational corporations in South Africa. More than anything else within the ecumenical movement PCR has been a testing ground for ethically grounded solidarity with the victims of ideology. South Africa's turn towards a new phase in its history in the 1990s has increasingly revealed how important, not so much in economic as in spiritual terms, the support of those groups and movements within the ecumenical family has been for the sustaining of the struggle of the majority people of South Africa against a system that denied their dignity.

Facing complex issues

The ambiguity and vulnerability of PCR became quite visible in the study on Violence, Non-violence and the Struggle for Social Justice, prepared by Church and Society and commended by the central committee in 1973 to the churches for study, comment and action **(116)**. It became clear that "commitment to a cause" is one thing and "complete identification with a political movement" another. A whole set of questions continues to besiege the Council and its member churches. Does the change of a particular social order necessarily imply its improvement? Will violent resistance attain the ends desired, after all the nonviolent possibilities are exhausted? Is violence to be equated only with radicalism and revolution, non-violence with gradualism and reform? Are Christians who live outside a particular conflict in a position to offer advice, whether towards violent or nonviolent strategies, to those within that situation who will be called upon to pay the price?

The rebels of Jesus' time challenged the Roman authorities and proclaimed the liberation of Jewish slaves. Jesus appealed to his followers to renounce force, not to resist the evildoer, to do good to those who hate, to bless those who curse and to pray for those who persecute. Yet the gospel of Matthew also records Jesus' words that he had not come to bring peace but a sword. Peace between oppressors and oppressed, as long as that oppression continues, is not possible. Jesus advised his disciples and friends to take up their cross and follow him. In his time crucifixion was a punishment for slaves, fugitives, outcasts and political insurgents. Tragically, the church has forgotten that the cross was an instrument of torture inflicted by the ruling class to maintain its power. Christianity spiritualized the carrying of the cross as an act of penance and self-abnegation.

How can we get beyond the heated yet sterile ecumenical debates around PCR and violence and nonviolence so as to develop a viable theology of action? Jesus' proclamation of the kingdom of God reveals a much deeper reality: that the cycle of violence and counter-violence is broken by his power as the crucified. The intricate issue of violence and nonviolence exists long before anyone takes up arms. It is at the heart of all human social life, particularly in the realm of racism. Especially white Christians should beware of using the term nonviolence, because it can well indicate an idolatrous desire to maintain the status quo of an oppressive society. All Christians have a long way to go towards an adequate understanding and practice of the power of the crucified.

That power challenges the apparently wise and prudent, yet in fact complacent and uncommitted emphasis on the part of many Christians that only peaceful and lawful forces can deal constructively with problems of racial injustice and lack of freedom. Not much courage is required to accuse so-called revolutionary Christians who call for a redistribution of political and economic power in the struggle against racism of romantic visions of justice, illusions of quick reform, "politicization" of religion and blind acceptance of secular, particularly Marxist ideologies. But the issue of power also challenges seemingly "revolutionary" Christians. Without continuous prayer for forgiveness and grace there is no guarantee that repentance actions will be more than cheap rhetorical exercises in political routine. Sensitivity to human suffering and right expression of Christian faith and ethics do not by themselves lead directly to the humanization of society. Christians in the forefront of the struggle against racism are caught again and again in the web of human inhumanity to other human beings; and they are vulnerable on all sides when the depth of their repentance is tested.

The criteria for the Special Fund to Combat Racism were adopted by the WCC central committee in 1969, regularly re-examined since then and reaffirmed with minor changes in 1976. The major elements of these criteria are:

— The purpose of the organizations must not be in conflict with the general purposes of the WCC and its units, and the grants are to be used for humanitarian purposes (i.e. social, health and educational purposes, legal aid, etc.).
— The proceeds of the fund shall be used to support organizations that combat racism, rather than welfare organizations that alleviate the effects of racism and which would normally be eligible for support from other units of the World Council of Churches.
— The focus of the grants should be on raising the level of awareness and on strengthening the organizational capability of racially oppressed people.
— In addition, the need is recognized to support organizations that align themselves with the victims of racial injustice and pursue the same objectives.
— The grants are made without control of the manner in which they are spent, and are intended as an expression of commitment by the PCR to the cause of economic, social and political justice which these organizations promote (*Minutes of the Central Committee*, Geneva, 1976, p.111).

The last paragraph does not imply that the WCC is unaware of how the money is spent. Besides making sure that the purpose of the organizations concerned does not conflict with the general purposes of the Council, the PCR maintains a continuing dialogue with the recipients of grants.

At a deeper level, the organizations receiving support through the Special Fund have clearly seen this instrument less in monetary terms than as a way of dramatizing and internationalizing their struggle against racism. While the grants do enable them to expand their humanitarian programmes, their greatest importance lies in their symbolic value as an ecumenical act of solidarity and their educational impact on the churches both in their own region and among the wider ecumenical constituency.

The theological and political principles undergirding the Special Fund have been affirmed time and time again. There are clear indications of well-planned and well-organized attempts to discredit the work and even the very existence of the WCC by deliberately

distorting the aims and nature of this programme. Many other criticisms of the Fund and the Council on social ethical grounds reflect a
failure to understand the need to risk concrete action when the signs of
the time demand it.

PCR and the Special Fund have made a unique contribution
towards people's awareness of the evil of racism. They have made it
possible for the WCC to interpret the struggles of the oppressed from
the perspective of the people directly involved in them. They have
been politically significant to the racially marginalized not only in
southern Africa but all over the world. They have demonstrated
ecumenical commitment to the cause of those exploited on the
ground of their colour. The Fund has helped to reveal the depth and
pervasiveness of racist attitudes and structures, reflected in and often
fostered by the media, and has encouraged many Christians and
churches in the poor countries to remain united with the victims of
racial oppression.

Consultations

Following a series of meetings in the late 1970s in Africa, Asia, the
Caribbean, Europe, Latin America, Southern Europe, Canada, South
Africa and the United States, the WCC held a world consultation on
racism in Noordwijkerhout, the Netherlands, in 1980. Its report, *Churches Responding to Racism in the 1980s* **(158)**, was adopted by the
WCC central committee meeting that year. It called on member churches "to declare as a fundamental matter of faith that the doctrine and
practice of apartheid is a perversion of the Christian gospel"; and "in
obedience to their faith, to examine in penitence their own involvement
in racism, wherever and in whatever form it occurs".

PCR also tackled the issue of racism in children's books, a
concern highlighted by the United Nations' designation of 1978 as
International Anti-Apartheid Year and 1979 as the International Year
of the Child. A workshop jointly sponsored by PCR and the WCC
Education office to promote non-racist and anti-racist children's
literature produced a set of criteria which have been used widely as
guidelines for the exposure of racist material, including that found in
religious textbooks **(168)**.

PCR's "Women Under Racism" programme, focusing on justice
and equality for women who are victims of both racism and sexism,

organized a global consultation in Geneva in 1986 on women under racism and casteism. The women called upon the churches to reverse the growing discrimination, repression and violence against them throughout the world and to enable their increased participation in the decision-making processes of church and society. They declared: "As Christians we believe that all human beings are created in the image of God, and oppression and violence done to any section of society is an act against God."

Indigenous people and their struggle for land rights have been an increasingly important focus for PCR. The United Nations defines indigenous peoples as "the existing descendants of the peoples who inhabited the present territory of a country wholly or partially at the time when persons of a different culture or ethnic origin arrived there from other parts of the world, overcame them and, by conquest, settlements or other means, reduced them to a non-dominant or colonial situation." Indigenous peoples are among the worst victims of racism today. While they remember with horror and bitterness what was done to them in the past, they often find themselves literally sacrificed in the name of national development and well-being, and in many cases their very survival is threatened. Expropriation of their land has meant the destruction of their beliefs, cultures and customs.

In 1985 PCR organized a meeting between international and South African church leaders in Harare, Zimbabwe. The declaration coming from that meeting challenged the churches to express solidarity with the victims of apartheid and called for "the transfer of power to the majority of the people, based on universal suffrage". Two years later a PCR-organized meeting in Lusaka, Zambia, brought together international church leaders and southern African liberation movements — the African National Congress (ANC), the Pan Africanist Congress (PAC) and the South West Africa People's Organization (SWAPO). The participants adopted the historic Lusaka Statement, which declared the South African government illegitimate. In 1989 an Eminent Church Persons Group visited the capitals of five European countries, Japan and the United States to call on those governments to impose comprehensive economic sanctions against South Africa, in order to force it to negotiate with the authentic leaders of the black majority.

Ecumenical work against racism is far from over. After the dramatic changes in South Africa in the 1990s, it will not be easy to infuse the Programme to Combat Racism with new vision, vigour and commitment to become anew a "cutting edge" and continue to be faithful to the mission of the gospel and the WCC. Foundations need to be shaken in order to overcome the prevailing inertia, struggle against the mood of powerlessness and resignation and shatter easy illusions about what it takes to satisfy people's quest for justice.

At the end of his article on "Racism" (in the *Dictionary of the Ecumenical Movement*, p.843), N. Barney Pityana, then director of PCR, struck a sobering note:

> PCR's method of operation has been radical. It seeks to get to the roots of this structural inequality. Unfortunately, one of the consequences of this approach has been to push the racially oppressed to the periphery of action for justice without acknowledging them as pro-actors in their struggle. Meanwhile, those who have the means, and may be even responsible for the racism, can be indifferent, paralyzed by guilt or a sense of powerlessness. A new and effective approach seems necessary — one which encourages partnership for effective action.

Equally down-to earth is Barbara Rogers in her book *Race: No Peace without Justice* **(166)**:

> At the height of the attacks on the Council and on its contributing churches, there was a substantial *rise* in contributions to the Special Fund. This increase in support, from the churches as well as from people and organizations that never had any contact with the ecumenical movement before, has been sustained since then. However, there still remains a very real problem of a crisis for the national "leadership" of the churches, and even of the World Council, battered as they are by the savage attacks they have been through.
>
> It is possible to criticize the church leadership for being hypersensitive. They seem to tremble before the criticism of a very small minority who are well known to be completely committed to the regime in South Africa, and who will never change their minds no matter what the facts of the case are. The World Council, too, seems badly shaken by the attacks and disinclined to enter any new areas which might be "controversial", indicating a failure of nerve which will simply encourage the racists to further attacks (p.viii).

XII

Inter-Church Aid, Refugee and World Service

Within the Life and Work movement the European Central Bureau for Inter-Church Aid was established in 1922 with offices in New York and Geneva. A pioneer venture in ecumenical relief, it began its work under the patronage of the Federal Council of the Churches of Christ in America and the Federation of Swiss Protestant Churches, later joined by other European churches. In 1944 it was merged into the Department of Reconstruction and Inter-Church Aid of the World Council of Churches (then in process of formation). Its name was changed at the third assembly of the WCC in New Delhi in 1961 to the Division (later Commission) of Inter-Church Aid, Refugee and World Service (DICARWS/CICARWS).

A memorandum drawn up by W.A. Visser 't Hooft and approved by the provisional committee of the WCC in 1943 said about the mandate of the Department:

> The paramount principle is that which is implied in the very existence of the World Council, namely that the task of reconstruction is to be conceived as an ecumenical task in which all the churches participate to the limit of their ability, and that the common objective is to rebuild the life of the whole fellowship of churches which finds expression in the World Council. If this ecumenical principle is taken seriously, this will mean that the churches will agree to coordinate their policies and activities in order to make certain that all needy churches receive adequate help, that churches will not confine their help exclusively to the churches belonging to the same denomination or confession and that the autonomy and desires of the receiving churches are taken into full consideration (*The Ten Formative Years, 1938-1948*, Geneva, WCC, 1948, p.33).

This was a timely and adequate statement. But several past shortcomings were difficult to correct and a number of emerging problems needed to be solved. It was no easy process to broaden the traditional concept — social and economic help given by a church to another of the same communion — into a vision of joint action in Christian solidarity across ecclesiastical and geographical boundaries. Persuading different Western churches to help different churches in Asia was not easy, for many denominations and confessions saw their own interchurch aid programme as an essential part of their confessional identity.

Until well into the 1950s interchurch aid was mainly limited to the reconstruction of Europe. Gradually it widened to all other continents, but it still took a long time for the realization to set in that common Christian stewardship must serve the whole human family, wherever it is in need, regardless of race, religion, tradition and culture. Another problem for the WCC was that some of its interchurch aid projects were overlapping and partly competitive with those of the International Missionary Council. Years of conferences and consultations were needed to sort out and define each other's respective responsibilities.

Probably the most difficult and enduring problem in inter-church aid is one which is not recognized in the memorandum of Visser 't Hooft: the sociological, psychological and not least theological problems that arise out of the relation between "giving" and "receiving" churches. It took more than fifteen years for the WCC to agree on and implement the concept of *sharing* resources ecumenically. For a long time, moreover, many people believed that mission and service are divided by a theological chasm. Mission was seen as the proclamation of the gospel, service as an outreach in human compassion. Mission seeks to convert, service to assist without intending to convert. But the dichotomy is more verbal than real. Some churches and Christians tend to conceive "mission" in a narrowly evangelistic sense. Others are inclined to restrict the role of service organizations largely to the relief of physical needs and general welfare work aimed directly at improving basic human living standards. The only way to deal with this tension is to unite the organizations of mission and service.

Whenever a major need develops, it will be met by the unified physical and spiritual resources of the ecumenical agencies on the international as well as the national level — for example, by Christian Aid (UK) or Church World Service (USA). These and other ecumenical institutions of diakonia are service arms of the churches. They are Good Samaritans ministering to hurting people along the roadsides of our troubled world. They seek to do God's work, not alone but with others, not well enough but nevertheless as well as they can. Instead of dulling consciences, they stir them.

Yet the well-organized ecumenical Christian charity in all parts of the world has been constantly threatened with misgivings, failures and objections. At its inaugural assembly in 1959 the East Asia Christian Conference made this significant statement:

> We strongly urge that the matter of giving and receiving be rethought. If inter-church aid is conceived as a giving of funds by wealthy churches for the bolstering up of the organization and material welfare of weaker churches, it is just as capable of creating self-righteousness on the one hand and dependence on the other as many other paternalistic programmes. Ecumenical inter-church aid must *not* be thought of merely as a giving by one group of churches and a receiving by others. We need to recognize that for every need, physical and spiritual, every Christian has an obligation to share. Our programmes must be so devised as to help us to understand that in the planning of projects those near at hand and those at a distance are *interdependent* in their ministry to human need. In this way we enter into a new understanding of the meaning of giving and receiving (*Witnesses Together*, ed. U Kyaw Than, Rangoon, EACC, 1959, p.103).

In a report from the Division of World Mission and Evangelism to the WCC central committee in Paris in 1962, the following opinion was expressed:

> The missionary movement shows too little sign of moving. The causes of this immobility are no doubt varied and complex. Among them are: (1) the fact that we have inherited a structure based upon the recent period of human history in which Christian missions were conducted exclusively by the people of the "Western" world. That period has ended, but many of our structures have remained unchanged; (2) the fact that we have not yet learned to see the missionary task as one common task for the whole people of God, in which the need of every part is to be the concern of all. Consequently

resources have not been available swiftly enough at the point where they are needed; (3) the fact that too many Christians regard the church as a source of privilege for themselves rather than as a place of responsibility for the neighbour, in whose service Christ is to be served. Consequently, congregations become self-centred and have even made it plain that converts were not welcome (*Minutes*, Geneva, WCC, 1962, p.88).

Both for the WCC and other sectors of the ecumenical movement the consultation on inter-church aid, refugee and world service in Swanwick in 1966 was decisive. In his concluding address Leslie Cooke, the director of the WCC's inter-church aid division, had a warning about the future:

There will be many who have been generous in their giving for relief who will become hesitant, if not resistant, when they realize that our aim is to change the *status quo*. They will think that the church has gone leftist, or socialist, or communist... There will be those among the rising generation, and in the churches of the developing countries, who are radical, who will say: "At last the churches are with us — they have espoused our cause, they have joined the revolution." Then there will come a moment when to the word "revolution" we will have to add the word "reconciliation", and these heralds of the new dawn will be disappointed and disillusioned as they see that the church cannot deploy into the long lines to face the enemies of change for violent battle. We shall face grave misunderstanding...

That we are now caught up to go beyond aid to challenge the structures of churches and society, even by the aid we give and the purposes to which we give it, is beyond doubt. That there is a price to be paid is also beyond doubt. The only two uncertainties are what the cost will be and whether we are prepared to pay it. We have to press on beyond co-operation to community... The overwhelming compulsion to move from co-operation to community derives from the fact that it is clear that many of the problems which face mankind can be solved only by the building of a world community. Perhaps the most significant contribution the churches can make is manifesting that they are a world community, that they in fact share a common life in the body of Christ (**175**, pp.127-31).

What has just been said can be applied to the overall involvement of the ecumenical movement in work for refugees. From the very beginning the WCC refugee programme did not distinguish (as did UN agencies and secular organizations) between refugees, displaced persons and "escapees" but took "need" as its criterion. It had liaison in Geneva with the National Catholic Welfare Conference, the Lutheran World Federation and the League of Red Cross Societies, as well as with other bodies that cared for refugees and displaced persons. Knowledge of legal requirements, sources of specialized help and the mandates of inter-governmental, international, governmental and voluntary agencies called for technical skills to which churches and national councils of churches seldom have access. Consequently, a centralized WCC refugee service became indispensable.

But the world refugee situation has seriously worsened since the 1970s, and in recent years the vast majority of the more than 15 million refugees in the world have fled from one country of the South to another. Countries which carry the main burden in hosting and helping refugees increasingly stress the need for greater burden-sharing through international solidarity. This has required from the churches an even sharper awareness of the root causes of refugee situations, more effective advocacy on behalf of the rights of refugees, alertness regarding xenophobia and racist trends, sharing of credible information and in some cases the granting of sanctuary to refugees.

During the 1960s two United Nations actions affected interchurch aid projects: the Food and Agriculture Organization (FAO) launched the first Freedom from Hunger campaign (1960-65), and the UN named the entire decade the first Development Decade. To those initiatives the churches and their aid agencies responded both nationally and through the WCC. This period saw a rapid expansion of interchurch aid into social, agricultural, medical and educational projects in the southern hemisphere. Support for "traditional" interchurch aid programmes became more difficult and complicated as the mandates of ecumenical partner agencies began to alter. For some agencies these changes were necessary because they had begun to receive significant government funding, which precluded support of projects which benefited primarily Christians. In the effort to avoid the donors setting the priorities, the World Council's role as an impartial broker became increasingly important.

As we saw in Chapter X, the WCC set up a specialized Commission on the Churches' Participation in Development after the Uppsala assembly. Its work would enable a comprehensive approach to questions of development, including study and research, education, technical and financial assistance. Nevertheless, a development component continued within the programmes and projects of CICARWS.

By the mid-1980s the optimism of the mid-1960s about the possibilities of development had given way to a mood of frustration and an awareness that the churches were also losing in the global struggle for justice. Against the backdrop of this increasingly alarming predicament, CICARWS convened a world consultation in Larnaca, Cyprus, in 1986 **(173)**.

Like Swanwick twenty years earlier, Larnaca marked a turning point in the ecumenical understanding of interchurch aid. There was relatively little discussion of development or aid projects; rather, discussions centred on the struggles for survival, liberation, dignity, justice, peace and reconciliation. The consultation underlined the importance of the local church as an agent of change, because it is there that attitudes regarding refugees, migrants, the poor and the marginalized are shaped and expressed. There also youth and women must secure more space for participation and involvement in decision-making.

The last paragraph of the Larnaca Declaration looks ahead to the approach of the third millennium with a vision and a commitment

> to work for justice and peace through our diakonia. We commit ourselves to implement a vision to identify ourselves and to be in solidarity with the people who are now in the process of struggling for peace based on justice. Our diakonia now and for the future must be based on mutual trust and genuine sharing. We recognize that people and churches on all continents have needs and that our diakonia must reach out to all those who suffer. We know the forces which confront us are many; we know that the road before us is long and painful. We know we can do no less than to pick up the cross and follow in the footsteps of the suffering servant, Christ our Lord. His victory over death gives us life and hope (pp.124f.).

Another world consultation, this one on the ecumenical sharing of resources (ESR), took place the next year in El Escorial, Spain, under the theme "Koinonia — Sharing Life in a World Community" **(184)**. ESR had begun as a study in 1976 after the Nairobi assembly, where interchurch aid, mission and development had been discussed in the wake of the debate about the call by several church leaders in Africa and Asia for a "moratorium" on outside personnel and assistance. The moratorium idea had raised fundamental questions about the selfhood of the receiving churches and the self-understanding of churches that were used to seeing themselves solely as senders or givers.

The understanding in the ESR study of what is meant by "resources" is a broad one, including spirituality, culture and human resources as well as finance. Calling for just relationships, based on equality and allowing mutual accountability, sharing of power and true interdependence, it requires holding together mission, development and service, which are often treated separately, both in Christian theology and in church organizational structures.

In his address to the consultation at El Escorial Konrad Raiser made two pertinent observations:

> It is vitally important that our commitment should not extend only to sharing in and between Christian churches and communities... A Christian congregation can only become a parable of shared life to the extent that it shares the goodness of God's creation with all human beings. In the course of the discussion in recent years there have been many stormy disputes as to whether sharing proves itself principally in fellowship and solidarity between Christians and churches or in solidarity with the poor in the struggle for justice and human dignity...
>
> Realism tells us that at the macro-level, relations between churches and the agencies they support will probably never measure up to the standard of comprehensive, mutual sharing, especially where the sharing of material resources is concerned. Nevertheless, these relations ought to be clearly and recognizably different from relations between governments, business corporations, etc. They should meet the fundamental requirement of justice. For only then can they keep the way open for the renewal that will lead to a sharing community. In their relations with one another, churches do not behave like autonomous states, business partners or pressure groups. As members of the body of Christ they live in a fundamental relationship to one another which binds them in mutual obligation (pp.21, 23).

It remains a real question whether ecumenical Christians can be enabled to understand that all service — to fellow Christians and to all fellow human beings alike — is participation in the redeeming ministry of Jesus Christ; in other words, that the aim of all their charity and aid is not only to change the status quo of the churches and humanity at large, but also to establish a universal community which is a foreshadowing of the kingdom of God.

It is primarily in the field of interchurch aid — much more than in the domain of a theological understanding of Christian unity or in the missionary realm of common witness — that the nations should be challenged to strive towards world community. This is not possible as long as the endless discussion on how to implement the sharing of Christian resources remains an end in itself. Matthew 25:31-46 makes it clear that acts of love and generous care are not a prerogative of world Christianity but the quintessence of all religious and secular communities. The only peculiar task of the churches is to manifest that proclamation, fellowship and service — kerygma, koinonia and diakonia — belong intimately together and condition one another.

XIII

Roman Catholic Social Thought

It has become evident in the ecumenical movement that serious research and continuous study are needed if the churches' witness in the area of social-ethical issues is to be worthy and effective. For a church to make a pronouncement on a specific problem is to open itself to the scrutiny of experts who will be quick to spot ignorance; to limit itself to generalities is to risk uttering pious platitudes to which no one will listen.

The Roman Catholic Church has never elaborated a complete doctrinal system in social-ethical issues. Rather, it has responded gradually to matters as they have arisen and to the religious and secular controversies surrounding them. Nevertheless, a developing coherence of Catholic social teaching can be detected in the more than 100 papal social documents, including encyclicals, since *Rerum novarum* was promulgated by Leo XIII in 1891.

A reliable reference work surveying systematically the social teachings of the popes from 1878 to 1953 in 19 thematic chapters is *The Church and Social Justice* **(186)**. In the introduction the editors succinctly describe the orientation and purpose of Roman Catholic social ethics:

> The social teaching of the Church is not a doctrine which can be put on the same level as liberalism, capitalism, socialism or communism. It is not a "model" of society which has been elaborated according to the view of the world held by one philosophy or another. It is a statement of the social implications of a religious faith. It makes no pretence of solving the technical problems of managing a society. It does not dispense with empirical methods of social analysis nor with the construction of theoretical or statistical models, nor even with the

imaginative drive of which the social spirit has need if society's progress is to be assured. What the Church deals with is the control and sometimes also the orientation of all these methods, all these means and all these projects of thought and of action, in the light of a view of man which rests upon faith in Jesus Christ, Man-God, in whose destiny all men are caught up (pp.xii-xiii).

The Gospel of Peace and Justice **(189)**, presented by Joseph Gremillion, is the most comprehensive and authoritative source on Catholic social teaching from John XXIII until 1975. In addition to the official texts of the 25 most important documents which set forth the historical development, this book contains nine valuable introductory chapters on such subjects as unjust power structures, liberation and reform, political power, population, resources and environment and the fate of the family in technological society. A third source which should be mentioned is *The Social Teaching of the Church* **(190)**, by John Desroches, which also includes the major conferences of the World Council of Churches, the Asian bishops conferences and the Christian Conference of Asia.

Major Catholic pronouncements

Two important documents, *Rerum novarum* and *Quadragesimo anno*, promulgated by Pius XI in 1931, launched and guided the Catholic social apostolate during its first seventy years. The former outlined relations between church and state, the right of peoples to determine their own form of government, the rights and duties of the state, management and workers, the protection of the labouring classes against exploitation and the promotion of their rights to receive just wages and to organize themselves. Forty years later Pius XI developed these principles, emphasizing the common good of society and the state's responsibility to promote the temporal well-being of all its subjects and introducing the concepts of social justice and social charity as essential to the building up of society.

Then, between 1961 and 1971, five documents of comparable substance and historical significance appeared: John XXIII's *Mater et magistra* (1961) and *Pacem in terris* (1963); the pastoral constitution *Gaudium et spes* from the Second Vatican Council and Paul VI's *Populorum progressio* (1967) and *Octogesima adveniens* (1971). This new readiness to speak out reflects the heightened awareness of the social mission of the church which has marked Roman Catholicism since John XXIII, as the urgent issues and pastoral needs of a fast-changing world became increasingly evident. *Gaudium et spes* was the first expressly social, cultural and political document to be proclaimed by an ecumenical council since Nicea in 325.

In the encyclical of 1961 John XXIII emphasized that true prosperity involves not only total national wealth but also its just distribution. The imbalance between developed and developing nations should be corrected through aid from the former to the latter. Advanced industrial nations should not, however, impose their sophisticated culture or seek political advantages, which would be another form of colonialism. The encyclical of 1963 proposed human dignity and freedom as the basis of world order and peace and pleaded for an end to the arms race, banning of nuclear weapons and general disarmament.

In his encyclical of 1967 Paul VI expressed the social conscience of the church in regard to poverty and wealth, denounced "the scandal of glaring inequalities not merely in the enjoyment of possession, but even more in the exercise of power", and declared that "the superfluous wealth of rich countries should be placed at the service of poor nations... The new name for peace is development."

Gaudium et spes represented a breakthrough in Christian thought. Discarding centuries of exaggerated dualism which had hampered the attempt of religion to relate to the secular order, it manifested a new awareness that an essential part of the Christian mission is to humanize political, social, economic, cultural and technological life. While church and world are not identical, neither are they in irrevocable opposition; for while the church transcends the world, it also exists in the world. Nor does the church have any ground for believing, pietistically or triumphalistically, that it is singularly well-equipped to perform the role of decisively transforming society.

In "Convergence and Divergence in Social Theology" **(197)**, Ronald Preston sums up four important features of *Gaudium et spes*:

> (1) It is not "churchy" in tone, but stresses both the dignity of the human person and the community of humankind. It argues for a fuller achievement of human rights, with Christians working with all men and women of good will to that end. Justice is the norm and love is to be the driving force. The church has been too conservative in the past and should be the servant of the truly human.

(2) It adopts a more flexible theology to cope with rapid social change. In particular it sees that a blanket condemnation of atheism is inadequate, including a blind anti-communism...

(3) The theology is less individualistic and more corporate in its concern for the universal common good and the structures of social life. The social rather than the individual nature of property is stressed, and the freedom of individuals and groups more in the principle of subsidiarity than in private property.

(4) There is a new respect for the autonomy of the secular; of ethics, of the social sciences and of the natural sciences. The church has not all the answers... It is "up to Christian communities to analyze the situation which is proper to their own country... and to draw principles of reflection, norms of judgment and directives for action from the social teaching of the church. This should be done in dialogue with other Christians and all men of good will" (pp.195f.).

In a commentary on *Gaudium et spes* **(188)**, Robert McAfee Brown registers several caveats:

> The statement that "the Church knows that her message is in harmony with the most secret desires of the human heart" (para. 21) illustrates a temptation throughout the document to assume that the gospel crowns the life of natural man, rather than being as well a challenge to and judgment upon that life... Although the final version is more realistic about man's sin than were earlier drafts, there needs to be more recognition of the pervasiveness of sin in men and human institutions, so that the hopes raised by the tone of the document will not be unnecessarily dimmed by the hard realities of the world. The ongoing power of evil is a theme to which more attention could have been given. If this [reaction] be Protestant pessimism, it is at least a pessimism we have learned from Scripture and tradition as well as from the daily newspaper (pp.315f.).

Despite such reservations there was general agreement both within and outside of the Roman Catholic Church that *Gaudium et spes* deserves special attention. In his survey of "The Ecumenical Movement and the Roman Catholic Church" **(201)**, Lukas Vischer observed that the document made an important ecumenical contribution:

> For was this not the point where divided churches could most easily co-operate together? Was it not here that the weight of our differences

was least in evidence? And might it not be that, when the churches faced together the questions of the time, they might also be shown ever new ways to greater unity? This had again and again been the experience of the ecumenical movement. The Constitution could therefore pave the way to a collaboration which might be of the greatest significance for the ecumenical movement (p.342).

Well-founded though it may have been at the time, this prediction of growing collaboration would prove within a decade to be premature and over-optimistic.

SODEPAX and JPIC

From 1968 to 1980 the joint committee on Society, Development and Peace (SODEPAX) operated as an agency co-responsible to the Holy See (through the Pontifical Commission on Justice and Peace) and the World Council of Churches (through the Commission on the Churches' Participation in Development and later through the Programme Unit on Justice and Service). Jointly announced as an "ecumenical experiment" with a three-year mandate, SODEPAX energetically took up its responsibilities from the beginning, setting up local and national groups and launching programmes on social communication, education for development, mobilization for peace, development research, theological reflection and interfaith dialogue. It organized large international conferences on development (1968), the theology of development (1969), the communication media in service of development and peace (1970), peace and the international community (1970) and the churches' role in the development of Asia (1970).

The more or less "official" version of the spectacular advance, long stagnation and painful liquidation of SODEPAX is that it became the victim of its own successes. Needing more staff to respond to demands from many parts of the world, it was unable to find sufficient outside funding and its parent bodies bore its costs reluctantly even as their worries grew that it was becoming a quasi-independent entity because of the diffuse nature of its programmes and its free style of operation.

The history of SODEPAX does reveal the problems of relations between the Roman Catholic Church, as a single universal and well-organized church, and the World Council of Churches, as a council of churches a few steps removed from the decision-making structures of its member churches. There was indeed concern about its possible competition with the Pontifical Commission on Justice and Peace on the one side and the WCC's sub-units on Church and Society and the Churches' Participation in Development on the other. The disappearance of SODEPAX was also bound up with the complicated question of whether the Roman Catholic Church would become a member of the WCC, which was still a vivid hope in many quarters in the early 1970s.

A quite different version of the fate of SODEPAX was given by the Jesuit George Dunne, its first general secretary, in his memoirs *King's Pawn* (Chicago, Loyola UP, 1990). Dunne sees the primary cause of the death of SODEPAX in 1980 as intrigues and power struggles among church officials on both sides, not the malfunctioning of church structures.

The Roman Catholic caution about offering precise "official" answers to contemporary social problems and political and economic crises has continued to cause tensions with the WCC, which tends to be more prepared to propose exact Christian analyses and solutions. Following the termination of SODEPAX, discussions in the Joint Working Group between the Roman Catholic Church and the WCC on collaboration in the field of social thought and action led to the formation of an interim structure, a Joint Consultative Group linking sub-units in the WCC Programme Unit on Justice and Service with the corresponding dicasteries in the Roman Curia. But this group too failed to yield satisfactory results.

In 1987 the WCC central committee, after a stormy discussion, invited the Roman Catholic Church to be co-inviter with the Council for the world convocation on Justice, Peace and the Integrity of Creation, to be held in Seoul in 1990. It took almost a year before a response was received from the Secretariat for Promoting Christian Unity, indicating that the Vatican could not accept this proposal for theological and ecclesiastical reasons. Some of the difficulty centred on the term "conciliar process" used in the recommendation from the Vancouver assembly that the WCC "engage member churches in a conciliar process of mutual commitment (covenant) to justice, peace and the integrity of all creation" (*Gathered for Life*, ed. David Gill, Geneva, 1983, p.255). In Catholic opinion the fact that this term was undefined meant that it was subject to imprecise understanding of what a council is. Furthermore, the relation between "conciliar process" and "conciliar fellowship" (the term from the 1975 WCC assembly in Nairobi) had not been clarified.

An unpublished document from May 1987 entitled "Proposals in View of Catholic Participation in JPIC" points to some of the theological problems which the Vatican saw in the materials being generated in the JPIC process. It spoke of

> an approach that seems to draw largely on a certain reading of the Old Testament and to lack the positive spirit of the New Testament, full of confidence and love, despite a clear awareness of sin and evil... There seems to be a negative reaction in face of the world, a feeling of unease in relation to creation and the world, almost a lack of confidence in God. It is a stress on fear and doom, which becomes almost apocalyptic. Despite the threats which have always menaced human existence and society, we can and must be confident, because the coming kingdom of God already transforms human hearts (Luke 17:21) and people's lives and the world...
>
> For the Roman Catholic Church (even under the cross of contemporary problems) a theology of the cross is not to be separated from a theology of glory... The emphasis in the report on resisting the forces that deny justice is also too strong. The Christian ideal is resistance to evil along with reconciliation, through justice, not simply resistance alone. Reconciliation is a scriptural notion which is an essential dimension of the gospel with a bearing on the Christian presence in the world.

While the Roman Catholic Church played a full part in the process leading to the European ecumenical assembly on JPIC issues in Basel in 1989, the final result at the global level of long and difficult negotiations was that only a small delegation of Roman Catholic observers — far fewer than the WCC had hoped — attended the world consultation in Seoul. The impact of this participation was fragmented, and the Roman Catholic Church continued on its own way of stating its position on social-ethical and political issues without consulting other churches.

Recent Catholic pronouncements

In *Laborem exercens* (1981) John Paul II argued that the current Western capitalist system can no longer provide people with the basic requirements of their existence and that what is needed is a planned economy based on Christian social principles and international coop- eration. The central idea of the encyclical is the priority of labour over capital — the belief that capital is meant to serve labour, which means it must serve those who make up the labour force. The violation of this principle lies behind the crises of unemployment, insecurity, inflation and growing poverty which appear in every society. In critical dialogue with Marxism, the pope emphasized that labour is the key to understanding people's historical vocation and the various projects of society. Through labour people create their social world, and in doing so they to some extent create themselves.

The explosive social, political and economic situation in Latin America and the resulting ferment in theology and church led the Vatican in the mid-1980s to address two documents to those who were elaborating and adhering to liberation theology, not only theologians and priests but also a great number of people in the so-called basic Christian communities. An *Instruction on Certain Aspects of the Theology of Liberation* (London, Catholic Truth Society, 1984), issued by the Sacred Congregation for the Doctrine of the Faith, warned against turning away from the official teachings of the Roman Catholic Church by adopting in contemporary theology Marxist prop- ositions, such as class struggle and the overthrow of the ruling class, which are incompatible with the Christian vision and vocation. Those who developed the concept of the church of the people — especially the poor — were accused of challenging "the sacramental and hierar- chical structure of the Church, which was willed by the Lord him- self... The denunciation of members of the hierarchy and the magis- terium as objective representatives of the ruling class has to be opposed." The clergy cannot take its origin from the people who "designate ministers of their own choice in accord with the needs of their historic revolutionary mission" (p.25).

Two years later, *The Instruction on Christian Freedom and Liberation* (Vatican, Polyglot Press, 1986) stressed the salvific and ethical dimensions of liberation, the necessity of the struggle for justice, the promotion of participation and the challenge of incultura- tion. Latin American theologians can in principle agree with the second document and expound their own theology without being threatened by the imposition of penitential silence. It is clear that a new and distinctive theology springing up in isolation from the Vatican threatens the unity of the Roman Catholic Church, but after the Vatican has taken an official position on it, a local theology may enjoy a measure of relative acceptance and relevance.

By its very nature the Sacred Congregation for the Doctrine of the Faith is oriented towards the past and reluctant to accept much change and innovation. This conservative theology tends to ignore the reality of evil and to minimize the effects of deception, injustice and upheaval in society and politics. The Congregation finds it difficult to conceive of the church as a place of searching and groping for where God is present in people's lives and for what fidelity to God demands of human beings in the present situation of economic injustice. Given the close relationship between the character of the socio-economic order and the personal virtue of individuals, any contribution the church can make to promote that order, according to the pastoral letter, constitutes an essential contribution to its overall mission of evangelization.

At the end of 1987 John Paul II issued his second encyclical devoted to Catholic social teaching, *Sollicitudo rei socialis* ("On Social Concern"), written to commemorate the twentieth anniversary of *Populorum progressio* (1967), in which his predecessor Paul VI had focused on the gap between the rich and the poor nations of the world. John Paul II observed that this gap has steadily widened: "One cannot deny that the present situation of the world, from the point of view of development, offers a rather negative impression" (para.13). The pope cited one indicator after another of a deteriorating situation: hunger, illiteracy, unemployment, massive debt, economic ruin, war, the expenditure on arms, the increase in refugees, the abuse of human rights. Solving the problems of underdevelopment will entail not paternalistic aid, but a deep change in the overall structure of relations between rich and poor countries. How this is to be achieved is a topic beyond the scope of the encyclical, but one of the critical factors, according to the pope, is the need for a profound awakening to the interdependence that is a feature of our common humanity. No concept is more frequently used in the encyclical than "solidarity". *The Logic of Solidarity* (eds Gregory Baum and Robert Ellsberg, Maryknoll, NY, Orbis, 1989) is a helpful collection of substantial essays on the pope's letter.

Centesimus annus, written in 1991 on the occasion of the cente-
nary of *Rerum novarum*, came at a time when state socialism in
Central and Eastern Europe and several nations of the south had
suffered a death blow. The anti-communist, pro-democratic and pro-
market developments of the late 1980s and early 1990s had radical
social, historical, ethical and theological significance not only for the
world, but also for the church. Despite the euphoria over new
freedom, it is evident that human community is disabled by the
consumerism, possessiveness and ecological damage which
dehumanize life in the non-socialist societies. *Centesimus annus*
sought not only to "manifest the true meaning of the church tradition",
but also to apply it to "an analysis of some events of recent history".
Moreover, it takes seriously secular thinking regarding economics and
politics in contemporary society. In speaking of "structures of sin" it is
also profoundly biblically oriented. A collection of critical commentaries is contained in *Rerum Novarum: One Hundred Years of
Catholic Social Teaching*, edited by John Coleman and Gregory Baum
(*Concilium*, 1991).

Structural and methodological divergences

There is very little literature on the differences in approach to
social ethics between the Roman Catholic Church and the World
Council of Churches. The superficial popular portrayal of these
disagreements in terms of a "conservative" Vatican over against a
"radical" WCC is inadequate and often mistaken. Yet there are
significant differences in theological method, ecclesial structure,
church-state relations and prophetic and priestly charisms which
continue to hinder the worldwide Christian community from making a
truly ecumenical witness together. Even in areas where convictions
seem virtually identical — human rights, religious liberty, development, racism, science and technology — little has emerged in the way
of common positions and joint actions. Not only is Roman Catholic
membership in the World Council still out of the question; the Holy
See remains reluctant to enter into cooperative relations in socio-
political areas.

The importance of the fact that the Vatican represents a single
church while the WCC is a council of many different churches should
not be minimized. The Vatican is the central office of one universal

community stressing its organic unity and hierarchical authority despite the many variations in Catholicism around the world. The WCC does not speak *for* its members, and it acts for them only in matters they entrust to it. They are not bound to accept its judgments. The Council often addresses statements *to* its member churches "for study and action", but they are not obliged to endorse them and can and sometimes do explicitly dissociate themselves from apparently controversial pronouncements.

Another important difference is that the Holy See operates in the diplomatic realm as a state. It has the formal apparatus of an independent nation, notably a diplomatic corps with accreditation to most of the world's governments. It enjoys special status at the United Nations and is a member of a number of specialized UN agencies. The World Council of Churches, since it is not a state, is related to the United Nations and its members as a non-governmental organization. The implication is that it has no real power.

A concise and useful book on the differences between the two would-be partners is Thomas S. Derr's *Barriers to Ecumenism* **(187)**, which is particularly helpful in its diagnosis of the structural obstacles and methodological differences in the approach to contemporary ecumenical social ethics. Derr observes that

> the statements of the Holy See... are likely to come, if they come at all, only at the end of a long and arduous process, and to tend toward generalities. The Vatican must keep in mind the effect of its actions on the local churches, which cannot disavow its directives. Often it is safer to say nothing or to speak vaguely... Its close relation to its churches shows in another way when local bishops insist, as they often do, that the Vatican take the lead on difficult issues. In effect, the local people "pass the buck" to Rome in order to avoid having to make the decision themselves. But then that decision from Rome, when it comes, must be aware of local sensibilities...
>
> This cautious manner of dealing with issues may have an effect on relations with the World Council. At least some people have detected a Catholic reluctance to agree to an ecumenical document lest they be committed to it. Keeping the World Council at arm's length, or at a conference table's length, becomes a way of life. Fear of being obligated can, however, be simply an excuse for avoiding closer

involvement with the World Council, whose members are not, after all, obligated by its positions (p.25).

The differing ways of approaching the world's crises and upheavals built into the two constituencies by their very composition will probably remain a source of friction. Conscious of its priestly vocation, the Vatican avoids visible impacts on ambiguous situations, preferring the traditional method of quiet diplomacy, which is inherently conservative, disturbing as little as possible the status quo to accomplish its immediate reconciling ends. The chief aim is to provide the given order with a greater human quality.

In contrast to this Roman Catholic pastoral style, Derr characterizes the style of the WCC as "prophetic":

> It is not a church with essentially pastoral functions, but a movement of change, willing to make mistakes as the necessary cost of keeping its dynamism. It *exists* to engage in demonstrative acts, to seize opportunities, to make public pronouncements on specific topics, lest by silence it appear to show unconcern. Its condemnations and denunciations are characteristically given to the press. Its tone, like that of its biblical prophetic models, is forceful and often blunt, eschewing the nuanced voice that the Holy See prizes. Its style alone would be an irritant to Rome, even where there was no substantial disagreement on the issue at hand (pp.18f.).

Mutual criticism is therefore inevitable, although it is practised mostly in polite silence and unofficial documents. The "this-worldly" activism of the World Council is played off against "other-worldly" Roman Catholic thought. Catholic critics charge that WCC statements belong more to the political than the moral order. Politics takes precedence over theology. The much-vaunted action-reflection model is insufficiently articulated and practised. It starts with actions of people without trying first to list solid agreements and refine distinctions. Critics of the Roman Catholic tradition object to its high level of abstraction and its focus on general principles rather than the unique features of particular situations. Its reluctance to identify salvation with any liberation within the present world leads it to overemphasize the conviction that the kingdom of God is reached by faith and membership in the church, and to underestimate the need for changing structures through social and political involvement.

These mutual criticisms echo old disputes over the relation of the new creation to history and the extent to which the transcendence of the kingdom relativizes historical accomplishments. The Vatican fears that the World Council is repeating the old error of liberal theology: seeing worldly improvements as a prelude to the coming of the kingdom. The WCC's reservation is that the sacred judgments of the Roman Catholic mind are irrelevant to secular situations.

Such contrasts are often overdrawn. Many Roman Catholics pay far more attention to the humanization of this world than to the destiny of the individual soul. Some bishops' synods have been quite direct about declaring that Christian love implies an absolute demand for justice, and that dedication to the liberation of human beings as they live in their world at present is of paramount importance. Nor is the theology of liberation regnant within the World Council of Churches, where participation in movements for social change is seen as a direct response to the love of Christ, not a precursor of a worldly utopia. Moreover, internal tension between radicals and conservatives is common to both partners in the dialogue and inhibits ecumenical cooperation. Derr's observation remains valid despite more recent insistence on the decisive function of the magisterium and of the pope's role within it:

> The period since Vatican II has been very unsettled, producing a crisis of identity and authority that has complicated ecumenical relations. The changes set in motion by the great council, so widely and deservedly praised, have been ill absorbed in the Church. The status given to national conferences of bishops and the new concept of collegiality have introduced decentralization into a body used to central authority. The new initiatives granted to the laity have limited the scope of clerical authority and reduced the dependence of the faithful on instruction from the top. The impulse the council gave to ecumenism was great, but led some people to go further on their own, even to intercommunion (p.33).

There is also a variety of influences which cause unrest within the World Council of Churches. Unfortunately the Council is sometimes unaware of these inner tensions and thus mutes necessary criticism. Adherents of an inclusive ecclesiology and advocates of a sound social theology, mistrusting each other, go their separate ways. Although no curia exists within the Council, some parallels can be drawn with the influence of the programme staff, who — more than the central committee, still more than the assembly — play a significant role in establishing priorities and deciding how they are carried out and who are brought in as members of commissions and committees. Greater frankness and honesty could help the would-be partners to a more sympathetic understanding of their mutual difficulties and the way to overcome them.

Natural law

According to Edward Duff, in his book *The Social Thought of the World Council of Churches* **(209)**, the "ethic of ends" and the "ethic of inspiration"

> express the deepest differences on the subject of social philosophy in the ecumenical community... The whole viewpoint of the "ethic of ends", or the natural law approach, supposes in men a capacity to apprehend the general pattern of correct personal moral existence and of a just social organization. The whole viewpoint of the "ethic of inspiration", or the new Reformation theology approach, rejects any continuity between man's sin-wrecked powers and the fulfilment of his ultimate responsibilities, between the puny constructions of human endeavour and the transcendent realm of the divine, between rational knowledge of present duty and the proper ordering of society on the one hand and the truths conveyed through the Word of God on the other (pp.100f.).

Since the option for the natural law as the single conceivable basis of social criticism and the preference for an "ethic of inspiration" approach to social questions are both found within the ecumenical movement, Duff concludes that "a manifestation of differing corporate traditions of the understanding of Christian life and faith... makes a synthesis of the social thought of the World Council of Churches impossible and a summary of its positions on social questions and international affairs somewhat inconclusive" (p.320).

On the contrast between "natural moral law" and "situation ethics", José Míguez Bonino makes a similar observation but comes to a quite different conclusion. In an article on "Social Doctrine as a Locus for Ecumenical Encounter" **(198)**, he writes:

The differences between these two approaches seem so great as to make them non-comparable. There is the obvious disparity of relating *a church* and a multilateral body of churches. Doctrinally, the Catholic Church has developed its social doctrine on the basis of "natural law" and increasingly of a theologico-philosophical anthropology, while the ecumenical movement has moved mostly with biblical and Christological models. In terms of style, the Roman Catholic Church has tried to articulate a comprehensive social doctrine while, by the very nature of its composition and mandate, the ecumenical movement has rather faced specific issues. Nevertheless..., there is here a rich and promising possibility of dialogue, common reflection and cooperation. The theological discussion within Catholic social thinking and in the churches represented in the ecumenical movement turns around some of the same foci. As one surveys the development of social doctrine in the Catholic magisterium, it seems that the efforts to relate classical insights of ("natural law") thinking and a biblico-theological framework are more and more evident (pp.396f.).

The long Roman Catholic tradition has been that of natural law — Thomistic, structural and rational. Scriptural injunctions that inspire Christian ethics were not used and integrated in the Catholic teachings. As developed by Thomas Aquinas, the concept of natural law holds that the human being can, by his or her own reason, gain considerable knowledge of the ethically good without reference to God's special revelation. Nevertheless, Aquinas himself, as well as later theologians even more convincingly, insisted that the limitations of imperfect human moral knowledge must be supplemented and perfected by God's special revelation, notably by the gospel of Jesus Christ, and that grace is necessary to observe the prescriptions of even the natural law in its entirety. The virtues of those who perform faith, hope and love can only be a reality of receiving pure grace.

Over the past century, Míguez Bonino notes, the notion of natural law has been sharply criticized from three sides:

Philosophically, positivism and existentialism have rejected the idea of an essential and immutable human nature, or even simply of human nature as such, thus undercutting the possibility of speaking of a universal law rooted in it. Second, the social sciences of anthropology and sociology have corroborated such criticisms by showing that there is nothing that can be called universal in moral precepts, considering the laws and customs of human societies across time and culture. If we would speak of a "universal moral principle", it would have to be so general ("do the good and don't do evil") that it would have no practical significance. Furthermore, modern science has "historicized" even biological human reality. Third, the Protestant theological opposition to the idea of natural law has been forcefully and radically expressed by Barth and other theologians with such strictures as "human self-justification" (Dombois) or "arrogance before God" (Schrey), on the basis that "it overlooks God's revelation in Christ" (Barth), that it is "a total interpenetration of creation and sin" (Helmut Thielicke), or that it has an implicitly deist view of a creation which "God, so to say, would have abandoned" (Regin Prenter, in *Dictionary of the Ecumenical Movement*, Geneva, WCC, 1991, pp.713f.).

Both the temptation of Protestantism to emphasize radical breaks with the past and the temptation of Roman Catholicism and Orthodoxy to emphasize continuity with it have their pitfalls. The ecumenical movement should become more comprehensive. The concept of natural law has certainly been used badly by those most attached to it, but it is hard to do without it in some form. In spite of religious opposition to it, natural law has gained support in secular thought in general and in legal thought in particular. Nevertheless, the meaning of natural law must be re-interpreted again and again. The fundamental elements of Thomism must be translated to suit the demands of the new social problems of our age. The unshakable rock of moral law must be consolidated by appeals to divine revelation and to authoritative teaching of the church. The Roman Catholic Church is moving slowly but steadily in this direction.

The World Council of Churches, on the other hand, needs to examine critically its fondness for moving from the Bible to judgments about the modern world without clarifying the intermediate steps. It is one thing to cite appropriate biblical comments on the serious predicament of society today; quite another to seek suitable texts from the Bible as pegs on which to hang Christian blame and condemnation. Biblical thinking, to be sure, is dynamic. The world is not a more or less well-ordered cosmos, but the field of God's ever new creative activity. The world process and its continuity are due not to the stability of a given order but to God's faithfulness in never forsaking the creation. Yet the natural law makes possible communication with other believers and non-believers on a just society and common norms of conduct.

This last point has often been dealt with inadequately in the ecumenical movement, precisely out of the desire to have a biblical-prophetic voice at its disposal in matters of justice, peace and creation. Saying that these concerns are universal and not just Christian requires the WCC to invite people of other living faiths as participants and not just guests or observers to its international conferences. Despite the ambiguity and complexity of the concept of natural law, it relates not only to issues for a Christian ethics that intends to be relevant to human reality, but also to the common response of all people to the problems of humanization of existence in a multi-religious, multi-cultural and multi-ideological world. While a common search for the healing of the world's ills is the best meeting point for religions in our time, that meeting can also surface what is most problematic about religions themselves. In his article "How Ecumenical Must the Ecumenical Movement Be?" **(198)**, Preman Niles elaborates this crucial issue.

Convergences and prospects for cooperation

The old ecumenical slogan "a united world is too strong for a divided church" is especially relevant in the context of the urgency of rapprochement between the Roman Catholic Church and other Christian churches. At the end of this century it should be clearer than ever before that the whole church needs the whole world, exists within it and with it. There must be a structure of dialogue between the church and the world. The church is not *of* the world and not *over* the world, but *in* the world, where it must minister and serve. Precisely here the traditional ecumenical terminology which spoke of "Church *and* Society" hints at a conceptual problem in social ethics. The church's role is rather one of service within the world. At the same time it is discovering the world, the church must help the world to discover the church, particularly when they are more separated from each other than ever before.

It would be a genuine ecumenical advance if all churches were to acknowledge that Christian social doctrine has borrowed many of its basic truths from "the world" and particularly from the scientific, economic, social and cultural advances of recent decades. Churches should frankly ask themselves, for example, whether their concept of the "image of God" has in fact contributed as much to arousing Christian convictions on freedom, creativity, human dignity, solidarity, justice and love as the words and actions of world leaders, scientists and sociologists.

Every church must rethink its structures in order to deal with such new social realities as secularization, global poverty, unemployment, the environmental crisis and new threats to justice and peace. Otherwise their institutional structures threaten to become irrelevant and their social message unfounded. The language they speak must be continuously renewed through active dialogue with those involved in social change.

In the present situation there are new possibilities of study and dialogue on positions which once seemed to be fixed. Facing the same problems in the world offers the possibility of drawing the churches closer together than they were before in order to deepen theological enquiries and work out a consensus which permits common action. An adequate theology of church in society today demands a complex methodology taking account of natural law, revelation, sociology and experience. Recognizing that the gospel must be proclaimed to the cultures of every time and place also means realizing that cultures change significantly. The generalizations of moral philosophy cannot simply be carried over from past cultures.

Commenting on the broad, complex and potentially divisive methodology and agenda of the WCC's programme on Justice, Peace and the Integrity of Creation, Ronald Preston notes in his essay on "Convergence and Divergence in Social Theology" **(197)** how greatly this process would have benefited from Roman Catholic cooperation at every level. He raises in this connection four important background questions:

> 1. What do we mean today by prophecy as distinct from biblical times? How far can the churches, sociologically considered, be agents of social change?
>
> 2. How far can analyses of the current situation by church-related groups overcome ideological differences?

3. What are the parameters of proper church commitments in areas of social ethics, as distinct from the role of the lay person as citizen?

4. What is the role of symbolic actions by churches and by individual Christians (e.g. covenanting), as distinct from the search for effective and appropriate actions for social change?

Then there is the empirical task of analyzing the facts and the trends, global and regional, and the process of checking and counter-checking in the course of seeing how far an ecumenical consensus emerges for the churches to commend to their constituency and to all persons of good will. This is particularly appropriate if it can be achieved at the middle level between general diagnosis and detailed policies... Nothing short of excellence will do... Roman Catholic cooperation is an almost indispensable factor in achieving it now. The Roman Catholic Church and the World Council of Churches may go it alone, but each will be much impoverished if they do (pp.202f.).

In his essay on "Social Doctrine as a Locus for Ecumenical Encounter" **(198)**, José Miguez Bonino makes four comments on the possibilities of ecumenical common and joint praxis in relation to the social area:

The churches cannot address society as if they were outside it, untouched by its struggles, unspotted by its sins and injustices, exempt from responsibility. The churches can only be *credible* if they recognize their involvement and, in the necessary reforms that they demand for society, endeavour to make the corresponding reforms in themselves. By recognizing their mutual accountability, this need for internal purification can be a part of the ecumenical dialogue and praxis.

The churches' pastoral task in relation to social issues is not only to provide their people with the doctrinal foundation and the pastoral guidance for understanding social questions but to challenge, stimulate, exhort them to commit themselves to an active witness and action...

In their social concern the churches must take responsibility for the implicit meanings and the social consequences of their pronouncements and actions as they are perceived, received and incorporated into the dynamics of a given time and society. It seems to me that this is one of the more difficult questions in relation to the churches'

— single or ecumenical — message and action in the social realm. We are, in fact, accustomed to believe that our word and action are direct and unambiguous; we say what we intend to say and do what we intend to do and everybody should understand it. If they do not, it is their responsibility. In the present state of our knowledge about human communication and social dynamics, nobody can claim that kind of objectivity... Our separation or unity are "social practices" which have meanings and consequences. This remark does not suggest an "easy" ecumenism or an indifference to doctrinal and ethical differences, but it does point to the need to bring back into the ecumenical discussion a concern about the social meaning of our separation which was quite strong — if perhaps somewhat naive — in the early stages of the ecumenical movement...

There are already *feasible* projects in the social area which can be the object of a joint/common ecumenical praxis, even at the global level. I think there is enough ecumenical doctrinal and ethical consensus among most of the Christian churches to say and do things together in relation to issues like torture, the foreign debt of the third world countries, the question of refugees or the growing international system of prostitution — to name some which seem to me very evident. I am well aware that there are historical, social and cultural obstacles... *But unless we begin a common social praxis at the points where it is possible, it is doubtful that we shall make progress in other areas.*

After a century in the modern ecumenical movement we know that practice does not necessarily unite. We know, moreover, that practice cannot be separated from doctrine. But we know also that common doctrine and practice are possible. The area of social doctrine and praxis is one of the dimensions of that possibility (pp.399f.).

Regarding a meaningful future of common reflection and concerted action, Thomas S. Derr strikes a more sedate note in *Barriers to Ecumenism* **(187)**:

It would be wrong to read this work as a catalogue of complaints about human folly in the face of the manifest value of ecumenical cooperation. We confront here tendencies built into the Roman Catholic Church and the World Council of Churches, ways of behaving almost inexorably pushing the would-be partners apart.

Reversal, if it happens, will require more than good intentions. Many more basic changes must first appear; perhaps most important, if one were to guess, a spreading experience of ecumenical cooperation at the local level. Common declarations at the summit are likely to lag behind common action in communities. The more is the pity, for effective unity at the top might inspire and not just follow united Christian social witness on the field (p.79).

Unfortunately, even in nations in the throes of violence, oppression, racism and economic injustice, churches often continue to issue separate statements because of denominational rivalry and divergent political life. It would be a clearer witness to the one God of righteousness and love if all churches were to speak with one voice on the same social issues. This urgency is stressed by Norbert Mette in his recent essay, "Socialism and Capitalism in Papal Social Teaching", in *Rerum Novarum: A Hundred Years of Catholic Social Teaching*, London, SCM Press, 1991 (*Concilium*, 5), pp.33f:

One significant change in papal social teaching has been the way in which — after *Populorum progressio* — it has increasingly taken into account the experiences of individuals and countries who find themselves on what Gustavo Gutiérrez has called the "underside of history" — the impoverished and oppressed, particularly in the southern hemisphere — and has called for their comprehensive liberation. In the new phase of an increasingly heedless "thorough-going capitalization" of all social spheres and forms of interpersonal life, one particular, much-needed contribution of church social teaching would be unswervingly to bring to bear the biblical "preferential option for the poor", allied with practical commitment to the dignity of all human beings and to social justice. All this, however, presupposes that the church and Christians are ready self-critically to concede and remedy their own entanglements in the capitalist system and thus in the "structures of sin".

If doctrinal purity and ecclesiastical rectitude are decisive for remedying entanglements in the capitalist system and making a preferential option for the poor, the churches cannot claim to be a part of the "underside of history". Only a deep solidarity with the threatened and broken world will reveal how narrowly the social teachings of the churches are still defined. The responsibility of the magisterium of the Roman Catholic Church is no exception. The insistence that "the unique church of Christ 'subsists in' the Roman Catholic Church" hardly suggests that other churches are in a position to produce valid social teaching. The basic ecumenical issue around which all social issues should be faced is a maximum effort to be jointly involved in the pastoral task of judgment and reconciliation. That task will show the way out of the impasse of being obliged to assign a full or partial ecclesial status to the respective ecclesiastical bodies. The fullness of the church subsists in its manifestation of Christ's redemption of the entire human race.

As this manuscript was being prepared for publication, an important new book, *Confusions in Christian Social Ethics: Problems for Geneva and Rome* by Ronald Preston, was published. Preston is critical of the activities of the World Council of Churches over the last decade and scarcely less so of much in Roman Catholic social ethics since the Second Vatican Council. He examines at considerable length various ecumenical slogans and theologies which have gained prominence and deals with the difficult question of method in Christian social ethics. His last chapter is a valuable look to the future of ecumenical social thought and practice, noting the present stalemate and summarizing the defects in recent documents, but also outlining a new programme and the possibility of reform by emulating the best wisdom of the past as new ground is broken.

XIV

Tentative Conclusions

The emphasis in the title of this concluding chapter must fall on the adjective "tentative", for the complex nature of the seventy years of international endeavours in ecumenical social ethics, which has been amply demonstrated in the preceding chapters, means any evaluation can be only groping and provisional.

Probably no one would deny that in the realm of social, economic and political policy the ecumenical movement does not have the credibility it once did. Its effectiveness on the international scene is less obvious than might have been expected at a time when religion (including Christianity) is once again playing an important role. One key reason for this is suggested by Gert Rüppell: the churches have generally failed to recognize the need for an "ecumenical learning" process concerned with the broader *oikoumene* and not just with the preoccupations of their own inner coherence — or, if they have seen the need, they have been unable to involve themselves effectively in it (*Einheit ist unteilbar*, pp.358-92).

Of the three streams through which international Christian efforts for unity in this century have flowed — mission and evangelism, faith and order and life and work (church and society) — it is the third which has encountered the most perplexities and contradictions. It has been turned upside-down by the discovery that the slogan "doctrine divides, service unites" of the earlier decades was simply mistaken. Moreover, there have continued to be shifts in dealing with world affairs from reliance on the competent guidance of Christian lay experts to prophetic denunciation of perceived injustice to churchly expressions of sympathy and solidarity in the face of suffering and defeat in so many parts of the world.

This final chapter selects a number of areas on the unfinished agenda of ecumenical social ethics and points to some of the innate tensions and ongoing conflicts between and within the Roman Catholic, Protestant, Orthodox and evangelical components of the ecumenical movement. In the process it will become clearer why ecumenical organizations, especially the World Council of Churches, are not only potentially valuable sources for guiding and enabling the churches but also at the same time fragile entities whose every position or resolution on socio-political matters is subject to reservations, suspicions and disagreements, often leading to new divisions.

Such discord is even more pronounced in the face of tensions within the ecumenical enterprise itself. The tendency to play off the concerns of faith and order, mission and evangelism and church and society against one another is ever-present. The old contrast between an "ontological" and "sacramental" conception of the church and a prophetic and functional conception of it seems insurmountable. It is very difficult, if not impossible, to accept at the same time that the church as a sign of God's kingdom is extended throughout humanity and that in its missionary calling the Christian community is entirely free to see salvation at work in all struggles for justice, human dignity and peace. Only when the world church escapes the temptation to flee into a vast international Christian ghetto will the ecumenical movement be able to relate responsibly to the stories of religions, cultures and peoples.

Criticism of social ecumenism

As the most visible international expression of the ecumenical movement, the World Council of Churches has been the target of constant criticisms from its very beginning. Some of these are based on deliberate or unintended caricatures and judgments made from a distance. Others reflect genuinely different theological, ecclesiological, institutional or political convictions. In any case, the socio-political objections are often the most passionate. Three types of criticisms can be distinguished.

The objection is often made that the WCC has increasingly subordinated concern for church unity to preoccupation with immediate social, political and economic issues. Moreover, especially in the

West, its public statements are denounced as tilting to the "left". Two books which develop this attack at length are *Christianity and the World Order* **(220)**, by E.R. Norman, and *Amsterdam to Nairobi — The World Council and the Third World* **(216)**, by Ernest W. Lefever.

The Norman book is a series of polemical essays which argue that "in identifying with a secular power or agency, the church runs the risk of losing its critical distance and of subverting its prophetic function, its capacity to judge all movements and systems by universal Christian standards". Lefever often quotes from Norman's work. His article, "The WCC: An Uneasy Alliance Between God and Marx?" (*Christianity Today*, September 1979, pp.25-28), from which the following quotations are taken, is a summary of *Amsterdam to Nairobi*.

In Lefever's view, the WCC moved from its early advocacy of a responsible society created by peaceful, democratic and constitutional means to a "qualified approval of violent and revolutionary change in the Third World", support in several cases for "terrorist groups" and "a more radical ideology that by 1975 embraced the concept and practice of 'liberation theology'":

> The ambiguity toward Marxism — a mixture of infatuation and fear — that characterizes the Third World ideology is evident in both secular and Christian circles in the West. This ambiguity stems from a profound confusion between ends and means — the ends of justice, freedom, order and plenty and the appropriate means for achieving these goals, or at least moving toward them. The Marxists have a clear-cut diagnosis and simple answers. They play upon Western feelings of guilt. These feelings are especially strong among upper-middle-class intellectuals and idealists — and it is mainly persons of this sort who founded and still shape the WCC.

Lefever argues that the WCC should encourage the "peaceful and lawful forces that are trying to deal constructively with the problems of poverty, injustice and lack of freedom", making pronouncements like papal encyclicals, "which instruct the faithful in basic moral precepts and relate those precepts to current realities". Although Christian communities are not competent in many complex economic and political issues, "the churches have frequently acted with superficial knowledge and with little understanding of either political theory or the dynamic of social structures... Trendy clergymen and laymen are often engaged in a thinly disguised rivalry with secular revolutionaries for 'relevance'."

A second kind of critique is exemplified well by Paul Ramsey's *Who Speaks for the Church?* **(221)**, an appraisal of the 1966 world conference on Church and Society and a weighty critique of the method of ecumenical social ethics. Ramsey is by no means entirely negative, and indeed describes much of the work of the conference as "astonishingly good". Ronald H. Preston in his essay "A Break-through in Ecumenical Social Ethics?" **(222)**, summarizes Ramsey's objections:

> Instead of *basic* decisions and action-orientated *principles* of ethical and political analysis, the [Geneva] conference continually went on to make particular pronouncements on policy questions based on assertions of "what God is doing in the world", which could be highly disputable, and without making clear the cost implications of the policies advocated. The result was, Ramsey maintains, that ill-thought-out solutions to particular problems which ought to be settled by prudence and worldly wisdom were put forward on an allegedly Christian basis. Christians who disagreed were implicitly put in the wrong and held to have a faulty conscience...
>
> Ramsey has a final criticism which is not well founded. He is altogether opposed to the method of churches sponsoring conferences whose members will not speak *for* them but *to* them, who are officially convened to speak unofficially. Geneva was an outstanding example of this. He says, "One can scarcely imagine a situation that to a greater extent invites irresponsible utterance." In this he is surely mistaken. Official church bodies, largely made up of dignitaries of various kinds and ecclesiastically-minded laymen... are not the best to investigate and reflect initially on the manifold empirical situation. Once other conferences and consultations have done their work, the official bodies can weigh it and speak *for* the churches. That was precisely the relation of Geneva to Uppsala. It is true that less official bodies may be tempted to irresponsibility; the remedy is to guard against it, not to abolish them (p.38).

Yet the central question posed by Ramsey and others cannot be ignored. Must the churches choose between uttering abstract, pious irrelevancies and offering lists of policy-making specifics which go beyond the facts or their competence? Or is there another choice? The history of ecumenical social ethics has shown that Christians and churches must take more radical steps in their involvement in international and national ethics if they are to correct the pretence that they are makers of political policy and get on with their proper task of nourishing, judging and repairing the contemporary moral and political ethos. The difficult question remains: what kind of concrete steps are possible and effective?

A third kind of criticism of ecumenical social thinking, coming from Jacques Ellul and others, is that the World Council of Churches has failed in its prophetic task by not foreseeing, for example, the diabolical effects of the use of atomic energy and bombs and not realizing that no war of liberation has ever led any people to freedom and well-being.

But prophecy is a rare phenomenon in the Judaeo-Christian tradition. Prophets are messengers of God in times of crisis who claim to have received a special revelation from God which offers a radical alternative to existing beliefs, ethical standards or religious, social or political structures. Since these structures are protected by political or ecclesiastical leaders, the prophets who stand in marked opposition to them are immediately accused of being "false prophets", which indicates that prophecy cannot avoid the ambiguities of any partisan involvement in a critical moment of history.

Whether the ecumenical movement as such should be called prophetic is open to debate. Certainly it has the role of reminding the churches of their shortcomings — lack of unity, slackness in mission, resistance to dialogue, insufficiency in sharing and solidarity. But to identify these exhortations with the charism of prophecy is a doubtful affair. Just as none should dare to call himself or herself a prophet without being prepared to carry the terrible burden of such a calling, so no one should designate from outside who or what is or should be prophetic. Prophecy is not a human enterprise of shrewd prediction but a divine practice of deep silence and sacrificial discipleship. In most cases, Christian institutions and movements cannot do more than help, console and strengthen their constituencies.

Violence and nonviolence

The ecumenical movement has recognized that the question of violence is to be taken seriously, not just as a subject of debate for ethicists but as an unresolved existential issue for the majority of the world's population. A major preoccupation of the WCC has been to listen to the voices of the downtrodden and suffering and to balance the vocations of pastoral care, solidarity and ethical guidance. It has continuously searched the wisdom of the Bible, agonized over the example of Jesus Christ and tried to learn lessons from church history and contemporary realities.

A major achievement was the study on *Violence, Nonviolence and the Struggle for Social Justice* **(116)** adopted by the WCC central committee in 1973 and commended to the churches for study, comment and action. This carefully crafted statement offered substantial guidance, and it remains the WCC's most substantial work on the subject. Unfortunately, it has not been consistently appealed to in subsequent instances of violent upheaval around the world. For example, in the controversy surrounding the Programme to Combat Racism and its support for liberation movements, the delicacy and danger of the choice for violent or nonviolent means of struggling against dominion and oppression was too often ignored, and it was taken for granted that support for the goal of justice and liberation would automatically be translated into support for the means chosen. It is to be hoped that the working out of the new WCC Programme to Overcome Violence (1994) — a major impulse for which came precisely from the persistence of violence in South Africa even after the steps towards dismantling apartheid and ensuring free elections with universal suffrage were evidently irreversible — will succeed in building on these solid earlier foundations by taking into account the lessons learned in the past 25 years, the realities of the full range of contemporary situations in which violence erupts and the need for continuous dialogue on these issues with the churches and Christian communities everywhere.

A helpful brief summary of the major contents of the 1973 statement is offered by David Gill **(115)**:

> Without taking a stance itself, the document lists three distinct points of view about methods of resisting oppression. The first understands nonviolent action as the only way consistent with obedience to Jesus Christ. The second sees violent resistance as a Christian duty in extreme circumstances, constrained by criteria similar to those traditionally applied to assessing a just war. "Not only must the cause be

just and all other possibilities exhausted, but also there must be reasonable expectation that violent resistance will attain the ends desired, the methods must be just and there must be a positive understanding of the order which will be established after the violence succeeds." The third point of view recognizes violence as a seemingly unavoidable element in certain situations in which nonviolence simply does not appear to present itself as an option (p.1056).

Gill notes that the document challenges several common misunderstandings. For example, it shows that nonviolent action is highly political, subject to "the compromise and ambiguity which accompany any attempt to embody a love-based ethic in a world of power and counter-power"; nor is it necessarily bloodless. Furthermore, most struggles for freedom and the government responses to them are neither solely violent nor purely nonviolent. With a warning that Christians should be wary of handing out gratuitous advice on behaviour to people far away in difficult situations, the document notes that "those near the top of the world's socio-economic pyramid must be particularly sensitive to the limitation their influence places on their giving moral counsel to others less well placed".

Gill notes finally:

Sharp questions are posed to all parties in the debate: those prepared to use violence, advocates of principled nonviolence, those who by whatever means work to bring down an existing power structure, the defenders of institutions that are under challenge, and Christians in countries where government is relatively responsive to pressures for change. Yet the most important question, says the statement, is raised not by any one of these groups to any other but by all of them together to the whole church, which is challenged to become wiser and more courageous in translating its commitment to Jesus Christ into effective engagement in the struggle for social justice (p.1057).

A consultation held at Corrymeela, Northern Ireland, in 1983 reviewed the 1973 statement. In its report, *Violence, Nonviolence and Civil Conflict* **(117)**, it affirmed the main thrust of the original document but noted major changes in both the international scene and the ecumenical debate. In many parts of the world, according to the Corrymeela report, mild optimism about the struggle for justice and peace had turned into deep pessimism, facing the churches with the question of how to articulate the gospel in a way that is free "from the illusion of facile optimism and the paralysis of faithless pessimism". With both pacifism and the just-war theory appearing to be inadequate positions in the ecumenical debate about revolutionary conflict, militarism and weapons of mass destruction, a broader focus on the variety of ways in which power is exercised and the constructive possibilities inherent in them is needed.

Liberation ecumenism and the critique of science and technology

The perplexing issue of violence and nonviolence is one of the points which manifests the chasm between the so-called developed and developing worlds. In the latter the discovery had to be made that theology must risk being partisan rather than simply critical if it is to mobilize the disenfranchised to secure their freedom and well-being. Out of the experience of suffering and struggle against oppressive powers, and with the eye of the poor, the theology of liberation was born and developed in Latin America. It is ecumenical in its origin, expression and intention, because it remains closely related to the life of various churches and especially to the basic Christian communities.

Although, as we noted earlier, the WCC itself has never explicitly discussed liberation theology, the general concern for liberation has been present in different forms, most explicitly in the theme of the Nairobi assembly: "Jesus Christ Frees and Unites". Liberation theology has also been implicitly present in some WCC programmes. As noted in Chapter XIII, the Vatican Congregation for the Doctrine of the Faith has issued two "instructions" concerning the theology of liberation — one a strong warning that "certain liberation theologies" may become reductionist or ideologized; the second establishing some principles for a right understanding of freedom and liberation.

Facing the spectacular and seemingly unlimited progress of science and technology, a pressing ethical question for many Christians — in the ecumenical movement itself — is whether the rich nations can move from their present over-consumption of limited natural resources to a society which is more just, in which people can take part in decision-making and creation is conserved and enhanced.

Some scientists say that the human race is living in an era of higher risk than at any time since humanity first established its precarious existence in the face of hostile natural forces. Obviously, to cease scientific experimentation is to cease to be human; yet the rash contemporary experimentation is more portentous than that of the past. Technology increases human powers to cope with and make use of nature. But many technological advances, particularly in weapons and economic productivity, have enhanced the power of some people to dominate others. Expertise possessed by a few is used solely for their own advantage.

The unequal distribution of scientific discoveries and technologies accentuates inequality. According to UNESCO, 97 percent of expenditures on research and development occur in the Western world and Japan. Research is directed primarily towards the projects of the rich and the powerful. And international transfer of technologies, even when it purports to help the poor, often chiefly serves the interests of wealthy corporations and mighty governments.

There are great tensions between ecumenism that strives for liberation and justice and ecumenism that seeks to control the use of science and technology. In his essay "From Oxford to Vancouver" **(211)**, Paul Abrecht offers the following criticism of liberation ecumenism:

> Liberation ecumenism has difficulty coping with the challenge of the modern scientific-technological worldview. The liberation socialist view of science and technology is as anachronistic as the capitalist-technocratic approach. The assumption is that a just and liberated society will always know how to use modern science and technology responsibly. But liberation thinking itself has been wedded to the modern scientific-technological worldview of unlimited domination of nature. Within the ecumenical movement liberation theologians have tended to downplay the importance of the questions posed by modern science and technology. Insofar as they have addressed these questions it has been mainly to demand that the industrially developing countries receive a just share of world scientific and technological power. The question of the future of societies dominated by such power has, for understandable reasons, been put aside in situations where social justice appears to be the primary issue. But in the larger ecumenical discussion, the science, technology, faith issue has become steadily more urgent...
>
> The "action-reflection" approach [in liberation ecumenism] becomes a sign of weakness rather than strength. It suggests that an

action commitment precedes reflection; that the reflection (in the form of conceptual and theological understanding) can never determine the action but can only strengthen or defend what is already decided. This forecloses the possibility of openness to the historical discipline of ecumenical scrutiny and creates doubts about whether liberation ecumenism is really ecumenical in spirit. It is prophetic but in the sectarian sense of that word: a movement that is not the united or uniting Christian force that it aspires to be (pp.165f.).

One group welcomes science and technology as products of human creative forces that liberate people from weakness, poverty and drudgery. Another sees them as dehumanizing powers that subject human beings to an impersonal fate and a meaningless existence. A third group evaluates them as neutral forces that can be used for good or evil, depending on the purposes of the users or the social system in which they function. The 1979 conference on Faith, Science and the Future, outlined in Chapter IV, challenged the modern scientific-technological worldview and many previously accepted social goals. But although it highlighted several crucial problems and questioned traditional Christian thinking, it could not solve the problems. The agenda for ethical inquiry into the diverse uses of scientific and technological skills extends far into the future.

Another critical voice is raised by Metropolitan Paulos Gregorios in *The Human Presence: An Orthodox View of Nature* (Geneva, WCC, 1978):

It is not technology and science and theology that need to be reconciled. It is rather these two attitudes — mastery and mystery — which have to be held in tension... Christ gave himself, with humanity and nature, to God in self-denying love, and thereby saved humanity and nature... Technology is the way of humanizing the world of matter in time-space, and thereby of extending the human body to envelop the whole universe. But that humanizing and extension, if it is to be salvific, must find its proper culmination in man's offering of himself and the universe to God in love. A secular technology of mastery of nature for oneself is the "original" sin of refusing our mediatory position between God and the universe, dethroning God and claiming mastery for the sake of indulging our own cupidity, avarice and greed. The mastery of nature must be held within the mystery of worship. Otherwise we lose both mastery and mystery.

The loss to our proper humanity caused by our technological civilization is greater than all the harm it has done through pollution, resource depletion and all the rest (pp.88f.).

The combination of these critical observations makes it clear that liberation theology aiming at human dignity and freedom from want and the project of trying on the basis of Christian faith to correct the excesses of science and technology are two very different concerns. In this global context the ecumenical movement finds itself in a baffling predicament. The demand for social and economic justice in the third world clashes with the claim of superiority of civilization in the first world. The humanistic spirit and scientific, technological and industrial power generated in the West have only one aim: to draw the whole world into itself. And the developing world cannot help accusing the affluent West of the heedless concupiscence of a consumer society. Thus the requirement of justice and equality and the lure of hedonism are irreconcilable. Christianity is squeezed between these extremes.

Whether they admit it or not, the churches in Europe and North America are part of the process of emphasis on the human and its creativity which reveals itself as a dangerous and destructive untruth and creates the technological spiral in which the human is lost. And whether they admit it or not, the mission-founded churches in the rest of the world have great difficulty understanding and coping with other religious and cultural traditions which are marked by a spirit of otherworldliness and a concentration on the Absolute and have tended to turn the human mind away from the material world and from practical and creative social activities.

No wonder that during ecumenical discussions of a Just, Participatory and Sustainable Society the uneasiness was expressed that the third world insists exclusively on the requirement of justice, the second world on the necessity of participation, and the first world on the urgency of sustainability. In this competition the first world remains in a position of advantage. Its passionate attachment to scientific and technological progress gives it good reasons to defend its attractive anthropocentrism, camouflaged by the glorification of an almighty Creator and a generous Redeemer. Justice and participation do not make up for its self-inflicted arrears. What prophetically inspired voice will succeed in denouncing the churches' social conditioning to maintain — consciously or unconsciously — the economic status quo and in suggesting a radical remedy for profound change? It remains to be seen whether the more recent emphasis on "threats to survival" — which is increasingly provoking, also in the Southern hemisphere, an ecological debate dominating justice questions — will be a corrective tool on the ideological level or remain at the level of activism.

Daring and sober-minded involvement

At the Uppsala assembly in 1968, W.A. Visser 't Hooft made his often quoted remark that "church members who deny in fact their responsibility for the needy in any part of the world are just as much guilty of heresy as those who deny this or that article of faith". Later, in his *Memoirs* **(226)**, he wrote:

> If I had known beforehand that this sentence would become so popular, I would have added a complementary phrase such as: "And church members who deny that God has reconciled men to himself in Christ are just as much guilty of heresy as those who refuse to be involved in the struggle for justice and freedom for all men and who do nothing to help their brethren in need." For it seems to me that the health of the ecumenical movement depends on our readiness to stand with equal firmness for these two convictions at the same time (p.363).

Still, the problem remains: with what conviction, with what means and to what extent are Christians and Christian communities involved in curing the ills of humanity? Does the ecumenical movement not overestimate its potential and underestimate its limitations for helping human beings in need? Do churches not sometimes use the world as a stage on which to prove that they have the right ethical convictions and know how to implement them?

David E. Jenkins put the problem bluntly in the *Humanum Studies 1969-1975* **(214)**:

> One of the factors which makes a big contribution to the dehumanizing effects of our present ways of working both within the WCC and within the churches is that although many of our activities are ostensibly responses to and aligned on the world "outside", in fact they are not, or only very indirectly. They are almost entirely

produced by and directed to factors in the *internal* environment of the WCC or of the churches concerned. For example, committees of the institution produce agendas for consultations which produce results for committees which then turn these into agendas for conferences. It is not the world which produces the agenda. It is, in fact, the tremors which the world's agenda sets up within the institution, and which are then transformed into the institution's concern, which produce the actual agendas that are worked on. And these agendas, of course, are mostly sterile as far as the world is concerned for the world has not actually been listened to, only reacted to...

As the world (the external environment) changes more and more and the institutions become less and less appropriate to life within it, the internal tremors do become more and more acute. They may reach a point at which a fresh attempt at real listening becomes not only desirable but essential for survival. This is the point at which repentance and renewal become a real possibility. But it is such a possibility for a limited period only...

It is not the role of the WCC, nor the churches, to be agents in the world of the whole work of God and to contribute to the work of men. Programmes therefore must be planned as limited means of carrying out roles that are enabling, initiating or entrepreneurial. Time and resources must be allowed for gaining awareness of what is being done in the world or the churches at large, and it must never be supposed that a WCC programme can justify the status of a truly representative programme. All programmes are "on behalf of", "in response to" and "in order to promote". They must not be given ontological or permanent status... (pp.61, 109f.).

In *Global Economy* (Geneva, WCC, 1987), Ulrich Duchrow insists that, since "the northern industrial countries... are growing steadily richer at the expense of the majority of the people in the countries supplying the raw materials, who are becoming steadily poorer", the basic economic issue of today should be declared a *status confessionis*. Already in 1977 at its assembly in Dar-es-Salaam, the Lutheran World Federation declared apartheid an issue of *status confessionis*. The term originated in the Formula of Concord (1577) and refers to vital matters which concern the cause of Christ himself and the very being of the church. Duchrow's severe denunciation of the Western economic system as a gigantic conspiracy threatening the continuation of life and human dignity is in turn

sharply criticized by Ronald Preston in "Christian Faith and Capitalism" **(211)**, pp.279-86.

In his account of the meeting of the WCC Commission on Faith
and Order at Louvain in 1971, *And Yet It Moves: Dream and Reality
of the Ecumenical Movement* (Belfast, Christian Journals Ltd, 1979),
Ernst Lange states forcefully:

> The focus of the theological criticism was not the centrality of the
> church for human destiny. What was emphasized far more was the
> eschatological proviso. Pessimism as to the possibilities of human
> development within history deepened. The principal role of the
> church was seen again in terms of eucharistic presence rather than in
> terms of its active intervention in the world. What divides the world
> divides the church, the church especially. Even the church is invaded
> by the *global class struggle* where questions are asked about "jus-
> tice", equality of opportunity, the redistribution of power and re-
> sources...
>
> The class division runs right through the church. So far as the
> "social question" is concerned, every single one of the churches has a
> skeleton — indeed many skeletons — in its cupboard, beginning with
> the failure of Christendom on the slavery question during the first
> Christian millennium. Nor is it merely a matter of Christendom
> having unfortunately been unable to escape completely from social
> influences... The churches have not just been the victims of world
> disorder, they have in many respects been themselves the wellspring
> of the disorder which subsequently destroys their own unity... Stored
> up in the realities of interdependence is a potential for conflict of such
> grotesque dimensions that any large claims for the church simply die
> on our lips (pp.95f.).

In taking up the theological theme of liberation, the world mission
conference in Bangkok in 1973 drew attention to the indissoluble
connection between the individual and social aspects of salvation and
to the necessity of responding to Christ and his missionary call to be
involved in the struggle for social justice, peace and full human life.
The conference section on "Salvation and Social Justice" stated:

> Within the comprehensive notion of salvation, we see the saving
> work in four social dimensions:
>
> (a) Salvation works in the struggle for economic justice against
> the exploitation of people by people.

(b) Salvation works in the struggle for human dignity against political oppression of human beings by their fellow men.

(c) Salvation works in the struggle for solidarity against the alienation of person from person.

(d) Salvation works in the struggle of hope against despair in personal life.

Mission under these conditions should be conceived of particularly in terms of what is required in obedience to Christ the liberator. This means an assessment of the political significance of remaining or withdrawing, and the likely impact of either course of action on issues of human dignity and freedom (*The Bangkok Assembly 1973*, Geneva, WCC, 1973, pp.89, 91).

The tensions and clashes among Christians over socio-political involvement outlined above are clearly grounded in different theological approaches. There is a general agreement that although the final realization of the kingdom is God's gift, human beings are liberated to participate actively in establishing at least a few signs of that kingdom. The incarnation demands that history and politics be taken absolutely seriously; and social justice is so central and so disturbing an issue that neutrality or aloofness is impossible.

But within that general agreement are those who attempt to view the entire history of Christianity and its present predicament and those who attack the churches' heretical maintenance of the status quo. In *The Contradiction of Christianity* **(215)**, David Jenkins articulates the first view:

Unless sinfulness is recognized as something shared in by all human beings, then there is no escape from the dehumanizing limitations of false and premature absolutes proclaimed by limited and partial agents of a partially understood historical process... The way to receiving the realities of God's salvation lies through the facing and accepting of his judgment... It is God who gives the presence, the relationships and the strength for that acceptance of judgment which is required for us to be changed into more human and hopeful ways of living and responding (pp.60,68f.).

The other group, particularly active in the ecumenical movement, accuses WCC member churches of being all too often accomplices in the unjust structures of society, engaging in acts of charity while being attached to the existing political and economic systems. Too often they exhort the world without rigorously examining themselves and their practices. Instead of issuing pious appeals for solidarity and generosity, churches should face the implications of a profound transformation of the structures of their life as well as that of society.

Out of their fundamental convictions this group supports the struggle for a more just international economic order, respect for human rights, efforts to halt the spread of militarism, the combat against racism and sexism around the world. A special concern is "God's preferential option for the poor". This identification is not because of some ontological or ethical quality of goodness which poor and oppressed people possess but because of their actual historical condition as victims of injustice. This understanding of "people" holds great revolutionary potential.

The first group will admit that the prophetic references to the plight of the poor certainly confirm as biblical the insight that discerning and creative judgment upon society as a whole comes from the poor. But even the notion of God's preferential option for the poor can be turned into an ideology which dangerously equates the struggle with and for the poor with the struggle for and of the kingdom of God. The hope for reaching a society without oppressors and oppressed is unrealistic. What the Bible has to say about the poor and God's controversy with his people reveals above all the perturbing ways of God himself in dealing with the human race. Forgiveness is the clearest evidence of God's power of love. It means reconciliation in spite of estrangement, reunion in spite of hostility, acceptance of those who are unacceptable and reception of those who are rejected. The other group will reply that this reasoning leads to pious resignation instead of costly and vulnerable involvement.

Theologians and lay Christians on both sides largely agree that the gap between Christian denunciation and concrete policy-making needs continuously to be bridged. If theological-ethical exhortations are not founded on careful, professionally informed and balanced analysis of political conflicts and social dislocations, they are likely to be illusory. But how can Christian communities be assisted to enlarge their moral horizon and to cope with differences of opinion on political and economic choices within their own ranks?

More fundamentally, what precisely is the function of the church in the modern world? If it declares, for example, that it must work for a just economic order and for liberation from the foreign debt bondage, what practical steps can give meaning to these general propositions? Could its assumption that it is conducting itself as "the church of the poor" in fact reduce its credibility because it does nothing to alter international economic mechanisms? Questions such as these not only relativize the difference in ecumenical economic and social positions; they also render both daring and sober-minded involvement in world affairs necessarily partial and provisional. Even between a faithful elaboration of a theology of judgment and hope and compassionate listening to the cries of anger and suffering in the world, unexpected discrepancies arise, weakening the already limited capacity of the ecumenical movement to give advice on what direction world society should move in.

The involvement of women

"The church must actively promote the redistribution of power, without discrimination of any kind, so that all men, women and young people may participate in the benefits of development" (*The Uppsala Report 1968*, p.50). This statement by the WCC's fourth assembly reflects the key position that the topic of women in church and society has had on the agenda of the WCC and the ecumenical movement from the outset. A report on this subject, based on responses to an extensive international survey of the situation in the churches, was presented to the first assembly in Amsterdam in 1948. In 1954 the Department on the Cooperation of Men and Women in Church, Family and Society was created. Even so, fifteen years later, only 9 percent of the voting delegates at Uppsala were women.

In 1974 the WCC women's desk sponsored a world consultation on "Sexism in the 1970s: Discrimination against Women" in West Berlin (the report was published by the WCC in 1975). A major issue was that women, who form more than half of the world's population, are disadvantaged and oppressed in all countries and suffer particularly in the underdeveloped nations. Women are considered liabilities rather than assets, and they suffer from an inferiority complex. This is not only a direct result of a long cultural and religious heritage; the most immediate and obvious reason is women's overall economic and political inactivity and their consequent dependence on men.

In his address to the Berlin gathering, Philip Potter, then general secretary of the WCC, observed:

> We have discovered in the struggle against racism that only the racially oppressed can really liberate themselves, and in the process they will help towards the liberation of the oppressors. This is what women are realizing all over the world today, especially as progress in realizing their rights has been slower than that of all other efforts at achieving human rights. They must, under God, take their destiny in their own hands... Neither men nor women will become truly human unless the disease of sexism is diagnosed and cured. It will be *one* world of women and men together or no world at all. And we are still a world in a state of becoming (p.33).

Subsequently, the four-year study on "The Community of Women and Men in the Church", co-sponsored by the Women's Desk and Faith and Order, touched many women and men around the world and elicited a good deal of grassroots participation between 1978 and 1981, when it culminated in a major conference in Sheffield, England. The study drew on the powerful critique of patriarchal structures in church and society by feminist theologians who stress the interconnectedness of life and deplore the dualism in much traditional thinking. A letter contained in the report of the Sheffield conference (*The Community of Women and Men in the Church*, ed. Constance F. Parvey, Geneva, WCC, 1983) summarizes some of the areas of learning highlighted by the conference:

— that for many women and men struggles against tyranny, militarism, economic exploitation and racism are the immediate task;
— that Christians in many places need to call on governments to overcome exploitation, particularly where women and men have become victims of wrong patterns of development, through cheap labour, migrant labour or tourist-oriented prostitution;
— that for many women and men there is real pain in the frustration of a church life controlled by male leadership, where, for instance, women feel called to the ministry of word and sacrament and ordination is not open to them, or where the church has not responded to creative developments in society (p.92).

In the aftermath of the United Nations Decade for Women (1975-85) and the recognition that much remained to be done regarding the situation of women also in the churches, the WCC inaugurated an Ecumenical Decade of Churches in Solidarity with Women at Easter 1988. Emphasizing activities at the local level, the Decade has sought to highlight a number of pressing issues that affect women around the world. One of them is the economically rooted suffering of women everywhere, addressed by the WCC's seventh assembly in Canberra in 1991:

> We are concerned about economic injustices to which women are subjected and the feminization of poverty. The major factor that contributes to it is the unjust global economic system exacerbated by the current recession and increasing burden on debtor nations, which places impossible demands on marginalized sections of society — particularly on women. Women's work is often unpaid and systematically undervalued, and they have limited access to the centres of economic and political power. This restricts their choices in work and education. Added to this, they experience sexual harassment and other forms of intimidation in their places of work (*Signs of the Spirit: Official Report, Seventh Assembly*, ed. Michael Kinnamon, Geneva, WCC, 1991, p.89).

Particularly in the years following the Canberra assembly, the discussion of violence against women, including domestic violence, sexual harassment and intimidation took a central place in the advocacy work of the WCC within the member churches. Another focal point during these years has been the need to increase the participation of women in the decision-making and policy-making of churches and ecumenical bodies, and to highlight the particular contributions they bring to the life of the churches, including the special insights of women theologians. In some contexts these goals are inextricably linked with the discussion of the ordination of women to the various ministries of the church. While the WCC itself, including among its members both churches which do and which do not ordain women, does not take an official position on this issue, the discussion has been a growing source of ecumenical tension, especially in relations among the Anglican, Orthodox and Roman Catholic churches. Meanwhile, even in those churches which do ordain women, experience has shown that women's gifts are far from being fully recognized and used and their role in decision-making often remains marginal.

The involvement of youth

Following the Evanston assembly in 1954, the Youth Department within the WCC's Division of Ecumenical Action tried out a new style of work to fulfil its mandate "to keep before the churches their responsibility for the evangelization of young people and their growth in the Christian faith". An overall study theme, "The Integration of Youth in the Life and Mission of the Church", served as a guiding principle of orientation and action. Through many debates and controversies, however, the very concept of integrating youth in the church came under increasing challenge. Integration within existing ecclesiastical structures was seen as an invitation to conform, denying young people the possibility of being at one and the same time relatively distant from and deeply involved in the Christian community so that they might become *critical* participants in it. Two events in 1960 — the Ecumenical Youth Assembly at Lausanne and the World Teaching Conference at Strasbourg — marked the beginning of a new period of rapid and radical change. Youth became increasingly caught in its own agonies, dilemmas and aspirations. Throughout the 1960s young people pressed hard for solutions but underestimated both the weight of tradition and prejudice in the churches and the innumerable complexities of an emerging global society.

Within the WCC the politicization of youth reached its climax at the Uppsala assembly in 1968. The high degree of consciousness and the intensity of engagement were beyond dispute. Young people had developed their own new methods of involvement to hammer home the urgency of common service to the suffering, the exploited and the poor. They saw the gulf between the affluent and the destitute, which cuts across all denominational and confessional boundaries. At another level, however, the youth participants in the assembly were as vulnerable as the adult delegates. In spite of their new and effective style of communication, their recommendations and proposals were no more to the point than the official decisions of the world gathering, reflecting an only imperfect grasp that identification with the victims of racial, economic and ideological oppression involves more than staging demonstrations and shouting slogans. In effect, too few of the youth participants were a visible part of the desperate predicament of the oppressed millions.

One further outcome of the turbulence created by the worldwide youth and student revolutions of the late 1960s, both within and outside the church, was a bitter ideological struggle which devastated the World Student Christian Federation between 1969 and 1973. As a result, the influence of the Student Christian Movement as an active contributor to international ecumenical social thought, which had been substantial for many years, virtually disappeared. The serious long-term consequences of this are summarized in the question: can the ecumenical movement itself be renewed if youth and student ecumenism are not revived?

Subsequent years have been marked by more far-reaching changes and unforeseen developments in the orientation, behaviour and commitment of youth. The new situation was made up of neo-conservatives, a silent and uninvolved majority, a confused and searching sector and a minority of social and political activists. A small percentage of young people have been passionately engaged in ecological movements and protests for the preservation of nature. Similarly, radical anti-war pacifism has increased among youth during the last two decades. European youth have come to be especially aware of the futility of relying on military force for security. But the counter-cultures of many young people have posed an even more fundamental challenge to the Western cultural tradition. Profoundly alienated from the adult church and the adult society, youth went its own way, leaving it to adults to tackle the problems of the world. In response, the older generation has too often fallen back on facile generalizations rather than attempting a careful assessment of what contemporary young people are saying.

The period of the counter-culture has already been superseded by a new period of "counter-counter culture". The majority of youth has become visionless and uninvolved. It prefers to be down-to-earth, sedate, modest, without illusions. It is sceptical of any social and political action, convinced that conflicts and strife in society will continue without leading to tangible results. It can see no cure for the various ugly forms of racism. Socialist and communist ideologies have failed; class struggle is an invention of outdated revolutionaries. But the capitalist system has not performed any better and is also in need of far-reaching change which is unlikely to come. The effects of worldwide unemployment will become increasingly disastrous. The only choice is to retreat into a personal environment which provides limited meaning and satisfaction. Whether youth as a silent and uninvolved majority will continue to live on the fringe of society and outside the confines of the established churches remains an open question.

Yet there are also a few pointers in another direction which should not be ignored. In 1974, a year prior to the WCC's Nairobi assembly, some 40,000 youth assembled for the opening of a Council of Youth in the tiny French village of Taizé, initiating a long-lasting process of consultation and communication which continues to this day. Globally, the population of the world is young, particularly in the countries of the South, where a distinctly new development of "youth movements" can be discerned — a third, and now global form of counter-culture. After a time of uncertainty, the World Council revitalized its youth desk and organized the first global ecumenical youth gathering in nearly 40 years in 1993. Given the observations above, however, the magnitude of its task of drawing the serious attention of the churches to the problems of the vast young majority of humankind should not be underestimated.

Interfaith dialogue

The effect of ecumenical social ethics on contemporary society needs to be clarified in the context of the dialogue among people of living faiths. Some Christian theologians have argued that in view of the need to resist the intolerable evils that infest the planet, all the world's faiths should accept a shared concern for justice as the starting point and guiding norm for their efforts at dialogue. Persons and institutions of different religious traditions should enter into a shared liberating praxis for the poor, the marginalized and the suffering, as well as a shared reflection on how that praxis relates to their religious beliefs. This could provide a workable means of better understanding and judging each other.

Having been engaged in interfaith dialogue as a way of life and not simply as a polite intellectual exercise, M.M. Thomas has argued "that the common humanity and the self-transcendence within it, more especially the common response to the problems of humanization of existence in the modern world, rather than any common religiosity, or common sense of the Divine, is the most fruitful point of entry for a meeting of faiths at spiritual depth in our time" (*Man and the Universe of Faiths*, Madras, Christian Literature Society, 1975, p.vi).

Recognizing the historical relativity of all religious forms and asking whether any religion has promoted the welfare of humanity better than the others, John Hick concludes that

> Each tradition has constituted its own unique mixture of good and evil. Each is a long-lived social reality that has gone through times of flourishing and times of decline; and each is internally highly diverse, some of its aspects promoting human good and others damaging the human family. In face of these complexities it seems impossible to make the global judgment that any one religious tradition has contributed more good or less evil, or a more favourable balance of good and evil, than the others... We may well judge that in some respects, or in some periods or regions, the fruits of one tradition are better than, whereas in other respects or periods or regions inferior to, those of another. But as vast complex realities, the world traditions seem to be more or less on a par with each other. None can be singled out as manifestly superior.

However, he adds, "Christianity has the distinction — and herein lies its genuine historical uniqueness — of being the first of the world religions to have been to a great extent transformed by modernity" (*The Myth of Christian Uniqueness*, Maryknoll NY, Orbis Books, 1987, pp.28,30).

Although the WCC's engagement in dialogue with people of living faiths has on the surface been generally accepted, considerable new difficulties developed with regard to the conciliar process of mutual commitment (covenant) to justice, peace and the integrity of creation. D. Preman Niles, who was in charge of monitoring the JPIC process until the WCC's seventh assembly, testifies to these confusions and reservations in his essay "How Ecumenical Must the Ecumenical Movement Be?" **(198)**:

> While agreeing with the fact that the concerns of JPIC are universal, many churches have difficulty in including "non-Christians" in what essentially is a Christian process. This conflict was evident in the discussions and decisions on JPIC in the Geneva meeting of the WCC central committee in 1987. It first said: "The concerns comprehended in JPIC are by no means limited to the constituency of the WCC or even the Christian world, so that the process will be greatly streng-

thened by the participation of others." Then it turned right around to declare: "The institutions and movements of other faiths would not be part of the conciliar process or the world convocation, except perhaps as observers. However, attempts should be made to engage them in dialogue so that their concerns and perspectives may be reflected in the JPIC process and the world convocation."

How do we include persons of other faiths and secular movements in a Christian process, named a conciliar process, when they do not share our faith even if they do share our commitment to the concerns of justice, peace and the integrity of creation? (p.455).

Here is the perennial ecumenical problem of the relationship between Christianity and other religions, which is not solved by attractive slogans such as "interdependence" or "interfaith cooperation" or the "world community of communities". The introduction of the final report of the Seoul convocation **(40)** states:

We make these affirmations as Christian people aware that many people of living faiths and ideologies share these concerns with us and are guided by their understanding of justice, peace and the integrity of creation. We therefore seek dialogue and cooperation with them, guided by a vision of the new future which is necessary for the survival of our planet (p.11).

But what do these sentences imply? Do they in fact deal with the far-reaching challenge which God's pluralistic world brings to the ecumenical movement? Has the WCC not consistently backed away from the summons to seek a new self-understanding in its relation to other religions?

In this context Hick's observation that only Christianity has been able to adapt to the conditions of advanced technological civilization and to incorporate its blessings and misfortunes merits close scrutiny, for this civilization has been built up by the powers of wealth, property, inventiveness, organizational skill, automation and control of the communications media. As the power of science grows, it more and more resists curtailment. In international relations, political power, organized in nation states, is only marginally affected by international organizations and world opinion.

In view of this accelerated process the ecumenical movement has had to face the issue of power and its effects. Power, it has affirmed, can be good as a vital human response to the Creator. It is also the source of evil in the world, as the desire for domination accompanying will to power knows no limits. As such it is destructive and rebellious against God.

But it has become ever clearer that a profound source of the world's crises is the excessive anthropocentrism in the interpretation given by the Christian tradition to the divine injunction to "subdue the creation" and to "have dominion over" all other creatures. Instead of insisting upon human accountability for the trusteeship of nature, Christianity took over a debased view of nature from classical civilization and concentrated exclusively on a theology of human history. Consequently, modern Christianity has been ill-prepared to meet the challenges of science and technology and to arrive together with them at an ecological awareness of the finite world. Theologies of nature and of the wholeness of God's creation, to be sure, are now rapidly being elaborated, but the question is whether they are not too fragmentary and too late to change the alarming global environmental situation.

In such a setting there are several reasons that the contributions of people of other living faiths become indispensable. As Christianity has obviously had great difficulty pulling itself out of the cultural morass it has co-created with Western secular society, a new confrontation must take place between anthropological theism and cosmological pantheism. Certain other religions can shed light on how Christian theology has indeed withdrawn from the field of cosmology by concentrating too intensively on human history, human existence and the relationship between human beings and God.

Asian religions in particular conceive humanity, nature and God in mutual dependence with all creation. The corollary of their affirmation of the fundamental unity of all existence is the truth of the inter-relatedness of life. Neither the role of nature nor the vision of the totality of life on earth as a living organism should ever be ignored. Only a worldwide environmental ethics can replace ignorance with knowledge, greed with generosity and lack of respect for the earth with an attitude of compassion and loving kindness for all life, including non-human forms of life and the inanimate world. Translated into contemporary language, this religious wisdom implies a concern for responsible stewardship of nature for the benefit of future generations and a less prodigal use of natural resources. Non-renewable goods must be used only if they are indispensable and then only with the greatest care for the sake of conservation.

But in view of a rapidly disintegrating world, the choice between theism or pantheism — philosophically speaking, between voluntarism and determinism — is misleading. Eastern pantheistic spirituality has its own pitfalls. It tends to marginalize humankind and consider it as a negligible factor. When humankind is dethroned, the question of human and personal identity may lead to resignation and to a new and even more disastrous self-containment. Ecological wisdom does not mean a return to nature-worship and magic.

It is especially in interfaith dialogue that the biblical alternative beyond anthropocentrism and cosmocentrism — a theocentric view of God as revealing himself both in creation and in true humankind — can be reaffirmed. There is no substantial difference between creation and salvation. If creation means that there is no owner of the world except the living God, then political, economic and ideological powers can and should be relativized and demythologized. Human creatures are to transcend themselves, to the glory of the Creator, by transcending their immediate interests, needs and understandings of other creatures.

Gert Rüppell (*Einheit ist unteilbar*, p.375) observes that ecumenical openness to the experience of other cultures has been hindered by the dominance of a kind of "church-parochialism" growing out of the universalism of the missionary movement. This can be transcended only through a process of ecumenical learning, in which the churches come to live in pro-existence with the other religions, ideologies and cultures surrounding them. In view of this, the ecumenical study process on gospel and culture, initiated at the world mission conference in Bangkok in 1973, reaffirmed by the WCC's Canberra assembly in 1991 and selected as the major focus for the 1996 world mission conference in Brazil, could potentially pave the way for a major ecumenical breakthrough. For by involving Christians in the discovery of the meaning of their own and other cultures and religions, the process could also have significant consequences for an enrichment of ecumenical social thought through interfaith dialogue.

Past, present and future

The history of the ecumenical movement in this century cannot simply be regarded in terms of a logical sequence from the past through the present to the future, but must be considered an open process in which the future holds in store the unfulfilled promises of the past. The relevance of ecumenical social ethics depends on an intimate knowledge of the successive stages of its development. The conditions of both the world and the church have radically changed, and more dramatic transformations should be anticipated in the years to come.

The 1920s were marked by a social idealism which generated a mood of optimism reflecting the spirit of the period after the first world war. The discovery of an international Christian fellowship transcending denominational and national antagonisms and of the obligation of the churches "to apply the gospel in all realms of industrial, social, political and international life" inspired the Life and Work movement with great hope and confidence. It perceived that the predominant ethos of pious individualism was no answer to the problems of the industrial revolution and world conflicts. Consequently, it sought to construct an ecumenical ethic based on the inspiration of various Christian social movements of the day. These were progressive movements, movements of indignation and protest against social evils, movements of reform and action. Although the Stockholm conference of 1925 endorsed many ideas of the social gospel movement, it was critical of several of the conclusions which the adherents of the social gospel drew from their insights.

During the 1930s the ecumenical movement found itself in an increasingly alarming international situation which was to lead inexorably to the second world war. The industrial countries were plagued by economic depression and social upheaval. Even worse was the rapid rise of totalitarian regimes. Mussolini's Italy, Hitler's Germany and Stalin's Soviet Union typified the form of society and government in which all aspects of personal and social life are subordinated to the absolute authority of a demonic centre of power. An exclusive value was attributed to the state, the national community and the dominant class. The struggle in the ecumenical movement to condemn totalitarianism as a destructive ideology was particularly fierce where groups of Christians and even churches supported their government and tried to justify it theologically.

The Oxford conference of 1937 clearly saw that totalitarianism becomes idolatrous by claiming for state, nation or race the total allegiance owed to God alone. This ideology reduces human beings created in the image of God to mere objects of the social system and prevents them from participating in the building up of a responsible and democratic society. But the maturing Life and Work movement did more than to challenge the elimination of political institutions, laws and traditions and the organized large-scale violence in the nations just mentioned. Experiencing the breakdown of prevailing liberal theology, the delegates at Oxford laid a solid basis for the social and political responsibility of the churches in matters of the state, international relations and the economic order. They succeeded in reaching a consensus in ethical approach and methodology.

Here it is worthwhile to repeat Paul Abrecht's description (cited in Chapter II) in his essay "From Oxford to Vancouver" **(211)**:

> By emphasizing the provisional character of all Christian efforts at social and economic policy-making, the Oxford conference helped avoid the danger of churches making ecclesiastical/theological commitments to contemporary social-ideological fashions. By its emphasis on cooperation with the social sciences and on the contribution of the Christian laity, it helped to prepare the way for a new type of Christian social thinking, avoiding the kind of ecclesiastical pontification and moralizing on social and economic issues which had so often in the past characterized the churches' thought and action (p.150).

Just as the weakness of the Stockholm conference has recurred in the history of the ecumenical movement, so the strength of the Oxford conference has periodically disappeared. Churches and Christian groups have regularly been overconfident about having the right ethical answers to the problems of modern society, thereby disregarding the sobering analytical experiences of the social sciences. Theological experimentalism, extreme contextualism in social ethics and total commitment to particular activist recipes for social justice have fragmented the ecumenical movement and hindered the fruitful dialogue between the so-called "experts" and the so-called "people" and weakened an effective ecumenical witness to the world at large.

An influential and convincing option in ecumenical social thought can be worked out only in and through the mutual challenge of different theological-ethical views.

From its inception the World Council of Churches amplified and applied the teachings of Oxford as it sought to establish the marks of a political and economic order compatible with Christian ethics and to transcend the East-West conflict by speaking pertinent words of peace and justice to both sides. It also faced the challenges of the post-war world such as a new arms race, support of the United Nations, racial conflicts and the problems of newly independent nations. At WCC assemblies, issues of social ethics were part of the agenda along with issues of faith and order and mission and evangelism; and social questions received their full share of attention in the intensive preparatory study for the Amsterdam and Evanston assemblies.

Though the churches of China were absent, the articulate delegates from Africa and Asia provided a constant reminder that hundreds of millions of people on those continents were demanding recognition. In the late 1950s the churches moved from an overemphasis on the concerns of the Western world to an equal concern for the Eastern and Southern parts of the globe, although the ecumenical movement did not really come to grips with the problems of these areas until the decolonization process was well underway. When the urgent need was felt to develop an independent regional ecumenical consciousness, Asian churches led the way, with churches in Africa and Latin America following their example.

Another outstanding feature of the late 1940s and the 1950s was the conviction that a common approach to the Bible would not only bring Christians nearer to each other, but would also enable them to make a common witness to their faith in the social and political realms. The contributions to *Biblical Authority for Today* **(205)** are a prominent example of an attempt to read and interpret Holy Scripture together in order to learn how "the church gets from the Bible to the modern world". In this diligent ecumenical exercise not only was the old liberal-orthodox antithesis considerably modified but a consensus was reached on the Lordship of Christ, whose universal sway over all powers is a central message of the gospel. It is in his name that the crumbling social structures of modern society are to be reconstructed and re-Christianized.

Questions about the authority and interpretation of the Bible have become considerably more complicated in recent decades. Roger Shinn offers the following contemporary wisdom:

> Since the Bible is for all our churches an important norm and testimony, we seek to validate our positions with biblical authority. The temptation is to use scripture as a convenient collection of prooftexts, from which we draw from time to time as a matter of convenience. That procedure often evades the requirements of an honest hermeneutic. There is, in fact, a distance between scriptures and ourselves, no matter how ardently we affirm a "biblical" faith. An example is economic ethics... The Bible may inform our identity, confront us with the grace and judgment of a righteous God and show us that the reign of God is always impinging on our world. All this shapes our economic ethics, sometimes decisively. But we cannot simply take directions literally from the laws of Leviticus and Deuteronomy on harvesting crops... When we appropriate biblical texts, we must not regard them as an answer book for our own perplexities. We must do our own thinking. That means we must acknowledge a wide hermeneutic arc from scripture to our present economic order... The WCC is not likely in the near future to agree on a single hermeneutic pleasing to all its members. What we can do is to acknowledge the hermeneutic issues and refrain from hurling selected biblical texts at those who differ from us (*One World*, no.194, April 1994, p.13).

Two distinctive trends marked the 1960s: the World Council of Churches became more truly universal, for it added many more churches from the third world and from the communist world to its membership; and the ecumenical movement was directly confronted with the global issues of development, revolution, technology and secularism.

The arrival of these Orthodox and third world churches, with their different points of view, meant that the tensions and conflicts of the world now became reflected in the social thinking of the WCC itself. No longer could theological and ethical consensus be based on the primarily Western and predominantly Protestant character of the ecumenical movement. The task was now much more complicated. Increased tensions came along with the increased challenges, and from the Geneva conference in 1966 onwards, a growing alienation could be sensed between the churches of the North and those of the South.

At the same time the theological perspective known as Christian realism was falling into decline. Though there was no clear unifying theological pattern in the 1960s, a new humanism or a theology of secularization came into considerable prominence. The church was asked to take a positive stand towards the world. While the 1930s and 1940s had stressed the dangers of secularism, especially in its totalitarian forms, the 1960s emphasized the positive aspects of secular society. While in the earlier phase the primary concern was for freedom and order, the central notion from the mid-1960s onwards became justice in its economic, social and political dimensions, and the concern for freedom was now expressed in terms of human dignity. A clear transition from study to action, translating consensus into specific commitments, resulted in an accent on the gospel-based bias towards the poor and oppressed and the need for them to participate in the political decision-making process.

Both the world conference on Church and Society in Geneva in 1966 and the WCC's fourth assembly in Uppsala in 1968 recognized that deep changes in world economic and political structures are required if global human justice and economic growth are to be achieved. The Geneva conference focused on how Christian social ethics should relate biblical and theological traditions to the fast-changing conditions of the modern world, the ambiguity of "revolution" and the need for a clearer statement of the theological ideas underlying a positive and critical response to the various demands for revolutionary change. The Uppsala assembly stated forcefully "that if our false security in the old and our fear of revolutionary change tempt us to defend the status quo or to patch it up with half-hearted measures, we may all perish" (*The Uppsala Report 1968*, p.45).

A succinct account of the trends in the 1960s is given by Paul Bock in *In Search of a Responsible World Society* (**206**):

> During this period there were changes in ethical thinking. Contextual or situation ethics received wide support while the ethics of principles, including middle axioms, declined in influence. According to contextual ethics, the Christian community needed to find what God was doing in each historical situation and to respond to his actions. It

would be difficult to find general principles valid for all parts of the world. Thus the proximate theological and ethical consensus of the previous period seemed to dwindle. Polarization was taking place between people of rich nations and people of poor nations, members of black and members of white races, advocates of reform and espousers of revolution, believers in situation ethics and believers in principle ethics, theologians with traditional perspectives and theologians with contemporary ones...

Ecumenical social thought has moved in the past half century from a Western-oriented to a universal movement; from a cooperation without agreement on theological foundations to a cooperation with considerable agreement; then back to cooperation with only limited agreement; from a somewhat humanistic social gospel to an orthodox theological foundation and back in the direction of humanism; from an optimistic view about the world to rather bleak views of secularism and back to more hopeful views of the secular world; from a responsible society to a responsible world society; from nonparticipation of the Roman Catholic Church in the ecumenical movement to dialogue and a close working relationship (pp.50f.).

Evaluating subsequent trends in ecumenical social thought is more difficult because of the closeness of this period and the debates surrounding it. Internally during the 1970s and 1980s, the WCC and its constituency continued the earlier pattern of gathering together to discuss urgent issues and engage in new policy-making. The agenda of successive WCC assemblies became ever more overcrowded; the debates on social, political and economic problems tended to be more general and diffuse and reports more descriptive and open-ended. Annual meetings of the WCC central committee were more concerned with structural, operational and administrative matters than with the reflection on theological and ethical issues that had taken place in earlier years. The forums for such discussions were the working groups and commissions for the various programmes, in which a single clear and persuasive opinion seldom emerged. With fewer and fewer independent, self-confident and visionary leaders, ecumenical discussions ended up in complexity and indecisiveness.

Complicating all this has been the emphasis on "doing theology" or "functional theology" and the "action-reflection" model. As Christians enter the struggle for justice, peace and the integrity of creation they must give a theological account of what they assert and do; in other words, they must determine the inner motivation and precise content of their action. In practice, the reflection tends to stop at the level of a basic theological motif, and idea and deed are only related in a general way. There is in effect a one-way street between praxis and theological reflection; there is little movement in the other direction — theological enrichment and correction of the course of action. The dialectic between theory and praxis — that the theory has something to say about the praxis as well as the praxis about the theory — is not recognized.

As a result, the conflicts between various theological-ethical perspectives and various political-ideological assumptions became more apparent, deepening the divisions over the substance of Christian social ethics. During the 1980s several churches which had supported the action approach began to raise questions about its presuppositions. They argued that the emphasis on identification with the poor and oppressed and the focus on the struggle against classism, racism and sexism were attractive ecumenical slogans and certainly "contextual" in terms of the period when these paradigms were developed. However, it was becoming obvious that this was an oversimplification of the problem of Christian action in society.

The 1979 MIT conference on Faith, Science and the Future and the international public hearing on nuclear weapons and disarmament in Amsterdam in 1981 had a timely and significant impact on these crucial world problems, but their findings and recommendations were soon forgotten and no internationally organized follow-up took place. The 1979 conference convinced the ecumenical movement that all present political and economic systems have made assumptions about technology and industrial planning which need thorough rethinking. The scientific-technological worldview and its accepted social goals were challenged, although the problems it has created remain unsolved. But the conference did help the churches to start questioning their traditional thinking about the effects of science in the secular world.

The 1981 hearing revealed the divisions within the churches on issues of peace and disarmament, illustrated by differing responses to the dilemma of nuclear deterrence. On the one side are those who believe that war may be morally justifiable and even necessary in the name of justice and thus accept deterrence on strict conditions and as a temporary expedient leading to progressive disarmament. On the other side are those churches for whom the traditional doctrine of just war has become totally invalid. The production, development, testing and deployment of nuclear weapons must be condemned as a moral evil in all circumstances. Christians who support the arms race are guilty of sin and disobedience to God and invite God's judgment on humanity. The attitude towards weapons of mass destruction should be determined solely by the Christian faith. It is a question of affirming or denying the gospel itself.

As was observed in Chapter IX, ten years after the Amsterdam hearing the long and frustrating debate on the Gulf War at the Canberra assembly revealed that the 1981 event had fallen into oblivion and that deep divisions over war, violence and peace still haunt the ecumenical movement.

No one can predict the direction in which ecumenical social ethics will move in the years ahead. The largely unexpected collapse of state socialism in the late 1980s and early 1990s is an unmistakable reminder that future developments in the world's affairs remain unpredictable and are in God's hands, not ours. What is clear is that the World Council of Churches and the ecumenical movement are at a crossroads, calling for totally new orientations and formulations. Merely reorganizing the programme structure, as the WCC did in 1992, is not the answer, because the problems go deeper than structure. The social and economic programmes which the WCC inherited from the Uppsala assembly in 1968 have, with some modifications and adaptations, remained virtually the same for twenty-five years and will have to be cast in a new mould in order to meet the new situation of a shaken and desperate world. Their permanency is being questioned in the debate about an ecumenical shift of paradigms. It is necessary to redefine, in the light of today's challenges and the history of almost 80 years, what of the past approaches is worthwhile maintaining and what must be cast away in order to find answers for the challenges of the 21st century. Risky as this task is, it must be undertaken, with the critical support and solidarity of the churches.

In all this it is fortunate that the time is largely past when the WCC was looked upon as a sort of ecumenical oracle of Delphi in the realm of social thought and action. Nor is there any reason to bewail the fact that recent Roman Catholic social pronouncements have carried considerably more weight than the statements of the World Council of Churches or that it is often the firm stands of Pope John Paul II on moral and ethical problems that garner most of the media's attention in this area.

In an essay entitled "Ecumenical Social Ethics for the Future" (*Ecumenical Review*, vol. 37, no. 1, Jan. 1985), Harry de Lange suggests that

> social thinking in the ecumenical movement is problem-oriented. We define and discover the problems the moment when men and women suffer from the injustices of political, technological and economic systems. In our common ecumenical view that biblical faith is not a metaphysical system, but a response to God's initiating action, expressing love and requiring justice in the midst of God's creation, there is a need for a bold new initiative by those who are responsible in the ecumenical movement. There is a need for an interdisciplinary approach to start a worldwide study, supported by regional groups of the same composition, to outline a new ecumenical social ethic (p.114).

This concern is expressed similarly by Roger L. Shinn in "A Venturing Social Ethic" (*ibid.*):

> The starting point of Christian ethics is the response of the historical Christian community to the God whom it recognizes in Christ and whose guidance it seeks in continuing history. The church "seeks" the kingdom of God... It struggles to find the ways of faithfulness in a world of conflict. Hence its ethic is not a deductive system, elaborated from a set of given propositions. It is a venturing ethic, the ethic of a people in pilgrimage — and therein lie its grandest possibilities and its perils. Faithfulness sometimes means constancy in the face of temptations; but faithfulness sometimes means innovation in response to new opportunities.
>
> In the twentieth century — more obviously, it seems to us, than in most of the past — the Christian community must relate itself to two kinds of reality: the social and the technical. The old realities of sin and grace, of divine and demonic promptings in history, of steadfastness in the faith and loyalty to a kingdom yet to come — these work themselves out in the midst of social and technical realities. Each of these realities requires attention in turn (p.135).

At the same time, the question arises more than ever before of the nature and destiny of the church vis-à-vis the world in regard to the eschatological future. More than ever before the WCC and its world-wide constituency are freed from the requirement of being always credible and immediately relevant. The ecumenical articulation of social truth is to be replaced by the courage *not* to be universally valid because the world has become permanently multi-political, multi-cultural and multi-religious. In a world of many cultures and many religions, a community of communities can be built up only by constant interaction and mutual correction.

The real test for the ecumenical movement in the years to come is whether it has the wisdom and the capacity to disentangle itself finally from the snare of the superior Christian civilization and the excessive anthropocentrism inherent in it. In no way does this imply that the ecumenical movement will be in a privileged position successfully to assist the North in remedying its scientific and technological predicament and the South in obtaining liberty, equality and dignity. But it does mean that, squeezed between these two, it has the obligation to stress that once creation is understood as a community of equal dignity and rights for all living things, human beings will see themselves no longer as the centre of history but as trustees of a history which belongs to God's earth.

In the entry on "Power" in the *Dictionary of the Ecumenical Movement* (Geneva, WCC, 1991), Charles West raises some pertinent questions for the evaluation of ecumenical social thought:

> The fundamental question is that of the relation between divine and human power. Can the world be redeemed by replacing the principalities and powers that now dominate it with others representing the people and the poor? Is the justice achieved by human struggle itself subject to the judgment of God and the correction of further struggle for the corruption which is present in its relative goodness? Are there resources in the Christian community to empower believers in their struggle against injustice while at the same time believing in and praying for divine forgiveness and transformation of us all? Will we learn in this light that human power is more ambivalent and more complex than we now imagine? Much work remains to be done in internal ecumenical struggle to clarify the relation of God's power in Christ to our own...

The power of God... is self-limited by covenant with the people of God, implicitly with the whole creation as well. It is an open-ended covenant filled with promise, a covenant redeemed even when human beings in their power struggles seek to destroy it. Under the risen Christ and looking to his coming, it is a promising covenant fulfilled in the service of one another and appreciative use of the creation around us. The exercise of power in this responsibility is an ecumenical art we are only beginning to learn (p.814).

Future ecumenical research may eventually clarify how the biblical call to human beings to subdue the earth and to exercise responsible stewardship and Christ's defeat of the dehumanizing powers illuminate such obdurate ethical problems as the vast political unwillingness to act with determination against world poverty, the alienation of large sectors of the population in industrial countries from effective participation in governing, the legitimacy of people's revolution, the claims of future generations on the earth's resources, the awful hazards of armaments as a method of securing peace. With courageous humility and humble courage, churches and Christians may become agents of God's healing in our ominous time.

Such humility and courage will increasingly challenge the "natural" relationship between the unity of the church and the renewal of human community which is too easily assumed in the ecumenical movement. Both the world and the church are continuously threatened by power struggles, domination and conflicts. That visible unity and the struggle for justice are not as closely related as the WCC sometimes seems to suggest has been unconsciously expressed in the Faith and Order study document *Church and World* (Geneva, WCC, 1990).

On the one hand, the text quotes a statement from the fifth international consultation of united and uniting churches in 1988:

The quest for visible unity is related, and must be seen to be related, to the overcoming of human divisions and the meeting of human needs. This does not mean that the unity of the church is only functional; it is also a direct reflection of God's own unity and unitive love. Relating unity to mission, service and sharing the sufferings of humankind is precisely an expression of the love of God which calls the church into being as the sign, foretaste and instrument of a new humanity in the kingdom of God.

This is followed, almost contradictorily, by the following:

> Thus, justice and unity... belong together. But despite the acknow-
> ledgment of this interconnection, justice (or any understanding of it),
> renewal and unity are, finally, not achieved by human endeavour.
> This ambiguity of the human situation must be recognized by Chris-
> tians as they listen to Scripture and Tradition affirming that only
> God's righteousness, God's justice for all humankind, can be the
> means for salvation and fulfilment; only God's righteousness, com-
> municated in the saving work of Christ, is the adequate vision and
> goal for the human quest (pp.39f.).

The gospel promise of renewal and abundant life for the whole
human community is not assured simply by endowing churches and
Christians with a broader and more holistic vision of the ecumenical
movement. It is not the classical search for church unity brought into
creative dialogue with the calling to mission, witness and service, but
rather the liberating recognition in Christ of the ambiguity of human
power, the complexity of power struggles and the contradiction of
corruptive power which intimately relates the church to the world and
leaves the ultimate victory over evil and injustice to the Lord of the
universe.

Ecumenical ecclesiology and ecumenical social ethics

Among the intricate ecumenical problems raised by Konrad Raiser
in his book *Ecumenism in Transition* is that of the relationship
between the ecclesiological significance of the World Council of
Churches and its engagement in a "conciliar process" of working for
justice, peace and the integrity of creation. Raiser notes that "all
traditional ecclesiologies are marked by their history of separation and
isolation. Thus traditional ecclesiological criteria are inadequate to
describe the WCC, which is a structure without precedent in the
history of the church" (pp.115f.).

But not only are old ecclesiologies searching for an effective
protection against the strong influences of the world, even the WCC
constantly faces the risk of isolation and separation from humanity.
For more than twenty years, the WCC Faith and Order study on "The
Unity of the Church and the Renewal of Human Community" (a
significant change of title from the original "The Unity of the Church

and the Unity of Humankind") has not got off the ground because of a failure to come to terms with its inherently interdisciplinary nature. Had the study been shared in a truly interdisciplinary approach to the theme, even if only within the WCC, the outcome might have been a completely different story. Instead, the solid and reassuring unity of the church has been played off against the ambivalent and improbable renewal of humanity; and the power of the churches — including the power of their fascination with the convergence document on *Baptism, Eucharist and Ministry* — prevents an inversion of the theme to "The Renewal of the Church and the Unity of the Human Community".

Whether one emphasizes the being or the doing of the Christian community in an ecumenical perspective, the temptation is ever-present of exchanging the powerlessness of the gospel for ecclesiastical power on the one hand and superior ethical behaviour on the other. But it is only together that "Faith and Order" and "Church and Society" will be able to shed new light from the gospel on the ambiguity of ethical questions and the limits of the ecclesiological significance of the church.

In February 1993, a consultation on "Koinonia and Justice, Peace and Creation" was held in Denmark under the sponsorship of the WCC programme units on Unity and Renewal, which includes Faith and Order, and Justice, Peace and Creation, which brings together many of the concerns once subsumed under Church and Society. The aim was to help bridge the considerable gap between these two ecumenical concerns. The consultation report (*Costly Unity*, eds Thomas F. Best and Wesley Granberg-Michaelson, Geneva, WCC, 1993) raises two central theological concerns: the church as moral community (ethics and ethical commitment are not just consequences of the life of the church, but essential elements of that life) and the assertion that the specific unity arising out of common social-ethical commitment and engagement has significance for the unity of the church. Yet large parts of the Christian tradition deny that anything other than the preaching of the word and the celebration of the sacraments can create the church, which is constituted by Christ in his Spirit. But the question remains whether the faithful response to this coming of Christ in the Spirit necessarily involves a commitment to discipleship. To say that moral unity cannot be generative of the church in the strict sense is to deny its importance.

Costly Unity has shown that the typical concerns of JPIC need to be thought through in the context of the concerns of Faith and Order and vice versa. Deep disagreements are still present and will remain, although these disagreements are not easy to articulate. It is important to find ways of promoting the sort of principled debate which can make this gap fruitful rather than trying to bridge it completely at once. In that attempt it is vital for both sides to continue to emphasize that it is solely the power of the powerless Jesus Christ which heals — both the disastrous divisions of the church and the passionately different approaches of Christians to the horrendous conflicts of the world. The more Christians rely on his mercy and forgiveness, the more they become authentic members of the ecumenical movement, which never subordinates the secular part of humanity to the Christian part.

Bibliography of Basic Literature 1910-1991

A complete bibliography can be found in *Classified Catalogue of the Ecumenical Movement*, 2 vols, Boston, G.K. Hall, 1972, 1st supplement, 1981. Also the two official histories of the ecumenical movement carry extensive bibliographies. For the period 1910-48 consult chapters 11 and 12 in *A History of the Ecumenical Movement 1517-1948*, eds Ruth Rouse & Stephen Charles Neill (London, SPCK, 1954. 4th ed. WCC, 1993). *The Ecumenical Advance: A History of the Ecumenical Movement 1948-68*, ed. Harold E. Fey (London, SPCK, 1970. 3rd ed. WCC, 1993) contains a comprehensive original bibliography and an updated systematic bibliography on WCC assemblies and the publications of all WCC sub-units in the area of ecumenical social ethics. Another important source of information is the reports of the WCC central committee to the successive assemblies: *From Evanston to New Delhi (1961)*, *From New Delhi to Uppsala (1968)*, *From Uppsala to Nairobi (1975)*, *From Nairobi to Vancouver (1983)*, and *From Vancouver to Canberra (1991)*.

OFFICIAL DOCUMENTS 1910-48

[1] *COPEC Commission Reports* (Conference on Christian Politics, Economics and Citizenship, Birmingham, April 5-12, 1924), 12 vols. London, Longmans, Green, 1924-25.

[2] *The Stockholm Conference 1925. The Report of the Universal Christian Council of Life and Work, Held at Stockholm, 10-30 August 1924*, ed. G.K.A. Bell. London, Oxford UP, 1925.

[3] *The Churches Survey Their Task*. The Report of the Conference at Oxford, July 1937, on Church, Community and State. London, Allen & Unwin, 1937.

[4] *The Churches in Action*. Newsletter of the Universal Christian Council for Life and Work and the World Alliance for Promoting International Friendship through the Churches. Quarterly. Geneva, 1931-38 (also in French and German).

[5] *Goodwill*. A Review of Interactional Christian Friendship. Quarterly. London, 1915-38.

[6] Life and Work: *Bulletin of the International Social Institute*. Occasional. Geneva, 1927-30.

[7] World Alliance for Promoting International Friendship through the Churches: *Minutes and Reports*, 1914-46.

[8] World Alliance for Promoting International Friendship through the Churches: *Handbooks*, 1916-46.

GENERAL WORKS 1910-48

[9] Brown, William Adams: *Church and State in Contemporary America*. New York, Scribner, 1936.

[10] *The Church through Half a Century: Essays in Honour of William Adams Brown*, eds Samuel McCrea Cavert & Henry Pitney Van Dusen. New York, Scribner, 1936.

[11] Ehrenström, Nils: "Movements for International Friendship and Life and Work" (1925-48). In: *A History of the Ecumenical Movement 1517-1948*, eds Ruth Rouse & Stephen Charles Neill. Geneva, WCC, 1986. 4th ed., pp.545-98.

[12] Horton, Walter Marshall: *Toward a Reborn Church: A Review and Forecast of the Ecumenical Movement*. New York, Harper, 1949.

[13] Hudson, Darril: *The Ecumenical Movement in World Affairs*. London, Weidenfeld & Nicolson, 1969.

[14] Karlström, Nils: "Movements for International Friendship and Life and Work (1910-25)". In: *A History of the Ecumenical Movement 1517-1948*, eds Ruth Rouse & Stephen Charles Neill. Geneva, WCC, 1986. 4th ed., pp.509-38.

[15] Keller, Adolf: *Church and State on the European Continent*. London, Epworth, 1936.

[16] Lee, Robert: *The Social Sources of Church Unity. An Interpretation of Unitive Movements in American Protestantism*. New York, Abingdon, 1960.

[17] Macfarland, Charles S.: *International Christian Movements*. New York, F.H. Revell, 1924.

[18] Macfarland, Charles, S.: *Steps toward the World Council: Origins of the Ecumenical Movement as Expressed in the Universal Christian Council For Life and Work*. New York, F.H. Revell, 1938.

[19] Temple, William: *Christianity and Social Order*. Harmondsworth, UK, Penguin Books, 1943.

[20] Visser 't Hooft, W.A.: *The Background of the Social Gospel in America*. Haarlem, T. Willink, 1928. Reprinted by Bethany Press, St Louis, 1962.

[21] Visser 't Hooft, W.A. & Oldham, Joseph H.: *The Church and Its Function in Society*. Chicago, Willett, Clark & Co., 1937.

WCC 1948-91

Sub-unit (department) on Church and Society

[22] Abrecht, Paul: "The Development of Ecumenical Social Thought and Action". In: *The Ecumenical Advance: A History of the Ecumenical Movement 1948-68*, ed. Harold E. Fey. Geneva, WCC, 1970, pp.233-60.

[23] "Church and Society: Ecumenical Perspectives. Essays in Honour of Paul Abrecht". In: *The Ecumenical Review*, vol. 37, no. 1, January 1985.

[24] "Fifty Years of Ecumenical Social Thought". In: *The Ecumenical Review*, vol. 40, no. 2, April 1988.

[25] *Statements of the WCC on Social Questions*. Geneva, WCC, 1956. 2nd ed.

[26] Turnbull, John W.: *Ecumenical Documents on Church and Society, 1925-53*. Geneva, WCC, 1954.

[27] *Background Information for Church and Society*, nos 1-39, 1951-69.

[28] *Anticipation*, nos 1-30, 1969-83.

[29] *Church and Society News Letter*, no. 1, 1984-

Responsible Society

[30] *The Arnoldshain Report 1956: A Regional Conference on the Responsible Society in National and International Affairs*. Geneva, WCC Division of Studies, 1956.

[31] "The Church and the Disorder of Society". Report of Section III. In: *The First Assembly of the WCC Held at Amsterdam August 22 to September 4, 1948*, ed. W.A. Visser 't Hooft. New York, Harper, 1949, pp.74-82.

[32] Muelder, Walter G.: *Foundations of the Responsible Society*. Nashville, TN, Abingdon, 1959.

[33] *The Responsible Society*. Geneva, WCC Study Department, 1949 (Christian Action in Society, 1).

[34] *Social Questions: The Responsible Society in World Perspective*: An Ecumenical Survey Prepared Under the Auspices of the WCC. London, SCM, 1954 (Evanston Surveys, 3).

Just, Participatory and Sustainable Society

[35] "Economics of a Just, Participatory and Sustainable Society". In: *Faith and Science in an Unjust World. Report of the WCC's Conference on Faith, Science and the Future at Cambridge, USA, 12-24 July 1979*. Vol. 2: Reports and Recommendations, ed. Paul Abrecht. Geneva, WCC, 1980, pp.125-134.

[36] *Energy for My Neighbour*: An Action Programme of the WCC. Geneva, 1978.

[37] "A Long-Term Concept of a Sustainable and Just Society". In: *Anticipation*, November 1974, no. 19.

[38] Paulos Mar Gregorios: *The Human Presence: An Orthodox View of Nature*. Geneva, WCC, 1978.

[39] "The Search for a Just, Participatory and Sustainable Society". In: *Central Committee, Minutes and Reports of the Thirty-First Meeting*, Kingston, Jamaica, 1-11 January, 1979, pp.16-18.

Justice, Peace and the Integrity of Creation

[40] *The Final Document on Justice, Peace and the Integrity of Creation, Seoul, Republic of Korea, 5-12 March 1990*. Geneva, WCC, 1990.

[41] *Integrity of Creation: An Ecumenical Discussion, Granvollen, Norway, February 25-March 3, 1988*. Geneva, WCC, 1988.

[42] "Justice, Peace and the Integrity of Creation". In: *The Ecumenical Review*, vol. 38, no. 3, July 1986, pp.251-341.

[43] Niles, Preman: *Resisting the Threats to Life: Covenanting for Justice, Peace and the Integrity of Creation*. Geneva, WCC, 1989.

[44] Report of the Committee on Unit II: "Justice, Peace and the Integrity of Creation (JPIC)". In: *Central Committee, Minutes and Reports of the Thirty-Eighth Meeting*, Geneva, 16-24 January, 1987, pp.50-57.

Rapid Social Change

[45] Abrecht, Paul: *The Churches and Rapid Social Change*. New York, Doubleday, 1961.

[46] *The Common Christian Responsibility toward Areas of Rapid Social Change*. Second statement. Geneva, WCC, 1956.

[47] *Dilemmas and Opportunities: Christian Action in Rapid Social Change*. Report of an International Ecumenical Study Conference, Thessalonica, Greece, July 25-August 2, 1959. Geneva, WCC, 1959.

[48] Vries, Egbert de: *Man in Rapid Social Change*. Garden City, NY, Doubleday, 1961.

World Conference on Church and Society, Geneva 1966

[49] *Christian Social Ethics in a Changing World: An Ecumenical Theological Inquiry*, ed. John C. Bennett. London, SCM; New York, Association Press, 1966 (Church and Society, 1). Also in French and German.

[50] *Responsible Government in a Revolutionary Age*, ed. Z.K. Matthews. London, SCM, 1966 (Church and Society, 2). Also in French and German.

[51] *Economic Growth in World Perspective*, ed. Denys Munby. London, SCM, 1966 (Church and Society, 3). Also in French and German.

[52] *Man in Community: Christian Concern for the Human in Changing Society*, ed. Egbert de Vries, 1966 (Church and Society, 4). Also in French and German.

[53] World Conference on Church and Society, Geneva, July 12-26, 1966: *Christians in the Technical and Social Revolutions of Our Time*. The Official Report. Geneva, WCC, 1967. Also in French and German.

[54] Ramsey, Paul: *Who Speaks for the Church? A Critique of the 1966 Conference on Church and Society*. Nashville, TN, Abingdon, 1967.

[55] Rendtorff, Trutz & Tödt, Heinz E.: *Theologie der Revolution: Analysen und Materialen*. Frankfurt am Main, Suhrkamp, 1968.

Faith, Science and Technology

[56] *Experiments with Man*. Report of an Ecumenical Consultation, ed. Hans-Ruedi Weber. Geneva, WCC, 1969 (WCC Studies, no. 6).

[57] *From Here to Where? Technology, Faith and the Future*. Report of an Exploratory Conference, Geneva, 28 June-4 July, 1970, ed. David Gill. Geneva, WCC, 1970.

[58] *Church and Society*: Three Reports of the Working Committee on Church and Society in Nemi, Italy, 20-26 June 1971. Geneva, WCC, 1971.

[59] "Report of an Ecumenical Consultation on Global Environment, Economic Growth and Social Justice", Cardiff, England, 3-8 September 1972. In: *Anticipation*, no. 13.

[60] "Science and Technology for Human Development: The Ambiguous Future and the Christian Hope". Selected Preparatory Papers for the 1974 World Conference in Bucharest, Romania. In: *Anticipation*, no. 17.

[61] "Science and Technology for Human Development: The Ambiguous Future and the Christian Hope". Report of the 1974 World Conference in Bucharest, Romania. In: *Anticipation*, no. 19.

[62] *Genetics and the Quality of Life*, eds Charles Birch & Paul Abrecht. Emsford, NY, Pergamon, 1975.

[63] *Science and Our Future*, ed. Paulos Gregorios. Madras, Christian Literature Society, 1978.

[64] *Faith, Science and the Future*. Preparatory Readings for a World Conference, Cambridge, Mass., 12-24 July, 1979, eds Paul Abrecht, Charles Birch & John Francis. Geneva, WCC, 1978.

[65] *Faith and Science in an Unjust World*. Report of the WCC Conference on Faith, Science and the Future, Cambridge, MA, 12-24 July, 1979. Vol. 1: Plenary Presentations. Ed. Roger L. Shinn. Geneva, WCC, 1980.

[66] *Faith and Science in an Unjust World*. Report of the WCC Conference on Faith, Science and the Future, Cambridge, MA, 12-24 July, 1979. Vol. 2: Reports and Recommendations, ed. Paul Abrecht. Geneva, WCC, 1980.

[67] *Manipulating Life: Ethical Issues in Genetic Engineering*. Geneva, WCC, 1982.

[68] *Science Education and Ethical Values: Introducing Ethics and Religion into the Science Classroom and Laboratory*, eds Bert Musschinga & David Gosling. Geneva, WCC, 1985.

International Affairs

[69] Barnes, Roswell P.: *Under Orders: The Churches and Public Affairs*. New York, Doubleday, 1961.

[70] Bennett, John C.: *Foreign Policy in Christian Perspective*. New York, Scribner, 1966.

[71] Bent, Ans J. van der: *Christian Response in a World of Crisis: A Brief History of the WCC's Commission of the Churches on International Affairs*. Geneva, WCC, 1986.

[72] *Christians in the Struggle for World Community*: Report of the Section on International Affairs Received by the Second Assembly of the WCC, Evanston, 1954. New York, WCC, 1954.

[73] Derr, Thomas Sieger: *The Political Thought of the Ecumenical Movement 1900-39*. Ann Arbor, MI, University Microfilms, 1972.

[74] Hamelink, Cees: "Towards a New International Information Order". In: *CCIA Background Information*, 1978, no. 7.

[75] Hudson, Darril: *The WCC in International Affairs*. Leighton Buzzard, UK, Faith Press, 1977.

[76] *International Affairs: Christians in the Struggle for World Community*. An Ecumenical Survey Prepared under the Auspices of the WCC. London, SCM, 1954 (Evanston Surveys, 4).

[77] Kramer, Leonard J.: *Man amid Change in World Affairs*. New York, Friendship, 1964.

[78] Nolde, O. Frederick: *The Churches and the Nations*. Philadelphia, Fortress, 1970.

[79] Thomas, M.M. & McCaughey, J.D.: *The Christian in the World Struggle*. Geneva, WSCF, 1951.

[80] *Toward World-Wide Christianity*, ed. O. Frederick Nolde. New York, Harper, 1946.

[81] *Churches in International Affairs*. Reports, 1970-.

[82] *CCIA Brief*, nos 1-19, 1959-69.

[83] *CCIA Background Information*, 1975-.

[84] *CCIA Newsletter*, 1975-.

Church and State

[85] Bennett, John C.: *Christians and the State*. New York, Scribner, 1958.

[86] *Church and State: Opening a New Ecumenical Discussion*. Colloquium held at the Ecumenical Institute Bossey, 19-25 August, 1975. Geneva, WCC, 1978 (Faith and Order Paper no. 85).

[87] *Church-State Relations in Ecumenical Perspective*, ed. Elwyn Smith. Pittsburgh, PA, Duquesne UP, 1966.

[88] Dickinson, Richard D.N.: *A Comparison of Concepts of the State in Roman Catholicism and the Ecumenical Movement*. Ann Arbor, MI, University Microfilms, 1959.

[89] Ehrenström, Nils: *Christian Faith and the Modern State: An Ecumenical Approach*. London, SCM, 1937.

[90] "Political Theology: A Documentary and Bibliographical Survey". In: *WCC Exchange*, no. 4, October 1979.

[91] *The Report of the Conference at Oxford, July 1937, on Church, Community and State*. London, George Allen & Unwin, 1937.

[92] Sanders, Thomas G.: *Protestant Concepts of Church and State: Historical Background and Approaches for the Future*. New York, Doubleday, 1964.

[93] Wolf, Donald J.: *Toward Consensus: Catholic-Protestant Interpretations of Church and State*. New York, Doubleday, 1968.

Human Rights and Religious Liberty

[94] Bent, Ans J. van der: "Human rights". In: *Vital Ecumenical Concerns: Sixteen Documentary Surveys*. Geneva, WCC, 1986, pp.243-60.

[95] Carrillo de Albornoz, Angel Francisco: *Religious Liberty*. New York, Sheed & Ward, 1967.

[96] Fonseca, Glenda Da: *How to File Complaints of Human Rights Violations: A Practical Guide to Intergovernmental Procedures*. Geneva, WCC, 1975.

[97] *Human Rights: A Challenge to Theology*, ed. Marc Reuver on behalf of IDOC International and the Commission of the Churches on International Affairs. Rome, IDOC International, 1983.

[98] *Human Rights and Christian Responsibility*. Report of the Consultation in St Pölten, Austria, 21-26 October, 1974. Geneva, WCC, 1974.

[99] *La liberté religieuse: Exigence spirituelle et problème politique*, E. Schillebeeckx, A.F. Carillo de Albornoz, etc. En annexe: Documents du Conseil oecuménique des Eglises. Paris, Centurion, 1965.

[100] "Militarism and Human Rights". Reports and Papers of a Workshop at Glion, Switzerland, 10-14 November 1982. In: *CCIA Background Information*, 1982, no. 3.

[101] Nolde, O. Frederick: *Free and Equal: Human Rights in Ecumenical Perspective*. Geneva, WCC, 1968.

[102] *Religious Freedom: Main Statements by the World Council of Churches 1948-75*. Geneva, 1976.

[103] *Religious Liberty: An End and a Beginning. The Declaration on Religious Freedom: An Ecumenical Discussion*, ed. John Courtney Murray. New York, Macmillan, 1966.

[104] *Religious Liberty in the Crossfire of Creeds*, ed. Franklin H. Littell. Philadelphia, Ecumenical Press, 1978.

[105] Weingärtner, Erich: "Human Rights on the Ecumenical Agenda: Report and Assessment". In: *CCIA Background Information*, 1983, no. 3.

[106] Zalaquett, José: "The Human Rights Issue and the Human Rights Movement: Characterization, Evaluation, Propositions". In: *CCIA Background Information*, 1981, no. 3.

Ideology and Ideologies

[107] Bent, Ans J. van der: *Christians and Communists: An Ecumenical Perspective*. Geneva, WCC, 1980.

[108] Bent, Ans J. van der: "Ideology and Ideologies". In: *Vital Ecumenical Concerns: Sixteen Documentary Surveys*. Geneva, WCC, 1986, pp.162-74.

[109] *Churches among Ideologies*. Report of a Consultation and Recommendations to Fellow Christians, 15-22 December 1981, Grand Saconnex, Switzerland. Geneva, WCC, 1982.

[110] *Faith and Ideologies: An Ecumenical Discussion*. Consultation at Cartigny, Geneva, 19-24 May, 1975, Organized by Faith and Order and Church and Society. Geneva, 1975.

[111] *Faith in the Midst of Faiths: Reflections on Dialogue in Community*, ed. Stanley J. Samartha. Geneva, WCC, 1977, pp.166-69 and 103-107.

[112] "Three Reports from Church and Society". Prepared by the Working Committee on Church and Society at Nemi, Italy, June 17-26, 1971. In: *Study Encounter*, vol. VII, no. 3, 1971, pp.15-20.

[113] *The First Assembly of the WCC Held at Amsterdam*, August 22 to September 4, 1948, ed. W.A. Visser 't Hooft. London, SCM, 1949, pp.77-82.

[114] *From Here to Where? Technology, Faith and the Future of Man*, ed. David M. Gill. Geneva, WCC, 1970, pp. 67-80.

Violence and Nonviolence

[115] Gill, David: "Violence and Nonviolence". In: *Dictionary of the Ecumenical Movement*. Geneva, WCC, 1991, pp.1055-58.

[116] *Violence, Nonviolence and the Struggle for Social Justice*. Geneva, WCC, 1973.

[117] *Violence, Nonviolence and Civil Conflict*. Geneva, WCC, 1983.

Peace and Disarmament

[118] *Before It's Too Late: The Challenge of Nuclear Disarmament*. The Complete Record of the Public Hearing on Nuclear Weapons and Disarmament, Amsterdam, 1981, eds Paul Abrecht & Ninan Koshy. Geneva, WCC, 1983.

[119] Bent, Ans J. van der: "Peace and Justice in the Ecumenical Movement". In: *Vital Ecumenical Concerns: Sixteen Documentary Surveys*. Geneva, WCC, 1986, pp.116-46.

[120] Booth, Alan R.: *Not Only Peace: Christian Realism and the Conflicts of the Twentieth Century*. London, SCM, 1967.

[121] *Christians and the Prevention of War in an Atomic Age: A Theological Discussion*, eds Thomas M. Taylor & Robert S. Bilheimer. London, SCM, 1961.

[122] "The Churches and the Nuclear Debate". 1977. In: *Anticipation*, no. 24.

[123] *Churches as Peacemakers? An Analysis of Recent Church Statements on Peace, Disarmament and War*. By Friedhelm Solms & Marc Reuver. Rome, IDOC, 1985.

[124] "Facing up to Nuclear Power, 1975". In: *Anticipation*, no. 20.

[125] *Facing up to Nuclear Power: A Contribution to the Debate on the Risks and Potentialities of the Large Use of Nuclear Energy*, eds John Francis & Paul Abrecht. Edinburgh, Saint Andrew, 1976.

[126] Hormann, Karl: *Peace and Modern War in the Judgment of the Church*. Westminster, MD, Newman, 1966.

[127] Macfarland, Charles S.: *Pioneers for Peace through Religion, Based on the Records of the Church Peace Union, 1914-45*. New York, Revell, 1946.

[128] *Pattern for Peace: Catholic Statements on International Order*, ed. Harry W. Flannery. Westminster, MD, Newman, 1962.

[129] *Peace and Disarmament*. Documents of the WCC presented by the Commission of the Churches on International Affairs, and of the Roman Catholic Church presented by the Pontifical Commission Iustitia et Pax. Geneva, WCC, 1982.

[130] "Peace in the Atomic Age". In: *Student World*, Special Number, 4, 1960, pp.405-503.

[131] Regehr, Ernie: *Militarism and the World Military Order: A Study Guide for Churches*. Geneva, WCC, 1980.

[132] "Report on the Conference on Disarmament, Glion, Switzerland, 9-15 April, 1978". In: *CCIA Background Information*, no. 4, 1978.

[133] "Report on the Consultation on Militarism, Glion, Switzerland, 13-18 November, 1977". In: *CCIA Background Information*, no. 2 , 1977.

[134] *The Security Trap: Arms Race, Militarism and Disarmament — A Concern for Christians*, ed. José-Antonio Viera Gallo. Rome, IDOC, 1979, 291p. Revised ed. 1982.

[135] *WCC Statements on Nuclear Weapons and Disarmament, 1948-81.* Prepared for the Public Hearing at Amsterdam, 23-27 November 1981. Geneva, WCC, 1981.

All WCC assemblies deal with issues of peace and disarmament. Consult also various publications of the Christian Peace Conference, Prague.

Development

[136] Bent, Ans J. van der: "Development". In: *Vital Ecumenical Concerns: Sixteen Documentary Surveys.* Geneva, WCC, 1986, pp.261-89.

[137] *Churches and the Transnational Corporations: An Ecumenical Programme.* Geneva, WCC, 1983.

[138] *Comprehensiveness in the Churches' Participation in Development: The Challenge of the Eighties.* Report of a CCPD Consultation, Crêt-Bérard, Switzerland, 28-31 January, 1981. Geneva, WCC, 1981.

[139] Dejung, Karl-Heinz: *Die ökumenische Bewegung im Entwicklungskonflikt 1910-68.* Stuttgart, Ernst Klett, 1973.

[140] Dickinson, Richard D.N.: *To Set at Liberty the Oppressed: Towards an Understanding of Christian Responsibilities of Development/Liberation.* Geneva, WCC, 1975.

[141] Elliott, Charles: *Patterns of Poverty in the Third World: A Study of Social and Economic Stratification.* London, Praeger, 1975.

[142] Fagley, Richard M.: *The Population Explosion and Christian Responsibility.* New York, Oxford UP, 1960.

[143] *Fetters of Injustice. Report of an Ecumenical Consultation on Ecumenical Assistance to Development Projects, Montreux, 26-31 January 1970,* ed. Pamela H. Gruber. Geneva, WCC, 1970.

[144] Gallis, Marion: *Trade for Justice: Myth or Mandate?* Geneva, WCC, 1972.

[145] Hürni, Bettina S.: *Development Work of the WCC.* Geneva, Médecine et Hygiène, 1974.

[146] *The International Financial System: An Ecumenical Critique.* Report of the Advisory Group on Economic Matters, Geneva, 1-4 November, 1984, ed. Reginald Green. Geneva, WCC, 1985.

[147] *Perspectives on Political Ethics: An Ecumenical Enquiry,* ed. Koson Srisang. Geneva, WCC, 1983.

[148] Santa Ana, Julio de: *Good News to the Poor: The Challenge of the Poor in the History of the Church.* Geneva, WCC, 1977.

[149] *Separation without Hope? Essays on the Relation Between the Church and the Poor During the Industrial Revolution and the Western Colonial Expansion,* ed. Julio de Santa Ana. Maryknoll, NY, Orbis, 1980.

[150] *Towards a Church of the Poor.* The Work of an Ecumenical Group on the Church and the Poor. Geneva, WCC, 1979.

[151] *To Break the Chains of Oppression*. Results of an Ecumenical Study Process on Domination and Dependence. Geneva, WCC, 1975.
[152] Ward, Barbara: *Spaceship Earth*. New York, Columbia UP, 1966.
[153] *World Development: The Challenge to the Churches. The Conference on World Cooperation for Development, Beirut, Lebanon, April 21-27, 1968*. The Official Report. Geneva, SODEPAX, 1968.
[154] "World Economic and Social Development". Section III. In: *The Uppsala Report 1968*. Ed. by Norman Goodall. Geneva, WCC, 1968, pp.39-56.

Several numbers of *CCPD Documents* deal with specific concerns and problems.

Racism

[155] Adler, Elisabeth: *A Small Beginning: An Assessment of the First Five Years of the Programme To Combat Racism*. Geneva, WCC, 1974.
[156] *Breaking Down the Walls: WCC Statements and Actions on Racism 1948-85*, ed. Ans J. van der Bent. Geneva, WCC, 1986.
[157] *The Churches' Involvement in Southern Africa*. Geneva, WCC, 1982.
[158] *Churches Responding to Racism in the 1980s*. Noordwijkerhout, Netherlands, 16-21 June 1980. Geneva, WCC, 1980.
[159] *Ecumenical Statements on Race Relations: Development of Ecumenical Thought on Race Relations 1937-64*. Geneva, WCC, 1965.
[160] Fuchs, Erika: *Antirassismus-Programm 1969-79*. Eine Dokumentation, hrsg. von Peter Karner. Wien, Evangelischer Oberkirchenrat H.B., 1979.
[161] *Die Kirchen im Kampf gegen den Rassismus*. Eine Materialsammlung, zusammengestellt vom Kirchlichen Aussenamt der EKD. Verantwortlich Lothar Coenen. Frankfurt, Lembeck, 1980.
[162] Oldham, Joseph H.: *Christianity and the Race Problem*. London, SCM, 1926.
[163] *Race Relations in Ecumenical Perspective*. WCC Secretariat on Racial and Ethnic Relations, nos 1-8, 1961-65.
[164] *Racism in Theology and Theology against Racism*. Geneva, WCC, 1975.
[165] Richardson, Neville: *The WCC and Race Relations: 1960-69*. Bern, Lang, 1977.
[166] Rogers, Barbara: *Race: No Peace Without Justice. Churches Confront the Mounting Racism of the 1980s*. Geneva, WCC, 1980.
[167] Sjollema, Baldwin: *Isolating Apartheid*. Geneva, WCC, 1982.
[168] *The Slant of the Pen: Racism in Children's Books*, ed. Roy Preiswerk. Geneva, WCC, 1980.
[169] Vincent, John J.: *The Race Race, London, Notting Hill, 1969*. London, SCM, 1970.
[170] *The WCC and Bank Loans to Apartheid*. Geneva, WCC, 1977.

Several numbers of *PCR Information* deal with specific concerns, problems and conflicts.

Inter-church Aid, Refugee and World Service

[171] Bent, Ans J. van der: "Interchurch Aid, Refugee and World Service". In: *Vital Ecumenical Concerns: Sixteen Documentary Surveys*. Geneva, WCC, 1986, pp.214-32.

[172] Bouman, Pieter: *Tears and Rejoicing: The Story of European Inter-Church Aid 1922-56*. Pieter Bouman, 1983.

[173] *Called to be Neighbours: Diakonia 2000*. Official Report, World Consultation of Inter-Church Aid, Refugee and World Service, Larnaca, 1986, ed. Klaus Poser. Geneva, WCC, 1987.

[174] *Contemporary Understandings of Diakonia*. Report of a Consultation, Geneva, Switzerland, 22-26 November, 1982. Geneva, WCC, 1983.

[175] *Digest of the 1966 World Consultation on Inter-Church Aid, at Swanwick, Great Britain*. Geneva, WCC, 1966.

[176] *Fellowship in Christian Sharing: The Story of Inter-Church Aid*, ed. James A. Ryberg. Geneva, WCC, 1951.

[177] *Empty Hands: An Agenda for the Churches*. A Study Guide on the Ecumenical Sharing of Resources for Use by Churches, Local Congregations and Other Groups. Geneva, WCC, 1980.

[178] *In a Strange Land: A Report of a World Conference on Problems of International Migration and the Responsibility of the Churches, held at Leysin, Switzerland, June 11-16, 1961*. Geneva, WCC, 1961.

[179] *Migrant Workers: A Test Case of Human Relationship*. Consultation on Migrant Workers in Western Europe, Bossey, May 29-June 4, 1965. Geneva, Churches Committee on Migrant Workers in Western Europe, 1965.

[180] *The Orthodox Approach to Diakonia*. Consultation on Church and Service, Orthodox Academy of Crete, 20-25 November, 1978. Geneva, WCC, 1980.

[181] *Refugees, a Global Concern*. Geneva, WCC, 1977.

[182] *The Role of the Churches in Social Service: An International Perspective*. Reporting a Consultation held at Mülheim, Germany, July 16-20, 1962. New York, National Council of Churches, 1963.

[183] *The Role of the Diakonia of the Church in Contemporary Society*. Report to the World Conference on Church and Society 1966. Geneva, WCC, 1966.

[184] *Sharing Life. Official Report of the World Consultation on Koinonia: Sharing Life in a World Community, El Escorial, Spain, October 1987*, ed. Huibert van Beek. Geneva, WCC, 1989.

[185] *Within Thy Gates. A Report of the Conference on Migrant Workers in Western Europe, held at Arnoldshain, Western Germany, June 10-15, 1963*. Geneva, WCC, 1964.

DIVERGENCES AND CONVERGENCES IN THE SOCIAL THOUGHT OF THE ROMAN CATHOLIC CHURCH AND THE WCC

[186] Calvez, Jean-Yves & Perrin, Jacques: *The Church and Social Justice: The Social Teaching of the Popes from Leo XIII to Pius XII (1878-1958).* London, Burns & Oates, 1961 (translated from the French: Eglise et la société économique).

[187] Derr, Thomas Sieger: *Barriers to Ecumenism: The Holy See and the WCC on Social Questions.* Maryknoll, NY, Orbis, 1983.

[188] *The Documents of Vatican II*, ed. Walter M. Abbott. London, Chapman, 1966 (see especially the Pastoral Constitution on the Church in the Modern World, *Gaudium et Spes*, pp.199-308).

[189] *The Gospel of Peace and Justice: Catholic Social Teaching since Pope John*, ed. J. Gremillion. Maryknoll, NY, Orbis, 1975.

[190] *The Social Teaching of the Church,* ed. J. Desroches. Madras, Sidma, 1982.

[191] John XXIII: *Encyclical Letter... on Recent Developments of the Social Question in the Light of Christian Social Teaching. Mater et Magistra.* Vatican Polyglot Press, 1961.

[192] John XXIII: *Encyclical Letter... on Establishing Universal Peace in Truth, Justice, Charity and Liberty. Pacem in Terris.* Vatican Polyglot Press, 1963.

[193] John Paul II: *Encyclical Letter... on Human Work. Laborem Excercens.* Vatican Polyglot Press, 1981.

[194] John Paul II: *Encyclical Letter... for the Twentieth Anniversary of Populorum Progressio. Sollicitudo Rei Socialis.* Vatican Polyglot Press, 1988.

[195] John Paul II: *Encyclical Letter... on the Hundredth Anniversary of Rerum Novarum. Centesimus Annus.* Vatican Polyglot Press, 1991.

[196] Paul VI: *Encyclical Letter... on the Development of Peoples. Populorum Progressio.* Vatican Polyglot Press, 1967.

[197] Preston, Ronald: "Convergence and Divergence in Social Theology: The Roman Catholic Church and the WCC". In: *The Ecumenical Review*, vol. 40, no. 2, April 1988, pp.194-203.

[198] "Rerum Novarum: One Hundred Years". In: *The Ecumenical Review*, vol. 43, no. 4, October 1991, pp.389-464.

[199] Stransky, Tom: "Social Encyclicals, Papal". In: *Dictionary of the Ecumenical Movement.* Geneva, WCC, 1991, pp.926-28.

[200] "Theology and Social Ethics: WCC and Roman Catholic Joint Discussion of Social Questions". In: *Study Encounter*, vol. 2, no. 2, 1966, pp.75-102.

[201] Vischer, Lukas: "The Ecumenical Movement and the Roman Catholic Church". In: *The Ecumenical Advance: A History of the Ecumenical Movement, volume 2, 1948-68*, ed. Harold E. Fey. Geneva, WCC, 1970, pp.311-52.

ECUMENICAL SOCIAL ETHICS

[202] Abrecht, Paul: "Christian Action in Society". In *The Ecumenical Review*, vol. 2, January 1950, pp.141-51.

[203] Abrecht, Paul: "From Oxford to Vancouver: Lessons from Fifty Years of Ecumenical Work for Economic and Social Justice". In: *The Ecumenical Review*, vol. 40, no. 2, April 1988, pp.147-68.

[204] Abrecht Paul: "The Social Thinking of the World Council of Churches". In: *The Ecumenical Review*, vol. 17, no. 3, 1965, pp.241-50.

[205] *Biblical Authority for Today: A WCC Symposium on "The Biblical Authority for the Churches Social and Political Message Today"*, eds Alan Richardson & Wolfgang Schweitzer. London, SCM, 1951.

[206] Bock, Paul: *In Search of a Responsible World Society: The Social Teachings of the WCC*. Philadelphia, Westminster, 1974.

[207] Crouch, Archie R.: *A Sociological Analysis of Factors in the Emergence of the WCC*. Dissertation, 1954.

[208] Doornkaat, Hans ten: *Die ökumenischen Arbeiten zur sozialen Frage*. Zürich, Gotthelf, 1954.

[209] Duff, Edward: *The Social Thought of the WCC*. London, Longmans, Green, 1956.

[210] "Ecumenical Social Thought in the Post-Cold-War Period". In: *The Ecumenical Review*, vol. 43, no. 3, July 1991, pp.305-76.

[211] "Fifty Years of Ecumenical Social Thought". In: *The Ecumenical Review*, vol. 40, no. 2, April 1988, pp.129-286.

[212] *Foundations of Ecumenical Social Thought*. Report of the Conference on Church Community and State at Oxford 1937, ed. J.H. Oldham. Philadelphia, Fortress, 1966.

[213] *From the Bible to the Modern World*. Report of Two Ecumenical Study Conferences on the "Biblical Authority for the Church's Social and Political Message Today", with addresses by L. Aalen, K. Barth, C.H. Dodd et al. Geneva, WCC Study Department, 1947.

[214] *The Humanum Studies 1969-75*. A Collection of Documents. Geneva, WCC, 1975.

[215] Jenkins, David E.: *The Contradiction of Christianity*. London, SCM, 1975.

[216] Lefever, Ernest W.: *Amsterdam to Nairobi. The WCC and the Third World*. Washington, DC, Georgetown University, Ethics and Public Policy Center, 1979.

[217] Mehl, Roger: *The Sociology of Protestantism*. London, SCM, 1970 (translated from the French: Traité de sociologie du protestantisme).

[218] Nelson, Claud D.: *Religion and Society: The Ecumenical Impact*. New York, Sheed & Ward, 1966.

[219] Niebuhr, H. Richard: *The Social Sources of Denominationalism*. New York, Holt, 1929.

220 Norman, Edward: *Christianity and the World Order*. Oxford, Oxford UP, 1979.

221 Ramsey, Paul: *Who Speaks for the Church? A Critique of the 1966 Geneva Conference on Church and Society*. Nashville, Abingdon, 1967.

222 *Technology and Social Justice: An International Symposium on the Social and Economic Teaching of the WCC from Geneva 1966 to Uppsala 1968*, ed. Ronald H. Preston. London, SCM, 1971.

223 Thomas, M.M.: *Towards a Theology of Contemporary Ecumenism*: A Collection of Addresses to Ecumenical Gatherings 1947-75. Geneva, WCC, 1978.

224 Visser 't Hooft, W.A.: *The Genesis and Formation of the WCC*. Geneva, WCC, 1982.

225 Visser 't Hooft, W.A.: *The Kingship of Christ: An Interpretation of Recent European Theology*. New York, Harper, 1948.

226 Visser 't Hooft, W.A.: *Memoirs*. London, SCM, 1973.

STATEMENTS OF CHURCHES ON SOCIAL ISSUES

227 Ellingsen, Mark: *The Cutting Edge: How Churches Speak on Social Issues*. Published for Ecumenical Research, Strasbourg, France, by WCC Publications, Geneva, and Eerdmans, Grand Rapids, 1993.

WCC Meetings and International Gatherings 1924-1991

For the many other consultations held since 1948 and not mentioned in this chronological record, consult *Six Hundred Ecumenical Consultations 1948-82*, by Ans J. van der Bent (Geneva, WCC, 1983). *Major Studies and Themes in the Ecumenical Movement* (Geneva, WCC, 1981) by the same author contains further information on the themes and concerns dealt with at various ecumenical gatherings. *Breaking Down the Walls*, edited by the same author (Geneva, WCC, 1986), contains a chronological record of ecumenical and WCC resolutions, statements and actions on combatting racism from 1937 to 1985.

1924	*Conference on Christian Politics, Economics and Citizenship*, Birmingham, England. COPEC Commision Reports: vol. I. The Nature of God and His Purpose for the World; vol. VII. International Relations; vol. XI. The Social Function of the Church; vol. XII. Historical Illustrations of the Social Effects of Christianity.
1925	*The Universal Christian Conference on Life and Work*, Stockholm, Sweden. 2. The Church and Economic and Industrial Problems; 3. The Church and Social and Moral Problems; 4. The Church and International Relations.
1934	*Universal Christian Council on Life and Work*, Fanø, Denmark.
1937	The Oxford Conference on Church, Community and State, Oxford, England. I. Church and Community; II. Church and State; III. Church, Community and State in Relation to Education; V. The Universal Church and the World of Nations.
1946	Creation of the *Commission of the Churches on International Affairs*, a joint agency of the WCC and the International Missionary Council.
1948	*First Assembly of the WCC*, Amsterdam, Netherlands. Section III. The Church and the Disorder of Society; Section IV. The Church and the International Disorder.
1948	The launching of an ecumenical study on *Christian Action in Society*.
1949	*WCC Central Committee*, Chichester, England. Central themes: Contemporary Issues of Religious Liberty; Christian Action in International Affairs.

1951   *WCC Central Committee*, Rolle, Switzerland. A central theme: The Role of the WCC in Times of Tension.

1953   *WCC Central Committee*, Lucknow, India. A central theme: The Asian Situation as a Concern of Christians Everywhere.

1954   *Second Assembly of the WCC*, Evanston, USA. Section III. Social Questions: The Responsible Society in World Perspective; Section IV. International Affairs: Christians in the Struggle for World Community; Section V. Intergroup Relations: The Churches amid Racial and Ethnic Tensions.

1954   The launching of an ecumenical study on the *Common Christian Responsibility toward Areas of Rapid Social Change*.

1955   The launching of a study programme on *Christians and the Prevention of War in an Atomic Age: A Theological Discussion*.

1956   *WCC Central Committee*, Galyatetö, Hungary. A main theme: The Churches and the Building of a Responsible Society.

1959   *International Ecumenical Study Conference on Social Change*, Thessalonica, Greece. Theme: Christian Action in Rapid Social Change: Dilemmas and Opportunities.

1960   *Cottesloe Declaration* of a Conference of WCC Delegates and Representatives of Churches in South Africa, Cottesloe, near Johannesburg.

1961   *Third Assembly of the WCC*, New Delhi, India. Section II. Service.

1963   *WCC Central Committee*, Rochester, NY, USA. A main theme: The Church's Responsibility in New Societies.

1965   *International Consultation*, Enugu, Eastern Nigeria. Theme: The Christian Response to the African Revolution.

1966   *Conference of the WCC Division of Inter-church Aid, Refugee, and World Service*, Swanwick, England. Theme: Inter-Church Aid in the Next Ten Years. Sections: I. Development Aid; II. Uprooted People; III. The Role of ICA in the Use and Training of the Churches' Manpower; IV. The Post-Herrenalb Situation.

1966   *World Conference on Church and Society*, Geneva, Switzerland. Theme: Christians in the Technical and Social Revolutions of Our Time. Sections: I. Economic Development in a World Perspective; II. The Nature and Function of the State in a Revolutionary Age; III. Structures of International Cooperation: Living Together in Peace in a Pluralistic World Society; IV. Man and Community in Changing Societies.

1968   *Consultation on Theological Issues of Church and Society*, Zagorsk, USSR.

1968   *Conference on Society, Development and Peace* (SODEPAX), Beirut, Lebanon. Theme: World Development — Challenge to the Churches.

1968   *Fourth Assembly of the WCC*, Uppsala, Sweden. Sections: III. World Economic and Social Development; IV. Towards Justice and Peace in International Affairs.

1969   *International Consultation on Racism*, Notting Hill, London.

1969   *WCC Central Committee*, Canterbury, England. Endorsement of an ecumenical study programme on the *Future of Man and Society in a World of Science-based Technology*. Endorsement of a *Plan for an Ecumenical Programme to Combat Racism*.

1970   *Ecumenical Consultation on Ecumenical Assistance to Development Projects*, Montreux, Switzerland.

1970   *Exploratory Conference on Technology, Faith and the Future*, Geneva, Switzerland.

1970   *Consultation on Christian Concern for Peace* (SODEPAX), Baden, Austria.

1971   *Consultation on the Human Environment and Responsible Choice*, Nemi, Italy.

1973   *WCC Central Committee*, Geneva, Switzerland. Acceptance of the Report on Violence, Nonviolence and the Struggle for Social Justice.

1973   *Assembly of the Commission on World Mission and Evangelism*, Bangkok, Thailand. Section II. Salvation and Social Justice.

1974   *World Conference on Science and Technology for Human Development*, Bucharest, Romania. I. The Significance for the Future of Pressures of Technology and Population on Environment, and of Natural Limits to Growth; II. Self-Reliance and the Technical Options of Developing Countries; III. Quality of Life and the Human Implications of Further Technological Change; IV. Human Settlements as a Challenge to the Churches; V. World Social Justice in a Technological Age; VI. The Theological Understanding of Humanity and Nature in a Technological Era.

1974   *Consultation (CCIA)*, St Pölten, Austria. Theme: Human Rights and Christian Responsibility. I. Equipping the Local and National Churches to Identify Human Rights Violations and to Protect the Victims; II. Equipping Regional Ecumenical Bodies and the WCC for More Effective Defence and Promotion of Human Rights; III. Promoting Greater International and Ecumenical Understanding and Cooperation for the Defence and Implementation of Human Rights.

1975   *Faith and Ideologies: An Ecumenical Discussion*, Cartigny, near Geneva. Consultation organized by Faith and Order and Church and Society.

1975   *Racism in Theology and Theology against Racism*, Geneva, Switzer-
       land. Report of a consultation organized by the Commission on Faith
       and Order and the Programme to Combat Racism.

1975   *Fifth Assembly of the WCC*, Nairobi, Kenya. Section V. Structures of
       Injustice and Struggles for Liberation; Section VI. Human Develop-
       ment: Ambiguities of Power, Technology, and Quality of Life.

1977   *Consultation on Militarism*, Glion, Switzerland, Commission of the
       Churches on International Affairs.

1978   *Conference on Disarmament*, Glion, Switzerland, Commission of the
       Churches on International Affairs.

1978   *Consultation on Political Economy, Ethics and Theology*, Zürich,
       Switzerland. Sponsored by Church and Society and the Commission on
       the Churches' Participation in Development.

1978   *Consultation of an Ecumenical Group of the Church and the Poor*,
       Ayia Napa, Cyprus. Organized by the Commission on the Churches'
       Participation in Development.

1979   *Conference on Faith, Science and the Future*, Massachusetts Institute
       of Technology, Cambridge, USA. Sections: I. The Nature of Science
       and the Nature of Faith; II. Humanity, Nature and God; III. Science
       and Education; IV. Ethical Issues in the Biological Manipulation of
       Life; V: Technology, Resources, Environment and Population; VI.
       Energy for the Future; VII. Restructuring the Industrial and Urban
       Environment; VIII. Economics of a Just, Participatory and Sustainable
       Society; IX. Science/Technology, Political Power and a More Just
       World Order; X. Towards a New Christian Social Ethic and New
       Social Policies for the Churches.

1981   *Ecumenical Perspectives on Political Ethics*, Cyprus. Report of a
       Consultation organized by the Commission on the Churches' Participa-
       tion in Development.

1981   *Public Hearing on Nuclear Weapons and Disarmament*, Amsterdam,
       Netherlands, organized by the WCC.

1981   *Churches among Ideologies*, Grand Saconnex, Switzerland. Report of
       a Consultation organized by the Sub-unit on Dialogue with People of
       Living Faiths and Ideologies.

1983   *Sixth Assembly of the WCC*, Vancouver, Canada. Issue 5. Confronting
       Threats to Peace and Survival; Issue 6. Struggling for Justice and
       Human Dignity.

1983   *Violence, Nonviolence and Civil Conflict*. Report of the Corrymeela
       Consultation, Ireland.

1985   *Harare Declaration* of a Conference organized by the Programme to
       Combat Racism.

1986   *World Consultation of Inter-church Aid, Refugee and World Service*, Larnaca, Cyprus. Theme: Called to be Neighbours: Diakonia 2000.

1987   *Lusaka Statement* of a Conference organized by the Programme to Combat Racism.

1987   *World Consultation on Koinonia. Sharing Life in a World Community*, El Escorial, Spain.

1988   *Consultation on the Integrity of Creation*, Granvollen, Norway.

1990   *World Convocation on Justice, Peace and the Integrity of Creation*, Seoul, South Korea.

1991   *Seventh Assembly of the WCC*, Canberra, Australia. Sub-theme 2. Spirit of Truth — Set Us Free; Sub-theme 3. Spirit of Unity — Reconcile Your People.

Index